INTEGRATION:

The Psychology and Mythology of Martin Luther King, Jr. and his (Unfinished) Therapy With the Soul of America

BY JENNIFER LEIGH SELIG, PHD

MANDORLA BOOKS

ISBN 978-0615630915

MANDORLA BOOKS
CARPINTERIA, CA
WWW.MANDORLABOOKS.COM

"The ultimate aim . . . is to foster and create the 'beloved community' in America where brotherhood is a reality. . . . Our ultimate goal is genuine intergroup and interpersonal living—*integration*."

~ Martin Luther King, Jr.

TABLE OF CONTENTS

INTRODUCTION

Sunday, January 24, 1954. At 11:00 a.m. on a cool morning in Montgomery, Alabama, a large crowd turned out at the Dexter Avenue Baptist Church to hear a 25-year-old young man from Atlanta, Georgia who had driven across the country to deliver a trial sermon to the congregation there. So impressed were they with his sermon that the young minister was invited that very afternoon to accept the position. After consulting with his new wife, the young couple accepted the offer and moved to Montgomery, a move that had a profound impact not just on the man and his wife, not just on the family they left behind and the family they would soon begin, not just on the congregation of Dexter Avenue Baptist Church, not just on Montgomery, Alabama, but on the nation—no, on the world as a whole. It put the man, Martin Luther King, Jr., in the right place at the right time to emerge as the leader of the Civil Rights Movement in the United States of America, and to enlarge into a leader for peace, equality, justice, and love for the world at large.

The sermon that earned him that place in the church and in history—"The Three Dimensions of a Complete Life"—was one he had preached before that morning, and was one he would preach again. It was a touchstone sermon for him during his life, and in this book, it serves as a touchstone sermon for us in examining what I would assert was the primary focus and goal of King's life: integration.

On a literal level, we all know King as a man who gave his life to the integration of black and white America during the Civil Rights Movement. But integration meant much more than that to King, and lived on a metaphorical level as well. Life was not complete, he believed, until each of us as individual souls had integrated our relationships with ourselves, with others, and with our God. As I'll show in this book, this was true not only for individuals, but for the nation at large, as King sought to integrate all three dimensions—the personal, the social/political, and the spiritual—into his work with the soul of the nation.

This book concludes with King's "Three Dimensions of a Complete Life" sermon, using the symbol of alchemy as a way to understand both the process and product of integration. But before we get there, I want to take you on a journey into the psyche, soul, and imagination of King himself. If we accept the truism that *the man is the message*, then it is important to explore to what degree *King himself* was an integrated personality.

This book is based upon the conceit that casts King as a "cultural therapist." It is my belief that just as therapists work with the psyche or soul of their clients to help them become more psychologically whole, healed, and integrated, so too are there people in any given culture who work with the psyche or soul of that culture to help it become more psychologically whole, healed, and integrated, often using the same psychological principles that work in one-on-one therapy. During the Civil Rights Movement, King put America on the couch, talked with her about her issues, challenged her to see her psychological dis-ease, and marched with her along the path toward healing, toward her own integration. Following the psychological truism that therapists can only take their clients as far toward their psychological health as they have been themselves, so too it is fair, and valuable, to look at King's psychological health for hints about why he was able to succeed, and where he might have failed, to heal his "client," the soul of America.

Before beginning this journey, a few words about myself and my perspective as it informs this book.

I was born in the 1960's in the United States of America—in fact, the calculator shows I was probably conceived right at the time of King's famous "I Have a Dream" speech at the March on Washington. I've always felt a deep affinity with that time period, and in particular, with the radical dream and vision of Martin Luther King, Jr. Thus, I write this book from the perspective of one who is unabashedly a devotee of King, but who understands, like King, that loving someone or something imperfect means that at times you may be called to offer gentle criticism. This leads me to confess two weaknesses of this book. First, I have certainly not offered criticism enough. Much of the shadow side of King's life and psyche is not explored in this book. For example, it has been argued that part of the failure of the Civil Rights Movement as a movement for integration was its failure to fully integrate women into the movement, and that King's ambivalence about women played a large part in this failure, something I mention here but do not take up in the body of this book. Added to accusations of misogyny are his well-known sexual infidelities, and the plagiarism of his dissertation and many of his speeches. While I will briefly comment on them in the book, I will not explore them in detail; they are well documented by others (for example, see Michael Eric Dyson's *I May Not Get There With You: The True Martin Luther King, Jr.*). A second weakness of this book is my position vis-à-vis history. I was only three years old when King was assassinated, and I have lived the Civil Rights Movement vicariously through research, reading, and travel, so the book is entirely composed of second and third-hand information filtered through a limited first-hand perspective.

I do not claim that this book contains *the* truth about *the* psychology of Martin Luther King, Jr. My background is in the discipline of depth psychology, where we take seriously the notion of the unconscious and thus, we know that all truths are only partial truths, that whatever we reveal always leaves something concealed. Depth psychology differs from mainstream psychology in that it does not reduce the psyche to the materialist, deterministic mind that can be explained away if only we find the right machine to peer inside of the brain and map its functions. Depth psychology seeks to return the root word *psyche* back to its original meaning as soul, not mind, and certainly not brain. It is more interested in the imaginative, polyvalent, metaphorical, mysterious unknown and ultimately unknowable psyche, and its goal is the interpretation of possible truths, not the revelation of The Truth.

In the last dozen years that I've spent with King and this book, I've followed the research approach called *interpretative inquiry*. Martin Packer described this approach as one that

> taps into our engaged practical understanding of an entity or phenomenon by adopting what seems an appropriate perspective. Interpretation is a matter of articulating this anticipatory sketch, letting an account of the phenomenon emerge gradually and become more explicit. An interpretative account opens up, lays out and articulates the perspective from which an event or interaction has been understood.

Using Packer's language, the entities I'm interpreting are King and America, the phenomenon is the Civil Rights Movement, and one perspective that seems appropriate to me is a depth psychological perspective with its close affinity to spirituality and mythology. The first chapter of this work views King's biography through the lens of psychologist C. G. Jung's theory of "the great personality," and it becomes the anticipatory sketch, while the subsequent chapters can be seen as the emerging of the perspective.

In choosing interpretative inquiry as a research approach, I am constantly aware—and want you to be too—that what I offer is only one interpretation among a host of other valid interpretations. Packer wrote, "No single account can include all the different forms understanding may take. Any text or interaction can be read in a multitude of ways." I am aware that there are other readings, other interpretations, other layers, and some of them may very well conflict with or even contradict the ones I offer here. This is par for the course with interpretative inquiry, according to Packer.

> To give an interpretive account covering all of them [ways of understanding a phenomenon] would require the impossible task of anticipating all the questions new readers could pose, all the concerns they might bring. The best we can do is grant that a better interpretation is one that uncovers more of the perspectives from which an interaction can be viewed. At no point can an interpretation be fully complete. It's always possible that a little more work will uncover a hitherto unsuspected perspective on things. In this way interpretive inquiry resembles the rest of life.

I stay humble, knowing this book is inherently incomplete, and I hope that others will add "a little more work" to it, uncovering new perspectives.

Jesse Jackson once said of King, "Thinking about him is like thinking about the prism, the sun shining through a glass from as many angles as you look. You know there is another set of rays, and as many angles as you think about Dr. King, there is yet another set of angles with which to analyze him." I hope you will find this angle illuminating, and I pray it does justice to the sun that is Martin Luther King, Jr., and the ongoing personal and cultural project that is integration.

I have another hope for this book, a hope that it won't be read only for insights into King, the Civil Rights Movement, and the American psyche at the time. While the book does offer this, it does not want to stop at interpreting the past, and in particular, this one man from the past. I also hope that others will take up this notion of "cultural therapy," of looking at our leaders and activists as cultural therapists, and will consider ways they can work with more psychological effectiveness and affectiveness toward cultural healing, transformation, and integration. The keys to the kingdom of psychological transformation needn't lie only in the inner chamber of the therapy room; they have the power to unlock groups, cultures, even nations, and unleash healing *en masse*. The more conscious and psychologically astute our leaders and activists are, the better the opportunities for positive cultural change and healing. And when a culture becomes healthier, the individuals within become healthier. So my goal in this book is not merely to reflect upon a healing moment from our collective past, but to offer a psychological path we can march on together toward a better collective future.

1 BIOGRAPHY:

"THE GREAT PERSONALITY" OF MARTIN LUTHER KING, JR.

In 1959, Swiss psychologist C. G. Jung surveyed the psychic landscape around him and saw little but chaos: the horrors of World War I and II, totalitarianism, upheaval in countries all over the world, the constant threat of nuclear war and total world annihilation, etc. Many "isms" were starting to be addressed on a global level, such as racism, colonialism, and imperialism, and all around the world people were asserting their rights to self-determination. Of the times, Jung wrote:

> A political, social, philosophical, and religious conflict of unprecedented proportions has split the consciousness of our age. When such tremendous opposites split asunder, we may expect with certainty that the need for a saviour will make itself felt. . . . Should something extraordinary or impressive then occur in the outside world, be it a human personality, a thing, or an idea, the unconscious content can project itself upon it, thereby investing the projection carrier with numinous and mythical powers.

At that very same moment, across the world from Jung in the less-than-United States, a human personality was being called to serve that function of a projection carrier with numinous and mythical powers: Martin Luther King, Jr. Jung said, "It is not for nothing that our age cries out for the redeemer personality. . . . The people always long for a hero, a slayer of dragons, when they feel the danger of psychic forces; hence the cry for personality." That personality could do what people themselves felt powerless to do: bring integration to a world torn asunder. Martin Luther King, Jr. answered the cry and quickly became his country's hero, its redeemer, its savior, and ultimately, its martyr.

Jung's Great Personality

Most of us know the basic outlines of King's biography, so I want to take us beyond those broad historical strokes and into a more psychological approach. Jung's definition of "the great personality" will allow us to reintroduce ourselves to King, and will illuminate some of the reasons, factors, and circumstances that led to his tremendous success. The fact that King *was* and *remains* a great personality is undeniable. King scholar James Ivory summarizes his legacy.

> Martin Luther King Jr. ranks as one of the most important and celebrated figures in the twentieth century. On the American scene, a national holiday has been named in his honor and is celebrated by millions each year. Countless scholarships, schools, bridges, streets, libraries, and churches bear his name. Plays, movies, books, and songs have been written about his life and his contribution to the struggle for human and civil rights. On the world scene, his influence extends beyond national boundaries as both his philosophy and method of nonviolent direct action have been embraced in many countries by social philosophers and leaders of protest movements. Without question, as a global figure of mythic-heroic proportions, King's life and thought continue to wield significant influence in struggles for political, economic, and social justice around the globe.

With the 2011 dedication of the Martin Luther King National Memorial in Washington D.C. (the only memorial to a person who is not a president), his influence promises to continue to spread into the 21st century and beyond.

Jung said of the great personality that he or she "acts upon society to liberate, to redeem, to transform, and to heal." Certainly this was King's goal; he wanted "To Redeem the Soul of America"— this he boldly declared as the motto of the Southern Christian Leadership Conference, an organization King helped found in 1957 to facilitate coordinated action of local protest groups.[1] He wanted

---

[1] King used the verb "save" ten years later in his 1967 speech "A Time to Break Silence" when he spoke out strongly against the Vietnam War. "In 1957 when a

to liberate both black and white people from the tyranny of racism, to redeem a country given over to the values of materialism and militarism, to transform a nation failing to match its deeds with its creeds, and to heal the split national psyche which privileged power over love, leading to injustice and inequality. King believed that her black citizens were "God's instrument to save the soul of America." He told them, "We can help America save her soul. Maybe God has called us here to this hour. Not merely to free ourselves but to free all our white brothers and save the soul of this nation." If black Americans were to free themselves and free white Americans, if they were to heal the soul of all of America, then King felt himself to be the leader of that movement. Once he began, he had to follow it through to the end, or to *his* end. He told his followers, "I can't stop now. History has thrust something upon me which I cannot turn away. I should free you now."

But how did one individual man become so great as to speak those inflated words, "*I* should free you now?" As Jung questioned, "But what has the individual personality to do with the plight of the many? In the first place he is part of the people as a whole, and is as much at the mercy of the power that moves the whole as anybody else." Yes, King was part of the people as a whole, for he was black too, subject to the same discrimination, the same segregation, as all black citizens were. But what distinguished him from other black Americans who did not become such renowned leaders? What, besides his name, made this man king above all others? What makes one man or woman among others the great personality? Why does one person become lifted above the morass and rise to such mythic status?

Jung himself raised this question, and then had a difficult time answering it: "All the usual explanations and nostrums of psychology are apt to fall short here." He believed that the great personality could not be explained by hereditary or environmental factors, not by seeds planted in childhood or any causal connections in adulthood, not by anything completely rational, external, or entirely explicable at all.

---

group of us formed the Southern Christian Leadership Conference, we chose as our motto: 'To save the soul of America.'"

The Making of a Great Personality: Rational Explanations

Many people take a rational approach to explain the rise of great personalities: biographers of King are no exception. Theologian James Cone represents the attitude of many King biographers in his assertion that

> to understand the history that Martin King made, it is necessary to know something about the circumstances that made him. Only through an investigation of his social, educational, and religious development, from birth to early adulthood, will we be able to understand the nature of his dream and the dimensions of his accomplishment.

Since Cone's approach—what we could call the developmental approach—is typical of most King's biographers, a close look at his "investigation" offers a composite description.

Cone opens his biographical sketch, "The Making of a Dreamer," with an essay King wrote at the age of twenty titled "An Autobiography of Religious Development."

> It is quite easy for me to think of a God of love mainly because I grew up in a family where love was central and where loving relationships were ever present. It is quite easy for me to think of the universe as basically friendly mainly because of my uplifting hereditary and environmental circumstances. It is quite easy for me to lean more toward optimism than pessimism about human nature mainly because of my childhood experiences.

King continued, "It is impossible to get at the roots of one's religious attitudes without taking into account the psychological and historical factors that play upon the individual." One of those historical factors that Cone and all King biographers emphasize is the importance of the church in King's life.

> The church was the dominant institution in the social life of Atlanta's African-American community, serving as the source for leadership development and also providing the moral values which leaders used to achieve justice for blacks. It also erected a protective shelter against the hostile white

world.

King's maternal grandfather and father were both leaders in that dominant institution, both ministers of the influential Ebenezer Baptist Church in Atlanta; both were also active community leaders in the civil rights arena. Both stressed "the economic, educational, and moral development of the black community" and "the spiritual values of justice, love, and obedience."

Self-worth and self-help were also accentuated. Though King's paternal grandfather was a sharecropper, King's father pulled himself up by his own boot straps and became a successful member of the black bourgeoisie, and though thrift was accentuated in the King house, Martin Jr. never knew want. He grew up in a predominately black middle-class "wholesome community" where crime was at a minimum.

Although King himself never experienced poverty while growing up, even during the Great Depression, he did recall seeing it around him:

> I was much too young to remember the beginning of this depression, but I do recall, when I was about five years of age, how I questioned my parents about the numerous people standing in breadlines. I see the effects of this early childhood experience on my anti-capitalistic feelings.

Though sheltered from personal poverty, his family was not able to shelter him from racism. However, if racism could be quantified, King saw and experienced relatively little in his youth. An early incident with racism when he was six-years-old left him shocked and "determined to hate every white person." For three years, he had played with a white boy whose father owned a store across the street from the King family home. However, soon after they both entered school, the boy broke off their friendship. King soon found out why: "His father had demanded that he would play with me no more" because Martin was black. To this incident, King attributed his first awareness of the race problem.

Later, King would see how his father dealt with that same race problem: by speaking frankly and refusing to be cowed. Once, in a shoe store, the clerk refused to fit King's father because he would not move to the back of the store. His father told the clerk, "We'll either buy shoes sitting here, or we won't buy shoes at all." He then took young King's hand and marched him out of the store. Of this incident, King noted, "My father had not adjusted to the system, and he played a great part in shaping my conscience." Another time, King Sr. was pulled over by a white police officer who made the mistake of calling him "boy." King's father retorted, "Let me make it clear to you that you aren't talking to a boy. If you persist in referring to me as boy, I will be forced to act as if I don't hear a word you are saying." King reported that the officer was stunned, and not knowing how to respond, quickly wrote the ticket and left. In addition to these examples of personal protest, King's father also modeled for him the importance of political protest: he was very active in civil rights issues, and, as the president of the NAACP in Atlanta for a while, led several battles against discrimination and segregation.

Though King wrote less about his mother than his father, her influence on him is clear. He described his mother as "very devout," "soft-spoken and easy-going," and "warm and easily approachable." She was also the child of a successful minister and grew up in comparative comfort; she was sent to the best schools and "in general, protected from the worst blights of discrimination." In spite of that protection, King noted, "My mother never complacently adjusted herself to the system of segregation. She instilled a sense of self-respect in all of her children from the very beginning," teaching them that they should always "feel a sense of 'somebodiness.'"

King took that sense of somebodiness to heart as a child. He wrote of himself, "I have always been somewhat precocious, both physically and mentally. My I.Q. stands somewhat above the average. So it seems that from a hereditary point of view nature was very kind to me." As Cone notes, "At an early age, he became fascinated by language, by the sound and power of words to arouse an audience. 'You just wait and see,' he told his parents, 'I'm going to get me some big words.'" When he was fourteen, he put those big words to use when he participated in and won an oratorical contest: his speech was called "The Negro and the Constitution." He skipped both kindergarten and twelfth grade and entered Morehouse College at the age of fifteen, the third generation in his family to attend the prestigious black college. He struggled a bit in his early years there; he was only reading at an eighth-grade level and was two years younger than his peers. His grades at Morehouse were mostly B's and C's, and when Lucius M. Tobin, a professor of religion at Morehouse, wrote a letter of recommendation for King to

Crozer Theological Seminary, he characterized King as "a little above the average in scholarship."

However, while this discussion of King's background shows him to be a very blessed child, even a slightly gifted one, none of it is enough to explain why he became the most celebrated African-American of the century, if not of our country's history; no doubt there were thousands of other black people who had similar backgrounds and similar advantages (including King's father), and many of these were also involved with civil rights issues long before King came onto the scene, and remained long after.

Some King biographers like Aldon D. Morris move beyond the personal and into the sociological realm: Morris argues that King's success "stemmed from the interaction of large social and historical factors with the unique combination of qualities that were deeply rooted in his own personality." Even if this interaction adequately answered the question "Why this man and no other?" it doesn't answer the question "Why this man *to this degree* and no other?"

The Making of a Great Personality: Irrational Explanations

Jung offered another explanation, beyond the "rational" realms of psychobiography, sociology, or history, as to why some become great personalities: the spiritual dimension.

> There is always something irrational to be added, something that simply cannot be explained, a *deus ex machina* or an *asylum ignorantiae*, that well-known sobriquet for God. The problem thus seems to border on the extra human realm, which has always been known by a divine name.

Richmond Smiley, a deacon at Dexter Avenue Baptist Church where King first ministered in his twenties, acknowledged the irrational or spiritual element that made King great: "I can't really understand it, except to say that perhaps it was an act of God." Arthur Henderson, a deacon at Ebenezer Baptist Church where King last ministered in his thirties, echoes this: "I will always believe that the Lord had his hands on Dr. King in everything that he did. He was guided by the hands of God." Many King biographers seem to believe this as well, and while they'll acknowledge the external and explicable factors that went into making the man, they ultimately point to the spiritual factor, to the hand of God, for at least a partial explanation.

For example, Nathan I. Huggins, a historian of African-American history, writes that King "represents something quite special to us, something that we will never understand. He contains a mystery." Part of that mystery, he argues, is King's relationship to God. Historians and social scientists are uncomfortable with attributing any of King's phenomenal success to his connection to the divine, because, in part, "we do not honor nonrational behavior. But this nonrational element, as all the very sophisticated social scientists will tell us rationally, is the basis, in the final analysis, of most behavior." We don't have the language, the "sophisticated means of analyzing and understanding the religious experience." He suggests we might turn to psychology to help, "but psychology is poor for this sort of thing because psychologists deal with religious experience, generally speaking, pathologically."

Jung's understanding of the psyche provides a notable exception to this generality, as does depth psychology in general. Jung did not define the experience of the numinous or the divine as pathological, but instead rather radically declared that those experiences are what heal patients *from* their pathology.[2] He wrote, "The fact is that the approach to the numinous is the real therapy and inasmuch as you attain to the numinous experiences you are released from the curse of pathology." Jung also attributed a good portion of the power of great personalities to their connection to the divine, which calls them to their vocation.

 What is it, in the end, that induces a man to go his own way and to rise out of unconscious identity with the mass as out of a swathing mist? . . . It is what is commonly called *vocation*: an irrational factor that destines a man to emancipate himself from the herd and from its well-worn paths. True personality is always a vocation and puts its trust in it as in God, despite its being, as the ordinary man would say, only a personal feeling. But vocation acts like a law of God from which there is no escape. The fact that

---

[2] Rudolf Otto coined the term "numinous" in 1917 in his book *The Idea of the Holy*. The word is based on the Latin term "numen," or active power of the divine. Numinous experiences are characterized by mystery, awe, a sense of sacredness, and spiritual intensity.

many a man who goes his own way ends in ruin means nothing to one who has a vocation. He must obey his own law, as if it were a daemon whispering to him of new and wonderful paths. Anyone with a vocation hears the voice of the inner man: he is *called.*

It is fascinating to examine King's greatness in the light of a vocational response to God's will, because in every way, the beginning of King's religious calling was unremarkable, more *normalized* than *numinous.*

The Vocational Response of the Great Personality

King joined the church at age five, not out of a religious feeling, but out of sibling rivalry: his older sister Christine joined one Sunday after a guest evangelist issued an invitation, and King did not want to be outdone. He admitted that "it is quite clear that I joined the church not out of any dynamic conviction, but out of a childhood desire to keep up with my sister." Because the church was a second home for him, it was easy to take it for granted, and he reported uncritically accepting everything he was taught until around the age of twelve. "But this uncritical attitude could not last long, for it was contrary to the very nature of my being. I had always been the questioning and precocious type. At the age of thirteen, I shocked my Sunday school class by denying the bodily resurrection of Jesus. Doubts began to spring forth unrelentingly."

King could not silence those doubts, and as a result, he initially turned his back on the family business of the church. Since he was raised with the ethic of serving humanity, he planned to be a lawyer or a doctor instead. However, at liberal Morehouse, "the shackles of fundamentalism" were removed; he met professors and took classes where he was able to reconcile his intellect with his religion, and he came to believe that being a minister could be both "intellectually respectable as well as emotionally satisfying." During his senior year of college, he decided to apply to the ministry; at the age of nineteen, he entered Crozer Theological Seminary. On his application to Crozer, in response to a question that prompted him to give his personal reasons for entering the ministry, he gave the first clear indication of the strength of his calling. "My call to the ministry was quite different from most explanations I've heard. This decision came about in the summer of 1944 when I felt an inescapable urge to serve society. In short, I felt a sense of responsibility which I could not escape."

His acknowledgment that his calling was different than most others refers to his lack of a direct calling from the Holy Spirit which many ministers experience, which he explored in "An Autobiography of a Religious Development."

> Conversion for me was never an abrupt something. I have never experienced the so called "crisis moment." Religion has just been something that I grew up in. Conversion for me has been the gradual in-taking of the noble ideals set forth in my family and environment, and I must admit that this in-taking has been largely unconscious.

After detailing his exciting days at Morehouse when he was introduced to a liberal approach to Christianity, King continued:

> It was in my senior year of college that I entered the ministry. I had felt the urge to enter the ministry from my latter high school days, but accumulated doubts had somewhat blocked the urge. Now it appeared again with an inescapable drive. My call to the ministry was not a miraculous or supernatural something, on the contrary it was an inner urge calling me to serve humanity.

Perhaps even more telling was something he wrote four months later regarding Edgar Brightman's book *A Philosophy of Religion*. In this book, Brightman argued that religion is an experience marked by "concern about experiences which are regarded as of supreme value" followed by "devotion towards the powers behind those values and the expression of the concern and devotion through symbolic rites." King reviewed the book, agreeing with Brightman's conclusions, and then ended his paper in this way: "How I long now for that religious experience which Dr. Brightman so cogently speaks of throughout his book. It seems to be an experience, the lack of which life becomes dull and meaningless." Here King confesses that he hadn't a powerful, first-hand experience of the divine, though he went on to say, "I do remember moments that I have been awe awakened; there have been times that I have been carried out of myself by something greater than myself and to that something I gave myself." Even then, King had to ask the question, "Has this great something been God?" He concluded by wondering, "Maybe after all I have been religious for a number of years, and am now only becoming aware of it."

In part it was those doubts, combined with the lack of a single immediate experience of conversion, which made King lean more towards a position teaching in a college or school of religion rather than preaching. Another part was his three-fold criticism of the black church. First, he was critical of the fundamentalism of the church, and could not see how the facts of science could be squared with the stories of religion. Second, he "revolted against the emotionalism of much Negro religion, the shouting and the stamping," saying that if blacks "as a people had as much religion in our hearts and souls as we have in our legs and feet, we could change the world." Third, he saw that many black ministers were "unlettered, not trained in seminaries" and he questioned whether religion could be intellectually stimulating in addition to emotionally satisfying. Some of those doubts were quelled for King at Morehouse under the influence of two educated men, president Benjamin Mays and professor George Kelsey, who made King "stop and think." King wrote of them, "Both were ministers, both deeply religious, and yet both were learned men, aware of all the trends of modern thinking. I could see in their lives the ideal of what I wanted a minister to be."

Although King decided to pursue the ministry, he still had his eye on becoming a professor like his Morehouse mentors, and thus in 1951 he entered Boston University's School of Theology to obtain his doctorate. After he finished his residential requirements for the Ph.D., and after his marriage to Coretta Scott, King decided it was time to settle down into a job. He debated the ministry versus teaching, and in fact, had offers from three churches *and* three colleges. He wrote, "I had had a great deal of satisfaction in the pastorate and had almost come to the point of feeling that I could best render my service in this area [though] I never could quite get the idea out of my mind that I should do some teaching."

After much soul-searching, he decided to accept the call to Dexter Avenue Baptist Church in Montgomery, Alabama, believing it was important to continue serving his native South, though he had offers in the North. During his first sermon as pastor of Dexter Avenue, he told his congregation that he came with "nothing so special to offer. . . . no pretense to being a great preacher or even a profound scholar. . . . No pretense to infallibility." Instead, he told them:

I come to you with only the claim of being a servant of Christ, and a feeling of dependence on his grace for my leadership. I come with a feeling that I have been called to preach and to lead God's people. . . I have felt with Jesus that the spirit of the Lord is upon me, because he hath anointed me to preach the gospel to the poor, to heal the brokenhearted, to preach deliverance to the captives and to set at liberty those that are bruised.

Though King reiterated here the original reason for his calling into the ministry—the urge to serve humanity—his feeling that "the spirit of the Lord" was upon him begins to suggest a more personal experience of the divine. Yet his language was still lukewarm compared to the man filled with divine fire he would later become.

But perhaps King had a sense that God was chasing him down in Montgomery, for it was there where everything fell into place, where a preacher of a church was made a leader of a movement, where a "slightly above ordinary" man was made into a myth of monumental proportion. For a year, King was an active pastor in his church, and took an interest in the community at large, joining the local branch of the NAACP and becoming vice-president of the Alabama Council on Human Relations, an interracial group that employed educational methods to improve relations between the races. He made good friends with fellow preacher Ralph David Abernathy and his wife, he completed his doctoral dissertation, and he became a new father when his daughter Yolanda Denise was born. And then, the infamous bus boycott began, and King had his first direct experience with the hand of God.

It was Thursday, December 1st, 1955 when Rosa Parks refused to move to the back of the bus and was arrested. Local black community members were quick to rally around Parks, and soon a call was made to Abernathy, who turned around and called King, suggesting they do something. According to Abernathy, King agreed that they *should* do something, but said he couldn't get involved, as he was preparing for his church's annual conference and didn't feel like he could spare any time.

He offered his church as a meeting place instead. King agreed to break away from his work for an hour or so to attend the meeting; during that meeting the boycott was planned for the following Monday, with another meeting to follow Monday night to assess the boycott's success and to plan for the next stage. At the meeting,

King grew more and more excited, and by the weekend, more and more involved; on Monday, he rose an hour before sunrise to watch the busses run and see how many black people were on them. He was thrilled to find not a single passenger. He went to court that day to witness Park's conviction, and to the mass meeting that night, where he was nominated as president of the newly formed Montgomery Improvement Association. When asked whether he would accept the nomination, he replied, "Well, if you think I can render some service, I will."

Those eleven humble words were to change the course of his life in unfathomable ways. He couldn't even fathom why he said yes: "The action had caught me unawares. It had happened so quickly that I did not even have time to think it through. It is probable that if I had, I would have declined the nomination." In fact, just three weeks earlier he had turned down the position of president of the local NAACP because he and Coretta agreed that after the completion of his dissertation, he now needed to pay more attention to his new church and his new family.

But accept he did, having no idea that the boycott would stretch on for over a year before reaching resolution. Within a month and a half, King had spent time in jail, and was the target of many threatening, blasphemous, and obscene phone calls and letters, as many as thirty to forty a day. In his book *Stride Toward Freedom*, King shared that at first he was able to take those incidents in stride, but "as the weeks passed, I began to see that many of the threats were in earnest. Soon I felt myself faltering and growing in fear." He also became fearful for his wife and his baby. Every night before he went to bed he was faced with uncertainty: every morning when he woke up, he would look at his wife and daughter, and say to himself, "They can be taken away from me at any moment; I can be taken away from them at any moment."

One night around midnight, King was ready to doze off when the phone rang. An angry voice said, "Listen, nigger, we've taken all we want from you; before next week you'll be sorry you ever came to Montgomery." King hung up, but couldn't sleep. He wrote, "It seemed that all of my fears had come down on me at once. I had reached my saturation point." He got up from bed, went into the kitchen, and heated a pot of coffee. He sat down at his kitchen table and prayed aloud in desperation: "I am here taking a stand for what I believe is right. But now I am afraid. The people are looking to me for leadership, and if I stand before them without strength and courage, they too will falter. I am at the end of my powers. I have nothing left. I've come to the point where I can't face it alone."

It was then that King "experienced the presence of the Divine as I had never experienced Him before. . . . It seemed as though I could hear the quiet assurance of an inner voice saying: 'Stand up for righteousness, stand up for truth; and God will be at your side forever.'" He was inalterably changed by the experience. "Almost at once my fears began to go. My uncertainty disappeared. I was ready to face anything." The immediate effect on King is clear; three nights later, when the front porch of his house was bombed, he was calmly able to quiet the crowd that gathered outside, reminding them of the importance of loving their enemies and sending them home with no retaliatory violence. Beyond the immediate effects, King attributed to that experience a deep and lasting effect: "Since that morning I can stand up without fear."

Jung wrote, "It is a very different thing when the psyche, as an objective fact, hard as granite and heavy as lead, confronts a man as an inner experience and addresses him in an audible voice, saying, 'This is what will and must be.'" That night's address by God made an indelible impression upon King; he would recount that story of midnight at the kitchen table his entire life. Over a decade later in 1967, the year before his death, he recalled it again in his sermon "Why Jesus Called a Man a Fool." There, his language was even more immediate than in the above initial account; there, the voice of God addressed him using the first person, not the third.

> And it seemed at that moment that I could hear an inner voice saying to me, "Martin Luther, stand up for righteousness, stand up for justice, stand up for truth. And lo I will be with you, even until the end of the world." And I'll tell you, I've seen the lightning flash. I've heard the thunder roll. I felt sin-breakers dashing, trying to conquer my soul. But I heard the voice of Jesus saying still to fight on. He promised never to leave me, never to leave me alone. No, never alone. No, never alone. He promised never to leave me, never to leave me alone.

King's voice on the recording of this sermon is chilling, so powerfully and passionately does he render his experience of the divine.

In the King materials this incident has become legendary and is commonly referred to as the "kitchen table incident." Some scholars label it the conversion experience King never had prior to entering the ministry: a "profoundly spiritual transformation" and "the most central and formative event in his life." David Garrow, the Pulitzer Prize-winning King biographer, calls it "the most important thing to grasp and appreciate in seeking to comprehend Martin Luther King's own understanding of his life, his role, his burden, and his mission." Garrow attributes King's ability to "go forward with feelings of companionship, self-assurance, and a growing sense of mission" to that midnight experience. Though King doesn't call it a conversion experience per se—perhaps viewing it more as confirmation than conversion—historian Nathan Huggins suggested that term.

> He never really says what it is; he describes it. Yet all the characteristics of that statement, that confession, make clear that it was a conversion experience. There are many examples in historical literature of individuals sitting in their closets, in their kitchens, on the bank, under a tree, wherever, and having this conversation with God. And God speaks to them and God tells them something.

"The original meaning of 'to have a vocation' is 'to be addressed by a voice,'" Jung wrote, so the kitchen table incident becomes the incitation and inspiration for King's vocational response thereafter.

In archetypal conversion experiences, according to Jung, "the archetypes come to independent life and serve as spiritual guides for the personality, thus supplanting the inadequate ego with its futile willing and striving. As the religious-minded person would say: guidance has come from God." King was distressed and suffering, not feeling like an archetypal hero as he faced the dissipation of his courage and the weakness of his will, and this made the voice a source of guidance and comfort, a welcome revelation. As Jung claimed, "To the patient it is nothing less than a revelation when, from the hidden depths of the psyche, something arises to confront him—something strange that is not the 'I' and is therefore beyond the reach of personal caprice. He has gained access to the sources of psychic life, and this marks the beginning of the cure." The cure that the kitchen table revelation provided King was the relinquishment of the fear of death, a relinquishment so complete, and so completely lasting, that Coretta quotes her husband as later saying, "If there is any one fear I have conquered, it is the fear of death."

Though this was the first time King was visited so directly and personally by the divine spirit, it was not the last. Another noteworthy incident when he "saw the light" was once again in Alabama, this time in Birmingham, seven years later. On Good Friday, King had promised to lead a demonstration and submit to arrest to call attention to the segregation and discrimination in Birmingham, and to the barbaric police brutality unleashed against peacefully protesting activists. However, the night before the planned demonstration, King received news "so distressing that it threatened to ruin the movement." The bondsman who had been providing bail money could no longer do so; therefore, the fifty people who planned to submit themselves for arrest with King could not be guaranteed the quick release they had been promised. Twenty-four of King's key advisers gathered around him the morning of Good Friday, advising him not to go to jail himself, as his presence was needed to raise funds to continue providing others with bail money. Yet King struggled with his conscience and his integrity. What would it mean if the local community saw him fail to practice what he passionately preached? On the other hand, he was torn by the thought of what would happen to the campaign, and to the three hundred people already in jail, if he couldn't raise the money to get them released so they could together continue on with the mission.

All eyes were on King, but his attention was turned inward. He walked to another room in the back of the suite. There, he recounted, "I thought I was standing at the center of all that my life had brought me to be." His "tortured mind" thought about what to do, and finally, "there was no more room for doubt." He whispered to himself, "I must go" and at that moment, "the doubt, the fear, the hesitation was gone." He participated in the march, submitted to arrest, and was placed in solitary confinement for more than twenty-four hours, during which time he literally could not see the light. On Easter Sunday, Coretta placed a call to President John F. Kennedy who had previously intervened on King's behalf, and Kennedy placed some calls to Birmingham that led to considerable improvement of conditions in jail for King.

By the next day, King had a visit from his friend and lawyer who "said a few words that lifted a thousand pounds from my heart"—popular performer Harry Belafonte had raised fifty thousand dollars for bail bonds, available immediately. King reported being silenced, feeling "a profound sense of awe."

> I was aware of a feeling that had been present all along below the surface of consciousness, pressed down under the weight of concern for the movement: I had never been truly in solitary confinement. God's companionship does not stop at the door of a jail cell. God had been my cellmate. When the decision came—in Room 30 on Good Friday—that we must commit a faith act, God was there. . . . In the midst of deepest midnight, daybreak had come. I did not know whether the sun was shining at that moment. But I knew that once again I could see the light.

If King had not committed that faith act, if he did not heeded "the still small voice" of God within who told him what he must do, not only might the Birmingham movement failed, but the world would have been bereft of one of the greatest documents of all time, King's "Letter from Birmingham City Jail."

King was eventually released from jail, but there was no escaping the strength and momentum of his vocation, particularly with his growing sense of cosmic companionship. Jung declared that vocation acts on the great personality "like a law of God from which there is no escape." Indeed, King had written some of the most prophetic words of his life when he expressed on his Crozer application that he could not escape his calling.

Choosing to be Chosen

Time and time again, King discussed how there was no escaping his burgeoning role: not in Montgomery, not in the South, not in the United States, and after he had won the 1964 Nobel Peace Prize, not in the world. He told his Dexter Avenue congregation, "History has thrust something upon me from which I cannot turn away."

> Unknowingly and unexpectedly, I was catapulted into the leadership of the Montgomery Movement. At points I was unprepared for the symbolic role that history had thrust upon me. But there was no way out. I, like everybody in Montgomery, was pulled into the mainstream by the rolling tides of historical necessity.

Later, when he accepted the Nobel Peace Prize, he told reporters, "History has thrust me into this position. It would both be immoral and a sign of ingratitude if I did not face my moral responsibility to do what I can in this struggle." Making it clear that he didn't seek out this position, he said,

> If anybody had asked me a year ago to head this movement, I tell you very honestly that I would have run a mile to get away from it. I had no intention of being involved this way. As I became involved, and as people began to derive inspiration from their involvement, I realized that the choice leaves your own hands. The people expect you to give them leadership. You see them growing as they move into action, and then you know you no longer have a choice, you can't decide *whether* to stay in it or get out of it, you *must* stay in it.

Thus, King's vocational response was not only inspired by the clear call from God, but also by the increasingly loud call of the community, a community which both inspired King and was inspired by him to ever-increasing action and involvement.

However, to say he was pulled or thrust into the mainstream and had only the choice to sink or to swim is misleading, and is dismissive of the vocational courage of the great personality. In every great calling, there exists both compulsion and choice, both freedom and destiny. Jung believed that "personality can never develop unless the individual chooses his own way, consciously and with moral deliberation. Not only the causal motive—necessity—but conscious moral decision must lend its strength to the process of building the personality." King knew this too. He called freedom "the chosen fulfillment of our destined nature." He knew that his personality was freest and most expressed when he followed his destiny. In this way, we can say that King *chose to be chosen*. Therein lies his greatness, for as Jung noted, "That is the great and liberating thing about any genuine personality: he voluntarily sacrifices himself to his vocation, and consciously translates into his own individual reality what would only lead to ruin if it were lived unconsciously by the group." Only if a person has the "greatest possible freedom for self-determination" can he or she make the greatest of all sacrifices, because a great sacrifice is by nature voluntary and conscious.

King told his wife after the events in Birmingham:

> This is not the life I expected to lead. But gradually you take some responsibility, then a little more, until finally you are not in control anymore. You have to give yourself entirely. Then, once you make up your mind that you *are* giving yourself, then you are prepared to do anything that serves the Cause and advances the Movement. I have reached that point. I have no option anymore about what I will do. I have given myself fully.

And by giving himself so fully, he gave the ultimate sacrifice—his own life—not unlike many other great personalities had done before him.

Remaining Faithful to the Call

One of those great personalities is Jesus, the life of whom Jung called "a sacred symbol because it is the psychological prototype of the only meaningful life, that is, of a life that strives for the individual realization—absolute and unconditional—of its own particular law." For Jung, one of the essentials of developing the great personality is "fidelity to the law of one's own being," or being faithful to the core of who you are and what you believe.

Two examples in particular best illustrate King's fidelity to his own inner laws: his faithfulness to the doctrine of nonviolence, and his denouncement of the war in Vietnam. Nonviolence was a doctrine King studied during college, especially as deployed by Gandhi in the Indian Independence Movement; King became convinced during the Montgomery Bus Boycott that it was applicable to the Civil Rights Movement as well. However, while nonviolence was never without its critics, those critics became very vocal as the Civil Rights Movement grew up and began to suffer casualties, as both political battles and physical lives were lost. The strongest critics, and those who stole the attention of many black supporters away from King and his peaceful movement, were Malcolm X, the Nation of Islam, and the Black Power Movement, all proponents of violence whenever necessary. Yet even when King felt his authority challenged, even with the power of his voice and vision waning on this issue, he held steadfast and true to the principle of nonviolence. He stated unequivocally, "I've decided that I'm going to do battle for my philosophy. You ought to believe something in life, believe that thing so fervently that you will stand up with it till the end of your days."

King lost followers as a result: black poet and activist June Jordan was one of them. In her essay about King, "The Mountain and the Man Who Was Not a God," she spoke for many involved in the civil rights struggle, stating that when King spoke about nonviolence, it was "then and there he lost me. Dr. King could not persuade me to adopt a posture that I felt was ignominious, abject, and suicidal." However, what follows next in her essay illustrates how people could still recognize King's greatness, despite vehemently disagreeing with his position of nonviolence.

> Nevertheless, and five years later, when I heard the news of Dr. King's assassination I knew that I had lost my leader: He could not take *me* where I did not wish to go but he had taken *himself* into the valley of death for my sake and he had *earned* his way to the uncontested mountaintop as the moral spokesman for all of the powerless and despised and impoverished. I might not agree with his tactics. But how could anyone quarrel with the monumental evidence of his colossal courage? I might not comprehend the relentlessly expanding context of his passionate concerns. I might resist the international, the multi-racial thrust of his vision. But how should anyone accuse Dr. King of insincerity, of cynicism, or trivial or selfish motivation?

What Jordan found so moving was King's fidelity to his own inner law, the law that had him refuse to do what might have been politically expedient in order to remain faithful to his inner beliefs. Jung noted that "a man can make a moral decision to go his own way only if he holds that way to be the best"; once King came to believe that nonviolence was the best way to achieve lasting peace in the world, he never wavered in that belief.

Jordan's essay hints at the second area where King was most faithful to his own inner law. The "relentlessly expanding context" of his "passionate concerns" undoubtedly refers in large part to his growing concern with the war in Vietnam. King had many reasons to oppose the war, not the least of which was the obvious conflict with his stance on nonviolence. However, when King initially began to speak out against Vietnam in 1965, he was immediately criticized on many fronts: by the black community, who saw King as "their" leader and couldn't understand why he would take on the cause of those halfway around the world; by his own SCLC, who believed he should not squander his energy or his political clout by taking what was then an unpopular stance against the war; by the media, who thought King was outside his area of expertise in criticizing a war he couldn't possibly understand; by the Johnson administration, who did not want a leader of King's stature speaking out against their policies; and by the American society in general, still deeply entrenched in its own anti-communist paranoia and taken-for-granted militaristic imperialism.

King largely held his peace after the backlash to his original comments, but by 1967 it was such an uneasy peace that he vowed to whole-heartedly protest the war. Garrow notes, "King knew full well that his new, aggressive stance on the war would harm him politically and might well damage SCLC financially." However, as King explained to a friend, "At times you do things to satisfy your conscience, and they may be altogether unrealistic or wrong, but you feel better." He thought America's involvement in Vietnam was morally unconscionable, and therefore, "I can no longer be cautious about this matter. I feel so deep in my heart that we are so wrong in this country and the time has come for a real prophecy and I'm willing to go that road." Garrow asserts, "More than anything else, the Vietnam War brought King face-to-face with what was becoming a consciously self-sacrificial understanding of his role and fate." After giving his most critical anti-Vietnam speech, appropriately titled "A Time to Break Silence," he was reproached by even his closest advisors. To them he admitted, "I was politically unwise but morally wise. I think I have a role to play which may be unpopular. I really feel that someone of influence has to say that the United States is wrong, and everybody is afraid to say it."

King did lose popularity then; as Jung forewarned, "To develop one's own personality is indeed an unpopular undertaking." Socrates with the hemlock, Jesus on the cross—King knew the company he kept. He told his dissenting staff,

> When I took up the cross, I recognized its meaning. . . . The cross is something that you bear and ultimately that you die on. The cross may mean the death of your popularity. It may mean the death of a foundation grant. It may cut down your budget a little, but take up your cross and just bear it. And that's the way I've decided to go.

Stanley Levison, one of King's closest friends and advisors, felt that King's "growing inclination to sacrifice himself to his larger mission" came from his understanding of his own particular role in history. King saw himself as "an actor in history at a particular moment that called for a personality, and he had simply been selected as that personality."

The Mythological Power of the Great Personality

Though King, like Socrates and Jesus, spend his life and lost his life over his fidelity to his own inner laws, it is that very fidelity that makes him stand out above the fray as the great personality. Jung called these personalities

> the legendary heroes of mankind, the very ones who are looked up to, loved, and worshipped, the true sons of God whose names perish not. They are the flower and the fruit, the ever fertile seeds of the tree of humanity. This allusion to historical personalities makes it abundantly clear why the development of personality is an ideal, and why the cry of individualism is an insult. Their greatness has never lain in their abject submission *to* convention, but, on the contrary, in their deliverance *from* convention. They towered up like mountain peaks above the mass that still clung to its collective fears, its beliefs, laws, and systems, and boldly chose their own way.

June Jordan was able to recognize, despite her criticisms, that "Martin Luther King, Jr. was not a god, but he was certainly a man of God. He was not a saint yet he lives on, miraculous: A mountain of a life."

"The ideal of personality is one of the ineradicable needs of the human soul," Jung stated, and therefore it is unsurprising that we would mythologize and deify a Jesus or a Buddha or any great personality because to do so shows "the enormous valuation that humanity places upon these hero figures and hence upon the ideal of personality." These figures are often seen as blessed or possessed by God or the gods, Jung noted.

> The miracle of a man being able to act otherwise than as humanity has always acted could only be explained by the gift of daemonic power of divine spirit. How could anyone

but a god counterbalance the dead weight of humanity in the mass, with its everlasting convention and habit? . . . All these attributes, which could be multiplied at will, show that for the ordinary man the outstanding personality is something *supernatural*, a phenomenon that can only be explained by the intervention of some daemonic factor.

Of course, like Jordan, there are people who are quick to point out then and now that King was just a man. King knew he was not a god but rather an instrument for God's will. He reminded himself before his first sermon at Dexter Avenue, "Keep Martin Luther King in the background and God in the foreground and everything will be all right. Remember, you're a channel of the gospel, not a source." However, for every person who pointed out that King was not a god, there was somebody else who stood and stands ready to mythologize him for his god-like powers and God-given gifts.

Poet and writer Maya Angelou's account of the first time she heard King speak paints a portrait of his supernatural powers and gifts. Angelou sat in a Harlem church where Ralph Abernathy had just finished introducing King.

The listeners didn't move. There was a yawning expectancy under the stillness. He was here, our own man, black, intelligent and fearless. He was going to be born to us in a moment. He would stand up behind the pulpit, full grown, and justify the years of sacrifice and days of humiliation. He was the best we had, the brightest and most beautiful. Maybe today would be the day we would find ourselves free.

The introduction was over and Martin Luther King, Jr. rose. The audience, collectively, lost its composure, pews scraped against the floor as people stood, rearing back, pushing, leaning forward, shouting. "Yes, Lord. Come on, Dr. King. Just come on."

A stout, short woman in red, standing next to me, grabbed me around the waist and squeezed. She looked at me as if we were old friends, and whispered, "If I never draw another breath, I could die happy."

She released me and caught the arm of a man on her right, pulling the arm to her breast, cradling it and whispering, "It's all right, now. He's right here and it's all right."

After King finished speaking, Angelou described the effect on the audience. "Strangers embraced tightly; some men and women wept openly, choking on sobs; others laughed at the waves of spirit and the delicious tide of emotion." Immediately after the meeting, Angelou was inspired to do something, anything, to be a part of the Movement. Eventually she took a job working for SCLC because, as she felt, "Martin Luther King was sacred" and she was called to serve him and his work in whatever way she could.

Other people felt the same sense of the sacred nature of King. R. D. Nesbitt was chairman of the pulpit committee that brought King to Dexter Avenue Baptist Church. Of King's time there, he recalled, "The young people just envisioned a new hope and a new day, and the old folks saw in him a black Jesus. They used to call him 'My boy' or 'My son.' They worshipped him." Black activist Steely Carmichael noticed, "People loved King. . . . I've seen people in the South climb over each other just to say, 'I touched him! I touched him!' . . . I'm even talking about the young. The old people had more love and respect. They even saw him like a God."

The Great Personality's Relationship With Death

"Cosmic companionship" was a phrase King often evoked during the Civil Rights Movement to elevate the struggle and inspire the strugglers. It appeared as early as the Montgomery Bus Boycott.

> We have the strange feeling down in Montgomery that in our struggle for justice we have cosmic companionship. And so we can walk and never get weary because we believe and know that there is a great camp meeting in the promised land of freedom and justice. And this belief, and this feeling that God is on the side of truth and justice and love and that they will eventually reign supreme in this universe.

King was so confident about this connection with a loving God that he was able to assure the people, with all sincerity, that God was on their side, that "the universe is under the control of a loving purpose, and that in the struggle for righteousness [we have] cosmic companionship." King felt a personal sense of cosmic companionship, as we explored earlier through the kitchen table incident and his experience in the Birmingham jail, but he felt it at other times as well. King was under the constant threat of death, from the beginning days of the Montgomery Bus Boycott in 1955 until the threats became real in 1968 in Memphis; for thirteen years he faced daily the unimaginable fear of his own violent demise. During a television interview in 1960, King explained how he was able to cope. "I don't think anyone in a situation like this can go through it without confronting moments of real fear. But I have always had something that gave me an inner sense of assurance, and an inner sense of security. . . . I have always felt a sense of cosmic companionship."

Jung argued that the ultimate danger to the great personality is death itself.

> But he who cannot lose his life, neither shall he save it. The hero's birth and the heroic life are always threatened. The serpents sent by Hera to destroy the infant Hercules, the python that tries to strangle Apollo at birth, the massacre of the innocents, all these tell the same story. To develop the personality is a gamble, and the tragedy is that the daemon of the inner voice is at once our greatest danger and an indispensable help. It is tragic, but logical, for it is the nature of things to be so.

Tragic, but logical, for while the world unconsciously calls for the voice and visionary message of the great personality, it cannot consciously stand to hear it for very long before a counter-force arises to kill the messenger.

Depth psychologist James Hillman also noted the connection between the great personality and death.

> The truer you are to your daimon [your guardian or guiding spirit], the closer you are to the death that belongs to your destiny. We expect the daimon to have prescience about death, calling on it before an airline flight or during a sudden attack of sickness. Is this my fate, and now? And when the demands of our calling seem undeniably necessary, again death appears: "If I do what I really must, it will kill me; and yet if I don't, I'll die." To be the calling or not to be, that still and again seems to be the question.

For King, once he affirmatively answered the question of his calling, he did not look back. He looked forward to a time when the demands on him might lessen, and he dreamed of becoming that college professor after all, but he was above all else dedicated to following his daimon, his destiny, and that daimon led him into ever-widening circles of involvement. Yet at the same moment when King first answered yes to his calling, answered yes to becoming a great personality, at that moment death entered the picture as well, and King somehow knew he must make his peace with it to fulfill his destiny.

One of the earliest times King spoke publicly of his own death was in Montgomery, just days before his numinous experience at the kitchen table. He was strained by those thirty or forty threats a day that came in the first month following the boycott. When a white friend warned him that there were plans being made to kill him, King seriously contemplated his own death. One night at a mass meeting, he found himself saying, "If one day you find me sprawled out dead, I do not want you to retaliate with a single act of violence." Soon after his experience at the kitchen table, when his house was bombed and he came outside to speak to the angry people gathered there, he told them, "Remember, if I am stopped, this movement will not stop, because God is with the movement." Two days after the busses were integrated, a shotgun blast ripped through the front door of King's house; no one was injured, but the next morning, King remarked to his Dexter Avenue congregation, "It may be that some of us have to die." Shortly after that, when a reporter asked King if the new spate of violence and bombings in Montgomery left him fearful, King replied no, explaining, "Once you become dedicated to a cause, personal security is not the goal. It is greater than that. What will happen to you personally does not matter. My cause, my race, is worth dying for." A little later, after having been jailed in Montgomery, King declared that he would continue to "stand up for what I think is right, even if it means further arrest, or even physical death."

King confronted his own death squarely for the first time in Montgomery and thereafter became comfortable speaking about it, continuing to do over the next thirteen years. Often he made the connection between being true to the daimon of one's vocation and the possibility of being killed for it. In the struggle in Albany in 1962, King said, "It may get me crucified. I may die. But I want it said even if I die in the struggle that 'He died to make men free.'" In the struggle in Mississippi in 1964, King described his feelings after hearing that a guerrilla group was plotting his death.

I was urged to cancel the trip, but I decided that I had no alternative but to go on into Mississippi, because I had a job to do. If I were constantly worried about death, I could not function. After a while, if your life is more or less constantly in peril, you come to a point where you accept the possibility of death philosophically.

In the struggle in Chicago in 1966, King reported,

> I'm tired of marching for something that should have been mine at first. . . . I'm tired of the tensions surrounding our day. . . . I'm tired of living every day under the threat of death. I have no martyr complex, I want to live as long as anybody in this building tonight, and sometimes I begin to doubt whether I'm going to make it through. I must confess I'm tired. . . . I don't march because I like it, I march because I must.

And, in the struggle in Memphis in 1968, the night before his own death, he said,

> Well, I don't know what will happen now. We've got some difficult days ahead. But it really doesn't matter to me now. Because I've been to the mountaintop. I won't mind. Like anybody, I'd like to live a long life. Longevity has its place. But I'm not concerned about that now. I just want to do God's will. And He's allowed me to go up to the mountain. And I've looked over and I've seen the Promised Land. So I'm happy tonight. I'm not worried about anything. I'm not fearing any man.

Coretta also had to face the very real possibility of her husband's death; she, too, faced it first in those early days in Montgomery. She told reporters then that she had "a recurring fear that her husband would be killed." In her autobiography, she noted how often her husband "talked about it [death] in his sermons and quoted again the phrase 'If a man has not found something worth giving his life for, he is not fit to live.'" In Coretta's first public statement after King's death, she reiterated the phrase.

> My husband often told the children that if a man had nothing that was worth dying for, then he was not fit to live.

He said also that it's not how long you live, but how well you live. He knew that at any moment his physical life could be cut short, and we faced this possibility squarely and honestly. My husband faced the possibility of death without bitterness or hatred. He knew that this was a sick society, totally infested with racism and violence that questioned his integrity, maligned his motives, and distorted his views, which would ultimately lead to his death. And he struggled with every ounce of his energy to save that society from itself.

Everywhere we look—this sermon and that speech, this private conversation and that public declaration—during every year of his abbreviated life, King gave testimony to his belief that when one accepts a calling, it must be followed, even to the death. For in Jung's description of the great personality,

> If he hearkens to the voice, he is at once set apart and isolated as he has resolved to obey the law that commands him from within. "His own law!" everybody will cry. But he knows better: it is the law, the vocation for which he is destined, no more "his own" that the lion that fells him, although it is undoubtedly this particular lion that kills him and not any other lion.

King certainly felt that sense of God-given destiny. As Andrew Young, one of King's closest friends, tells us, "I think that Martin always felt that he had a special purpose in life and that that purpose in life was something that was given to him by God, that he was the son and grandson of Baptist preachers, and he understood, I think, the scriptural notion of men of destiny." Coretta came to believe that her husband knew his destiny was intricately connected with his death. "Martin was driven by a sense of urgency. Looking back now, I feel that he had to complete his life's work early because of his ultimate destiny of becoming a martyr, so that God's will and His creative purpose might be fulfilled."

At some point he went from facing the idea of his *possible* death to accepting the idea of his *probable* death, from knowing he *might* be killed to knowing he *would* be killed, and the "particular lion" that would kill him would be the very lion he was trying to save. Coretta was with King when President Kennedy's death was announced on television. He was quiet for a while, and then he told her, "This is what is going to happen to me also. I keep telling you, this is a sick society." He shared his belief in his imminent death not just with his wife, but with his inner circle of followers. According to Young, King knew "that as the leader of the Movement he would be killed and that he talked about it 'all the time.'"

Conclusion

Martin Luther King, Jr. embodies the description of Jung's great personality, most particularly in the inexplicable spiritual element, or what could be called the touch of the divine on his life; in his sense of vocation; in his willingness to break with convention and follow his own inner laws; in the people's need to deify him; and in his special relationship with destiny and death. As Jung wrote, in times of crisis and chaos, the people call for a great personality, for a hero, a redeemer, and a savior, and King answered that call, thus becoming the great personality bent on saving and redeeming the soul of his beloved country.

2

SPIRITUALITY:

KING'S FOUR PSYCHOTHERAPEUTIC GIFTS OF GRACE

As we explored in the last chapter, in 1957, when King was only 28 years old, he declared his mission via the Southern Christian Leadership Conference's mission statement—"to redeem the soul of America." The ministerial profession has always seen its mission as one of redeeming or saving souls, so this statement is only lofty in scope and scale; we might expect most ministers to be focused on saving the souls of their individual parishioners, not the entire country.

Of course, King was concerned about the individual souls of his parishioners, but after the success of the Montgomery Bus Boycott, he was catapulted behind a more public pulpit, as the country outside of the church clamored for his voice and vision. So in 1957 he answered that call in a most unusual way—he took on a traditionally therapeutic role by accepting a position as an advice columnist for *Ebony* magazine (we'll explore his columns in the next chapter).

Or perhaps it is *not* so unusual, for the mission of the minister and the therapist are quite similar, particularly if the therapist is a depth psychologist, a branch of psychology that has been quite comfortable with the word "soul." Though therapists might be less comfortable with the word "save" and might prefer to use "heal" or "cure" or "tend" or "care for," the minister and the therapist both have in common their desire to work with the transformation of the psyche or soul. Of course, the end goal might be different: the ultimate end goal of a minister may be saving souls from an afterlife spent in hell, while therapists are more concerned with healing a soul from whatever particular hellish conditions they might be living in this life here and now.

Both goals were important to King. He believed that religion at its best "deals with both earth and heaven, both time and eternity. Religion operates not only on the vertical plane but also on the horizontal. It seeks not only to integrate men with God but to integrate men with men and each man with himself." And yet, when examining the total arc of his life, King focused more on bringing heaven down to people on earth than on bringing people on earth up to heaven: as a preacher and as an advice columnist, he did not advise people about what to do to get into heaven, but rather, advised people about what to do to make their lives on earth more heavenly. When he moved onto the national stage, he termed this heaven on earth "the beloved community" and counseled an entire country, even the world, on its creation. His goal, as we'll see throughout this book, and specifically focus on in the last chapter, was always integration: the integration of each individual with him or herself, the integration of individuals with each other, and the integration of individuals with their God.

Given this goal and King's background as a minister, it is not surprising that he would combine psychology and religion in his work with his congregation and his country, practicing what we might call *spiritual therapeutics*, or *therapeutic spirituality*. In fact, King was a great supporter of therapy long before it became popular and commonplace. In his advice column, there were times when he recommended that people seek the counsel of their minister or pastor, but he often suggested they see a traditional therapist. The ideal, of course, would be a therapist with a religious sensitivity, or a minister with a therapeutic sensitivity. Jung would agree.

The Therapist as Minister: The Minister as Therapist

The basic contention of Jung's 1932 essay "Psychotherapists or the Clergy" is that a minister and a therapist have the same aim in "rightly seeing in the cure of souls the real purpose of his existence." Psychological disorders and neuroses of all kinds can be ultimately understood "as the suffering of a soul which has not discovered its meaning." For Jung, the rediscovery of meaning was the cure for the soul's malaise. For this reason, Jung was critical of his peers such as Sigmund Freud and Alfred Adler for focusing too much on the instincts as a source of suffering—for Freud, the sexual instinct, and for Adler, the power instinct—and not focusing enough on the soul's meaning. He accused them of performing "psychology without the psyche [the Greek word for spirit or soul], and this suits people who think they have no spiritual needs or aspirations."

For Jung, it wasn't the instincts that were thwarted but rather the soul itself. In fact, he stated, all the patients who consulted him who were in the second half of life (he defined this as the age of thirty-five and older) shared the same basic problem: they had lost their religious outlook on life. "It is safe to say that every one of them fell ill because he had lost what the living religions of every age have given to their followers," and this despite their religious background, creed, or membership in any particular church. Because he believed that "healing may be called a religious problem," he saw the therapist as a modern-day medical priest.

> Man is never helped in his suffering by what he thinks for himself, but only by revelations of a wisdom greater than his own. It is this which lifts him out of his distress. Today the eruption of destructive forces has already taken place, and man suffers from it in spirit. That is why patients force the psychotherapist into the role of a priest, and expect and demand of him that he shall free them from their distress. That is why we psychotherapists must occupy ourselves with problems which, strictly speaking, belong to the theologian.

However, despite the fact that psychology as a whole had denied the religious aspect of life and even classified religion as pathological (as did Freud and his followers), Jung saw more and more people leaving the church and seeking their healing through the medical science of psychology and psychiatry. Jung conducted his own survey as to why this was so, and he concluded that the majority of people believed that the clergy lacked psychological knowledge and insight, and might be blinded by their "dogmatic and traditional biases." Therefore, Jung called "for the clergyman and the psychotherapist to join forces to meet this great spiritual task."

As we'll see in the next chapter, King was conversant with this theory of Jung's, and he agreed that the main problems were religious after the age of thirty-five. King knew the rising popularity of secular therapy; he obviously believed in its potential efficacy or he wouldn't have recommended it to the readers of his advice column. However, like Jung, he also knew that therapy was a limited venture if the therapist did not have a spiritual bent. He offered the following explanation.

Many of our abnormal fears can be dealt with by the skills of psychiatry, a relatively new discipline pioneered by Sigmund Freud, which investigates the subconscious drives of men and seeks to discover how and why fundamental energies are diverted into neurotic channels. Psychiatry helps us to look candidly at our inner selves and to search out the causes of our failures and fears. But much of our fearful living encompasses a realm where the service of psychiatry is ineffectual unless the psychiatrist is a man of religious faith. For our trouble is simply that we attempt to confront fear without faith; we sail through the stormy seas of life without adequate spiritual boats. One of the leading physicians in America has said, "The only known cure for fear is faith."

Jung might have said the same himself. He acknowledged what a fearful, overwhelming task it was to face the dark and powerful unconscious, whether it was the unconscious within oneself or a meeting with the dark unconscious in others. He wrote, "Man has never yet been able single-handedly to hold his own against the powers of darkness—that is, of the unconscious. Man has always stood in need of the spiritual help which each individual's own religion held out to him. The opening up of the unconscious always means the outbreak of intense spiritual suffering."

Because Jung and King so easily melded the roles of minister and therapist, it is easy to imagine both taking a different path, with Jung becoming a minister and King becoming a therapist. In fact, Jung's father was a minister, and Jung once considered the profession himself, but decided instead to become a medical doctor. As we saw in the last chapter, King once planned on becoming a medical doctor, and given the therapeutic nature of his ministry, quite conceivably he might have chosen to specialize in psychiatry.

Or perhaps not. King always wanted to be a big voice with big words, and the big audience of the church fulfilled that ambition. "No one has the ears of as many people as the man who occupies the pulpit," he wrote, particularly in the black community. Certainly a therapist would never reach as many people directly as a preacher could, nor was therapy then or now as popular within the black community as it was within the white. Besides, King saw the therapeutic potential of the pulpit, believing it "an important single force in shaping public consciousness and in motivating and inspiring people to act responsibly in the social, political, and economic arenas of life." Therefore, on many a Sunday and in many a sermon, King took the role of group therapist, using the pulpit instead to diagnose and offer treatment for what ailed the psyches of his parishioners: we will examine four of those sermons in Chapter 4. He was concerned with saving souls, surely, but he was also concerned with transforming and liberating souls, with helping his congregation and his country to live up to their potential and promise as children of the divine who were now living an earthly existence.

The Four Spiritual Graces

Jung believed that religion's greatest gift was giving people what they need to live a meaningful life: faith, hope, love, and understanding. He called these "the four great gifts of grace" which can both heal the suffering and liberate the soul of humanity. The tricky part, wrote Jung, is that

> these four highest achievements of human endeavor are so many gifts of grace, which are neither to be taught nor learned, neither given nor taken, neither withheld nor earned, since they come through experience, which is an irrational datum not subject to human will and caprice. Experiences cannot be *made*. They happen.

In other words, much of a client's or congregant's psychological healing and liberation cannot be willed by the therapist or clergy; somehow, he or she must find a way to facilitate the experience, to "help the sufferer to attain the liberating experience which will bestow upon him the four great gifts of grace and heal his sickness."

Besides providing experience, Jung believed there was a second way for therapists to promote healing and liberation: they must possess those four graces themselves, which their clients can then experience through contact with them. But those people are rare, Jung thought. He asked, "And where are the great and wise men who do not merely talk about the meaning of life and of the world, but really possess it? One cannot just think up a system of truth which would give the patient what he needs in order to live, namely faith, hope, love, and understanding." In other words, these qualities must not be mere intellectual possessions of the mind, but must be embodied by the therapist. Jung continued, "The way to experience, moreover, is anything but a clever trick; it is rather a venture which requires us to commit ourselves with our whole being."

The brilliance of King as a great cultural healer and liberator lies in those two-fold talents. Not only did he offer the country opportunities to experience the spiritual graces of faith, hope, love, and understanding, but he possessed those himself in abundance and committed himself to them with his whole being, repeating them tirelessly in words and modeling them courageously in deeds.

Because these four great gifts of grace can be considered the foundation of King's spiritual psychotherapeutics, we'll explore each of them in turn here, looking at how he modeled each grace for the country and how he provided people opportunities to experience those graces themselves.

Faith

In one of King's most beloved sermons, "A Knock at Midnight," he opened with Jesus' parable from Luke 11: 5-6. A weary traveler knocks on the door at midnight, but the homeowner has nothing to offer him. Jesus asks, "Which of you who has a friend will go to him at midnight and say to him, 'Friend, lend me three loaves; for a friend of mine has arrived on a journey, and I have nothing to set before him.'" King began his interpretation by noting, "It is midnight in the parable; it is also midnight in our world, and the darkness is so deep that we can hardly see which way to turn." He layered this midnight underworld with three levels: there was darkness in the social, the psychological, and the moral realms. Extending the parable, he saw modern man knocking on the door at midnight as a traveler, desperate for deliverance in the symbolic form of bread. "The traveler asks for three loaves of bread. He wants the bread of faith. . . . There is also a deep longing for the bread of hope. . . . And there is the deep longing for the bread of love."

King wanted to be that kind of friend, one who without question or complaint would devote his life to feeding those three loaves of bread to his weary country at midnight, beginning with the first loaf of faith. King offered three levels of faith upon which his listener could find the solace of certitude and place his trust: faith in a God who is just and good, faith in the goodness of humanity, and faith in the transformation of the world into a new social order.

On the first level, King recognized that especially for ex-slaves and the children of ex-slaves living at midnight in the underworld, it was sometimes difficult to have faith in a God who is just and good.

Midnight is a confusing hour when it is difficult to be faithful. The most inspiring word that the church must speak is that no midnight long remains. The weary traveler by midnight who asks for bread is really seeking the dawn . . . . Faith in the dawn arises from the faith that God is good and just. When one believes this, he knows that the contradictions of life are neither final nor ultimate. He can walk through the dark night with the radiant conviction that all things work together for good for those that love God.

He offered them an experience of that dawn; the early victories of the Civil Rights Movement were like the beginning rays of light in the long struggle with night—and he never failed to give God credit for that light. For example, speaking during the Montgomery Bus Boycott, he said, "We have moved all of these months in the daring faith that God is with us in our struggle. The many experiences of days gone by have vindicated that faith in a marvelous way. Tonight we must believe that a way will be made out of no way." King often repeated this definition of faith: the belief that *a way will be made out of no way.*

King taught a faith in God and the ultimate goodness of the world, preaching that "we [keep] going with the faith that as we struggle, God struggles with us, and that the arc of the moral universe, although long, is bending toward justice." Often he talked about God as "a creative force in the universe," and he offered faith in that force.

When our days become dreary with low-hovering clouds of despair, and when our nights become darker than a thousand midnights, let us remember that there is a creative force in this universe, working to pull down the gigantic mountains of evil, a power that is able to make a way out of no way and transform dark yesterdays into bright tomorrows.

As we explored in Chapter 1, King felt as though he and the Movement worked with God in "cosmic companionship," a comforting concept that could bolster faith.

The second level of faith King offered was in the goodness of humanity. Many people have noted the unusual strength of King's faith in humanity: sociologist Michael Eric Dyson went so far as to call it a genius "for making people believe that they had a moral gift they had forgotten, or never knew they possessed, and for making them proud to contribute to the moral good." Photojournalist Flip Schulke and author Penelope McPhee stated in their book *King Remembered*, "At the root of King's civil rights conviction was an even more profound faith in the basic goodness of man and the great potential of American democracy. He evoked the best in Americans."

Many black Americans struggled in particular with having faith in white humanity. Some had given up entirely. Author James Baldwin wrote in 1955, "The Negro himself no longer believes in the good faith of white Americans—if, indeed, he ever could have." But King stressed to black America the importance of faith in white America, and demonstrated that faith by his actions.

Though King had a couple of experiences with racism early in life that shook his faith in white people, it was always restored. Early in his college days, he joined an Intercollegiate Council dedicated to racial justice, working in partnership with white people for the first time. He said of that experience, "I had been ready to resent the whole white race, but as I got to see more of white people, my resentment was softened, and a spirit of cooperation took place." Instead of thinking of white people as evil, King preferred to think of them as ignorant, and therefore, the job of black people was "to awaken the dozing conscience of many of our white brothers." In his "I Have a Dream" speech, King warned black America not to fall prey to a "distrust of all white people, for many of our white brothers, as evidenced by their presence here today, have come to realize that their destiny is tied up with our destiny and they have come to realize that their freedom is inextricably bound to our freedom."

He held onto his faith vehemently: in 1966, when Black Power was on the rise and the attitude of many in the Civil Rights Movement was turning against nonviolence and cooperation, he was attacked internally for his inclusion of white people in marches and protests. He sat down with the leaders of the counter-movement and reminded them of "the dedicated whites who had suffered, bled, and died in the cause of racial justice, and suggested that to reject white participation now would be a shameful repudiation of all for which they had sacrificed," and he backed his words with action by refusing to participate in any march or protest where white people were excluded. This was a brilliant move on King's part because it allowed black Americans to come into contact with good white Americans who shared a commitment to their cause. Thus, King was not merely talking about having faith, or demonstrating his own faith, but he was facilitating an encounter so black people could directly experience the spiritual grace of faith.

Even when it was difficult to have faith in white people, even when they did heinous things like bombing the church in Birmingham and killing four little black girls, King was able to model the retention of faith, counseling at the girls' funerals, "We must not lose faith in our white brothers. Somehow we must believe that the most misguided among them can learn to respect the dignity and worth of all human personality." While Malcolm X and the Nation of Islam were calling them "white devils," King refused to demonize white people, reminding black America that "we must never forget that there are some white people in the United States just as determined to see us free as we are to be free ourselves." When black people were tempted to look at all white people as evil, he suggested they look at the whole of the situation, where they would discover "that some of the most implacable and vehement advocates of racial equality are consecrated white persons." At the foundation of King's faith in his white brothers and sisters was his belief that *all* people were the beloved children of the same God. It was this belief, coupled with his own experiences, which allowed him to accept the Nobel Peace Prize by saying, "I accept this award today with an abiding faith in America and an audacious faith in the future of mankind."

Finally, King offered faith not only in God and humanity, but faith in the process of transformation itself. In a book that was highly influential for King, theologian Walter Rauschenbusch in *Christianity and the Social Crisis* discussed the importance of this kind of faith.

> If any new principle is to gain power in human history, it must take shape and life in individuals who have faith in it. The men of faith are the living spirits, the channels by which new truth and power from God enter humanity. To repent of our collective social sins, to have faith in the possibility and reality of a divine life in humanity, to submit the will to the purposes of the kingdom of God, to permit the divine inspiration to emancipate and clarify the moral insight—this

is the most intimate duty of the religious man who would help to build the coming Messianic era of mankind.

King offered the country this "faith in the possibility and reality of a divine life in humanity," speaking unabashedly of his faith in the creation of the beloved community on earth.

As much faith as he had, it was not Pollyannaish; it was tempered with a very real sense of how painful, and painfully slow, the process of transformation might be. He said,

> I confess that I do not believe this day is around the corner. The concept of supremacy is so imbedded in the white society that it will take many years for color to cease to be a judgmental factor. But it is certainly my hope and dream. Indeed, it is the keystone of my faith in the future that we will someday achieve a thoroughly integrated society.

He offered faith that by the end of the century, we would have come a long way towards achieving that society. For the time being, he urged people to "walk on in the days ahead with an audacious faith in the future."

King, in speaking his faith, living his faith, and allowing others to experience faith themselves, offered the entire country a spiritual gift. In doing so, he was both clergy and therapist, for offering faith to one's clients is crucial in supporting them in their own transformational processes. In the words of psychologist Maurice Friedman, "The therapist embodies for the patient a loving inclination of the world that seeks to restore the patient's dispirited and mistrustful self to a new dialogical meeting with the forces of nature and history." Certainly King embodied that loving inclination, and as a result Jesse Jackson said of him, "He challenged us to be better people than we thought we could be. He refused to allow us to lose faith and give in to cynicism."

Hope

Closely aligned with faith is hope, "the second loaf of bread" King offered his weary country at midnight. If the opposite of faith is cynicism, the opposite of hope is despair, and though King acknowledged the pain, the suffering, the sadness, and the difficulty of maintaining hope sometimes, he never allowed his "clients," be they congregation or fellow citizens, to sink into despair. While he never discounted how hard the struggle would be, he never publicly

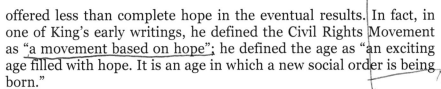

offered less than complete hope in the eventual results. In fact, in one of King's early writings, he defined the Civil Rights Movement as "a movement based on hope"; he defined the age as "an exciting age filled with hope. It is an age in which a new social order is being born."

Over and over again he delivered the same message: "We have difficult days ahead in the struggle for justice and peace, but I will not yield to a politic of despair. I'm going to maintain hope." He set about to "hew out of the mountain of despair the stone of hope,"[3] and when that stone got heavy and threatened to roll back down the mountain, his Sisyphusian effort would push it back up again. While a minister may be expected to inspire faith in his congregation, a man like King could inspire hope in the secular world as well. Long time King friend Richard Smiley said, "He became a symbol, and disenfranchised people across the world were looking at this symbol. In this symbol they saw hope." Across the world, people saw what *Jet* magazine saw when it deigned King "a symbol of divinely inspired hope."[4]

King spoke often on hope, defining its many angles for his listeners. "Genuine hope," in his definition, "involves a recognition that what is hoped for is already here. It is already present, in the sense that it is a power which drives us to fulfill that which we hope for . . . hope is a final refusal to give up. . . . It means going on *anyhow*." This is a crucial definition, for it allowed King to see the presence of hope anytime people took action, regardless of the outcome. Thus, during the Civil Rights Movement, the marchers he galvanized were able to experience hope themselves, regardless of the actual outcome of the march. Given the difficulties—indeed, the uphill battle—that they faced, it was important that King make this distinction between effort and outcome.

"Realistic hope," in another of his definitions, "is based on a

[3] Indeed, this statement itself is hewed onto the monument to King at the National Mall in Washington D.C.

[4] Because the focus of this book is on King's therapy with the soul of America, I won't discuss his inspirational effect on citizens of other countries beyond a few nods here and there, but of course he has been terribly influential to international liberation movements. His concerns were never merely national; see King, *"In a Single Garment of Destiny": A Global Vision of Justice*, edited by Lewis V. Baldwin, for an exploration of the global nature of King's leadership.

willingness to face the risk of failure and embrace an in-spite-of quality." Through this definition King taught people to say to their adversaries, in spite of how you treat me, I will still love you because I have hope. In spite of whether you beat me or not, I will not hit you back, because I have hope. Using this "in-spite-of" philosophy, King could take any situation in which despair would be a natural response, and reframe it as hopeful instead.

"Hope," as he further defined it, "is something of the tension between present and future." Hope allows us to keep acting in the present because we have the hope of changing the future. This is good therapeutics; psychologist Karen Horney advised that "the analyst must realize and explicitly convey to the patient that his situation is hopeless only so long as the status quo persists and is regarded as unchangeable." What King did so brilliantly was to repeat over and over again that the status quo *was* changing and would continue to change if people only hoped and turned that hope into action. For King, the collective nature of action was crucial, for hope, in another definition, "always has a 'we' quality. And this is why hope is always contagious."

Despair, too, is contagious. King believed that so many people were drawn to the Nation of Islam and the Black Power movement out of their own despair and demoralization, and King offered the best tonic for both: the restoration of hope.

Recall from the last chapter Maya Angelou's story of hearing King speak in the Harlem church in 1960. Angelou summarized what King conveyed to the audience that night.

 We, the black people, the most displaced, the poorest, the most maligned and scourged, we had the glorious task of reclaiming the soul and saving the honor of the country. We, the most hated, must take hate into our hands and by the miracle of love, turn loathing into love. We, the most feared and apprehensive, must take fear and by love, change it into hope.

Angelou and her friend were buoyant with hope that they decided to join the movement immediately.

Angelou's anecdote allows us to see three aspects of the power of King's hope: first, how contagious King's hope was; second, how his hope led others to an experience of it for themselves; and third, how it inspired people to do something with their hope, moving them not just to *feel* but to *act*. One of the problems inherent in a lack of hope is demoralization, and demoralization can lead to depression, one quality of which is the inability to act. And this was what King was able to do—to release people from some degree of their demoralization, and free them psychologically to take action that could transform the very situation that was causing their demoralization in the first place. And he was able to do so without disregarding their feelings of depression, or minimizing their very real problems and concerns.

Reflecting back on that time, Angelou wrote, "Martin King had been a hero and a leader to me since the time when Godfrey and I heard him speak and had been carried to glory on his wings of hope." On those wings of hope an entire era soared. Angelou described the time.

> The period was absolutely intoxicating. The streets were filled with people who were on their toes, figuratively, with alertness. There was a promise in the air, like a delicious aroma of a wonderful soup being cooked in the kitchen on a cold day when you are hungry. It really appeared as if we were going to overcome racism, sexism, violence, hate. So while it was strident, it was hopeful and it was as if there was a heaven in the air. It was a wonderful time.

The time period she refers to is the late 1950's through the early 1960's. However, there was a shift in the middle to late 1960's, and the Civil Rights Movement changed, shifting its attention away from an exclusive focus on the South to the problems occurring in the North. King realized the period of time between 1954 and 1965 offered some legislative and judicial victories, particularly in the South, but it didn't do much to change the lives of million of black Americans living in the Northern ghettos. He feared that some of the changes made were surface changes rather than substantive changes, and he admitted, "We raised the hopes tremendously but... we were not able to really produce the dreams and the results inherent in that hope. We as leaders lifted the hope. We had to do it. It was a fine thing to do. But we were not able to produce," and as a result, some responded with "deep despair and deep frustration and the deep sense of alienation." In Angelou's analysis, "I think that it was a hope that died aborning."

King tried to restore hope again by suggesting that all

movements go in cycles, that it was natural to take some steps backward after a large step forward, and that the psyche sometimes responds to uncomfortable changes by a stubborn re-entrenchment in the status quo. Still, King noted, "Hope is the final refusal to give up," and he declared, "I can't lose hope. I can't lose hope because when you lose hope, you die." So instead of losing hope, he offered this: "The only healthy answer lies in one's honest recognition of disappointment even as he still clings to hope, one's acceptance of finite disappointment even while clinging to infinite hope." King himself fell victim to disappointment and depression during this same time period—we'll explore this more in Chapter 7.

King acknowledged that he made some mistakes and missteps, that he might have raised the hope index too high without being able to fulfill on the promise. Still hope was one of the greatest spiritual gifts of grace he offered the country—in word, deed, and experience. James Cone thought it was his greatest contribution during the Movement.

> Martin King's greatest contribution was his ability to communicate a vision of hope in extreme situations of oppression. No matter how difficult the struggle for justice became, no matter how powerful were the opponents of justice, no matter how many persons turned against him, King refused absolutely to lose hope, because he believed that ultimately right would triumph over wrong. He spoke of this hope to the masses throughout the world, inspiring them to keep on struggling for freedom and justice even though the odds were against them.

Love

The third spiritual grace and the last of the three loaves of bread King wished to offer his country at midnight was love, and as the Bible verse says, "And now these three remain [faith, hope, and love]. But the greatest of these is love."

For King, the value he embraced above all others was love, agreeing with the apostle Paul that it is "the greatest of all virtues." He lavished praises upon love, calling it "the most durable power in the world" and "the highest good" and "the *summon bonum* of life"; he called it "the only absolute" and "the key that unlocks the door which leads to ultimate reality." He not only wanted to move "the ethics of love to the center of our lives," he wanted to put love at the center of the Civil Rights Movement itself: "Love *must* be at the forefront of our movement if it is to be a successful movement." And he was not afraid to declare his own love for humanity. In one sermon, he said, "As I look into your eyes, and into the eyes of all of my brothers in Alabama and all over America and all over the world, I say to you, 'I love you. I would rather die than hate you.'" It is of little wonder then, with such an emphasis on the value of love, that writer bell hooks would come to call King "a prophet of love."

Not only did King verbalize the value of love and express his love, but he also embodied it in his actions. As Gandhi said, "A coward is incapable of exhibiting love; it is the prerogative of the brave." King made it clear that everyone should interpret the courageousness of his actions as the exhibition of love. During the Albany movement, he spoke these words at a rally:

> You hear it said some of us are agitators. I am here because there are twenty million Negroes in the United States and I love every one of them. I am concerned about every one of them. What happens to any one of them concerns all directly. I am here because I love the white man. Until the Negro gets free, white men will not be free. I am here because I love America.

In a very radical way, he did not divorce social activism and politics from love, but in fact, believed that love should inform *all* social activism and politics. He preached to America,

> but even more, Americans, you may give your goods to feed the poor. You may give great gifts to charity. You may tower high in philanthropy. But if you have not love it means nothing. You may even give your body to be burned, and die the death of a martyr. Your spilt blood may be a symbol of honor for generations yet unborn, and thousands may praise you as history's supreme hero. But even so, if you have not love your blood was spilt in vain.

He called for leaders who were "not in love with money, but in love with justice. Not leaders in love with publicity, but in love with humanity." He called for *everyone* to fall in love with humanity: "this call for a world-wide fellowship that lifts neighborly concern beyond one's tribe, race, class and nation is in reality a call for an all-embracing and unconditional love for all men."

For a man to speak so boldly and so unabashedly on behalf of love indeed does require some bravery. Our culture is uncomfortable with love, author Diane Ackerman has argued.

> As a society we are embarrassed by love. We treat it as if it were an obscenity. We reluctantly admit to it. Even saying the word makes us stumble and blush . . . Love is the most important thing in our lives, a passion for which we would fight or die, and yet we're reluctant to linger over its names. Without a supple vocabulary, we can't even talk or think about it directly.

King was well aware of the lack of "supple vocabulary" when speaking about love; thus, he was always careful to define his terms, explaining that when he called for love to be raised into the social and political domain, he meant the "creative, redemptive sort of love." Not sure his audience would understand what he meant by this description, he often educated them about the many kinds of love, offering them the vocabulary they would need to think about it differently. To accomplish this purpose, he turned to the Greek language and its three terms for love: eros, philia, and agape. I quote this particular passage from his sermon "Loving Your Enemies" as representative of dozens of similar sermons and speeches on the same topic:

> The Greek language, as I've said so often before, is very powerful at this point. It comes to our aid beautifully in giving us the real meaning and depth of the whole philosophy of love. And I think it is quite apropos at this point, for you see the Greek language has three words for love, interestingly enough. It talks about love as *eros*. That's one word for love. *Eros* is a sort of aesthetic love. Plato talks about it a great deal in his dialogues, a sort of yearning of the soul for the realm of the gods. And it's come to us to be a sort of romantic love, though it's a beautiful love. Everybody has experienced *eros* in all of its beauty when you find some individual that is attractive to you and that you pour out all of your like and your love on that individual. That is *eros*, you see, and it's a powerful, beautiful love that is given to us through all of the beauty of literature; we read about it.

Then the Greek language talks about *philia*, and that's another type of love that's also beautiful. It is a sort of intimate affection between personal friends. And this is the type of love that you have for those persons that you're friendly with, your intimate friends, or people that you call on the telephone and you go by to have dinner with, and your roommate in college and that type of thing. It's a sort of reciprocal love. On this level, you like a person because that person likes you. You love on this level, because you are loved. You love on this level, because there's something about the person you love that is likeable to you. This too is a beautiful love. You can communicate with a person; you have certain things in common; you like to do things together. This is *philia*.

The Greek language comes out with another word for love. It is the word *agape*. And *agape* is more than *eros*; *agape* is more than *philia*; *agape* is something of the understanding, creative, redemptive goodwill for all men. It is a love that seeks nothing in return. It is an overflowing love; it's what theologians would call the love of God working in the lives of men. And when you rise to love on this level, you begin to love men, not because they are likeable, but because God loves them. You look at every man, and you love him because you know God loves him. And he might be the worst person you've ever seen.

Agape, King believed, was the most effective form of love to catalyze the kind of psychological transformation and healing the country needed. There were three important qualities of agape on which he focused: first, it is an imitation of the love God has for humanity; second, it is the only love that is realistic for one's enemies; and third, it is transformational and redemptive.

First, King was drawn to agape because of its unconditional nature; agape is not earned, but is given through grace. Thus, it is an imitation of the love of God and Christ for humanity, he said.

The divine love, in short, is sacrificial in its nature. This truth was symbolized . . . by the death of Christ, who, because of his unique relation to God and his moral perfection, made this truth more efficacious than any other martyr. . . . Some of life is an earned reward, a commercial transaction, *quid pro quo*, so much for so much, but that is not the major element. The major element arrives when we feel some beauty, goodness, love, truth poured out on us by the sacrifices of others beyond our merit and deserving. It is at this point that we find the unique meaning of the cross. It is a symbol of one of the most towering facts in life, the realm of grace, the sacrificial gifts bought and paid for by one who did what we had no right to ask.

Agape is precisely so powerful a love for just those reasons: it is a love we have no right to ask for, a love beyond our deserving, and a love that is freely given. God modeled that love, particularly its sacrificial nature, by offering the crucifixion of his son, and as a result King believed you were imitating God when "you love every man because God loves him." He also taught that we should love everyone because we are all made in the image of God; loving someone then becomes a way of loving God. He said, "And when you come to the point that you look in the face of every man and see deep down within him what religion calls 'the image of God,' you begin to love him in spite of—no matter what he does, you see God's image there." Agape is then both an imitation of the love of God, and a way of loving God himself.

Secondly, King believed that embracing agape was the only way to follow Jesus' commandment to love one's enemies, a commandment that King viewed as "an absolute necessity for the survival of our civilization." He preached that "Jesus was very serious when he gave this command; he wasn't playing." For King, there were two very important reasons to love one's enemy.

> Hate for hate only intensifies the existence of hate and evil in the universe. If I hit you and you hit me and I hit you back and you hit me back and go on, you see, that goes on ad infinitum. It just never ends. Somewhere somebody must have a little sense, and that's the strong person. The strong person is the person who can cut off the chain of hate, the chain of evil. . . . Somebody must have religion enough and morality enough to cut it off and inject within the very structure of the universe that strong and powerful element of love.

King knew there was nothing healing about hate, that it simply propagated and expanded the division between people.

While his first reason not to hate deals with its negative effects in the universe, his second moves into the negative effects in the individual: in his words, "hate distorts the personality of the hater."

> We usually think of what hate does for the individual hated or the individuals hated or the groups hated. But it is even more tragic, it is even more ruinous and injurious to the individual who hates. You just begin hating somebody, and you will begin to do irrational things. You can't see straight when you hate. You can't strand upright. Your vision is distorted. There is nothing more tragic than to see an individual whose heart is filled with hate.

If the hatred doesn't cease, King warned, that individual "becomes a pathological case" and the hate will destroy "the very structure of the personality of the hater." He constantly denounced hate.

> Never hate, because it ends up in tragic, neurotic responses. Psychologists and psychiatrists are telling us today that the more we hate, the more we develop guilt feelings and we begin to subconsciously repress or consciously suppress certain emotions, and they all stack up in our subconscious selves and make for tragic, neurotic responses. And may this not be the neuroses of many individuals as they confront life that there is an element of hate there. And modern psychology is calling on us now to love.

But even before modern psychologists began calling on us to love, King noted that "the world's greatest psychologist"—Jesus— taught the same thing in his commandment to love our enemies.

King also acknowledged the obvious: that loving one's enemies is extremely difficult for most people, that "many would go so far as to say it just isn't possible to move out into the practice of this glorious command." And this is why he turned to agape, because it offered a distinction between loving and liking that was absolutely crucial.

> And it's significant that he [Jesus] does not say, "Like your enemy." Like is a sentimental something, an affectionate

something. There are a lot of people that I find it difficult to like. I don't like what they do to me. I don't like what they say about me and other people. I don't like their attitudes. I don't like some of the things they're doing. I don't like them. But Jesus says love them. And love is greater than like. Love is understanding, redemptive goodwill for all men, so that you love everybody, because God loves them. You refuse to do anything that will defeat an individual, because you have *agape* in your soul.

Besides allowing people to love someone without having to like them, King also found agape useful for making another distinction: that of hating the sin while loving the sinner. With agape, "You come to the point that you love the individual who does the evil deed, while hating the deed that the person does." In this way, agape allowed black people to dislike certain white people and hate acts of segregation and discrimination while still holding love for the white race. In turn, he felt strongly that love was crucial to the redemption of those very white people that black people disliked, and the transformation of those very acts they hated. And this is the third reason for loving your enemies, that "there is a power there that eventually transforms individuals. . . . If you love your enemies, you will discover that at the very root of love is the power of redemption."

King did not make much of a distinction between transformation and redemption, for in his mind, transformation was redemptive, and redemption was transformative, and both transformation and redemption were made possible by the catalytic effects of love. He said, "And I'm foolish enough to believe that through the power of this love somewhere, men of the most recalcitrant bent will be transformed. And then we will be in God's kingdom." This illustrates love at its most powerful: not only can it transform the individual who loves and the individual who is loved, but also an entire community. He spoke unequivocally about this power: "I believe firmly that love is a transforming power that can lift a whole community to new horizons of fair play, good will and justice." For that reason, he wanted love at the center of the Civil Rights Movement; in his words, "the only way to ultimately change humanity and make for the society that we all long for is to keep love at the center of our lives."

King did this, kept love at the center by making love so central to his speeches, sermons, writings, and all his actions in the Movement, and combining love with faith and hope as his primary spiritual and therapeutic gifts of grace. He believed these three gifts, which he symbolized as loaves of bread for the poor and hungry, would offer both sustenance and deliverance from the darkness of the social, psychological, and moral order. He also offered the fourth of Jung's psychotherapeutic graces through his emphasis on understanding.

Understanding

The fourth and final spiritual grace was called understanding in Jung's essay, but it is used synonymously with meaning. Jung stated simply, "The soul longs to discover its meaning." This is a basic human need, a hunger: "In the same way the body needs food, and not just any kind of food but only that which suits it, the psyche needs to know the meaning of its existence." Jung believed that we can survive any "what" if we have a "why." One role of the therapist, then, is to help his or her clients to understand their why, the meaning of their lives and their suffering.

In this, too, King was masterful. He provided a noble purpose to the civil rights struggle; he gave it the most powerful of meanings. And he did so in several different ways, a varied approach that was sure to strike the chords of meaning and make everyone feel instrumental by giving them a "why" which appealed to their particular temperament.

One of the early ways King achieved this was by taking the key strategies of the Civil Rights Movement—love, suffering, and nonviolence—and elevating them to powers that could save the world. Regarding love, he preached that "it is love that will save our world and our civilization, love even for enemies." He urged, "We must discover the power of love, the power, the redemptive power of love. And when we discover that, we will be able to make of this old world a new world." Regarding suffering, King called for his supporters to see it as a virtue because "to suffer in a righteous cause is to grow to our humanity's full stature." Suffering offered a person "the opportunity to transfigure himself and American society." Regarding nonviolence, King said over and over again that "the choice is no longer between violence and nonviolence; it is either nonviolence or nonexistence." Nonviolence was meaningful not just to America, but to the whole world: "By following this method, we may also be able to teach our world something that it so desperately needs at this hour."

This was the second way King helped people understand the struggle, by connecting it to a worldwide movement. He acknowledged that in one sense, the Civil Rights Movement was "a special American phenomenon which must be understood in the light of American history and be dealt with in terms of the American situation," but, he added, "On another and more important level, what is happening in the United States today is a significant part of a world development." He called the era "a major turning point in history," one "of offensive on the part of oppressed people. All peoples deprived of dignity and freedom [are marching] on every continent throughout the world." Consciously or unconsciously, black Americans had "been caught up by the spirit of the times, and with his black brothers of Africa and his brown and yellow brothers in Asia, South America and the Caribbean," were moving toward the promised land of freedom. During one speech, King called upon his listeners "not to be detached spectators, but involved participants, in this great drama that is taking place in our nation and around the world," a drama he called "the widest liberation movement in history." King often traveled to other countries and came back with reports of how people there were inspired by what was happening in the United States, adding credence to his message. So did being awarded the 1964 Nobel Peace Prize, which he believed was recognition that the black struggle in the United States was both part of a worldwide struggle and served an exemplary leadership role in that struggle.

King was astute in helping black citizens to understand their unique role in transforming the South, the United States, and the world. King framed the time period as "a great hour for the Negro. The challenge is here. To become the instruments of a great idea is a privilege that history gives only occasionally." He continued: "Arnold Toynbee says in *A Study of History* that it may be the Negro who will give the new spiritual dynamic to Western civilization that it so desperately needs to survive." In fact, he wrote that "the Negro may be God's appeal to this age, an age drifting rapidly to its doom." King repeated these ideas time and again, especially in the early years of the Movement—that black Americans were God's chosen people with spiritual power and a spiritual mission to transform an epoch and to save the world.

The third way King added meaning to the movement was by connecting its participants to great people throughout history who had also struggled for a righteous cause. They could be like the biblical prophet Amos, he told them, crying out for justice and righteousness. They could be like Abraham Lincoln, working for his vision of a united country. They could be like Jesus, loving his enemies and willingly sacrificing himself for their redemption. They could be like Thomas Jefferson, dedicating his life to the realization of great principles. They could be like the apostle Paul, giving up his life to spread the good word of "a higher and more noble order." And in this struggle, they were connected in cosmic companionship with the highest force of all—God.

For those not convinced by spiritual arguments, he offered them a more civic meaning and understanding. He wrote, "History has thrust upon our generation an indescribably important destiny—to complete a process of democratization which our nation has too long developed too slowly." He reminded people, "We are here in the general sense because first and foremost we are American citizens and we are determined to apply our citizenship to the fullness of its meaning. We are also here because of our love for democracy." He assured them, "We will win our freedom because the sacred heritage of our nation and the eternal will of God are embodied in our echoing demands." In combining God's will with American civic democracy, he echoed back to the founding of the nation by its first white citizens who believed that God had called them to create a great "city on a hill" to shine as a beacon of light for all the world. This struggle was no less than the fulfillment of that first dream.

Not only was the American dream at stake, but also America's reputation in the world. King called democracy "our most powerful weapon for world respect and emulation" and he ennobled the Civil Rights Movement with multiple meanings when he stated, "How we deal with this crucial situation will determine our moral health as individuals, our cultural health as a region, our political health as a nation, and our prestige as a leader of the free world. The future of America is bound up with the solution of the present crisis."

As if all this were not meaning and purpose enough to help the Civil Rights Movement's participants to understand and appreciate their special role in history, King added one more layer. When black participants were criticized as being self-serving and power-grabbing during the movement, King quelled that criticism.

There comes a time when we move from protest to

reconciliation and we have been misinterpreted by the press and by the political leaders of this town as to our motives and our goals, but let me say once again that it is our purpose, our single purpose to create the beloved community. We seek only to make possible a city where men can live together as brothers.

As we will explore in detail in Chapter 7, the beloved community was King's vision for the truly integrated society.

Conclusion

While King also made it clear that participating in the Civil Rights Movement could provide personal meaning and purpose to each individual, aiding in his or her own transformation and self-realization, he was at his most brilliant in providing people with a larger understanding of and context for the struggle. If Jung was right that people can survive any "what" if they have a "why," King gave plenty of whys, including the biggest whys of all: to save America, to save the world, and to create God's kingdom on earth. Though it might seem inflated for one man to claim so much on behalf of one Movement, King was completely sincere. Not only did he believe it himself and dedicate his life to the actualization of his belief, but he also called upon people from all over America and the world to experience this transformation for themselves. He combined his understanding of the meaningful role of the Movement with faith, hope, and love, believing along with Jung that these "the four great gifts of grace" could heal the suffering of individuals and liberate the dis-integrated soul of humanity.

3

TEACHINGS:

"DEAR DR. KING": KING'S STINT AS AN ADVICE COLUMNIST

In the last chapter we explored how King as a minister and Jung as a therapist found ways to bring the two professions together, with Jung shepherding clients through their spiritual crises and King shepherding both church and country through their psychological crises. Both men also briefly took on the writing roles of the other's profession: Jung once wrote a lengthy sermon titled "Seven Sermons to the Dead" ("VII Sermones ad Mortuos") and King once wrote an advice column. We turn to that advice column in this chapter, and several of King's more psychological sermons in the next, but before we do so, it's important to briefly examine King's background and education in psychology, his "credentials," so to speak, as a lay psychologist.

King's Psychological Credentials

First, though it is difficult to know the exact degree of King's study of psychology in general, and depth psychology in particular, we can learn much from studying his college transcripts and papers, as well as his references to psychology sprinkled throughout his sermons and speeches. He took his first college psychology course in the 1945-1946 school year during his second year at Morehouse College: "General Psychology" from Joseph L. Whiting, for which he received a "C." The following semester, he took "Educational Psychology" from the same professor and received the same grade. In 1946-1947, he took "Social Psychology" from Walter R. Chivers and received a "B." He also took classes in sociology and philosophy where he might have bumped into psychological thinkers.

Perhaps the most interesting reference to depth psychology from that time comes from a paper King wrote for George Davis's class, "Religious Development of Personality." There King reviewed a book called *Personality, Its Study and Hygiene* by Winifred V. Richmond. He wrote of the greatest impression the book made on him: "the deeper insight it gave me into the psychological theories that I heretofore scorned."

> This was the first time that I was able to read the psychologies of Freud and John Watson with a degree of objectivity. I had read Joshua Liebman's *Peace of Mind*, and even he was unable to convince me that there was any truth in Freud. But now I am convinced. It is probably true that the basic facts of Freud and Watson are correct, notwithstanding the fact that their bias had conditioned what they observed. I am now willing to admit that they discovered new continents and new areas that had for centuries been overlooked. No one can observe human personality objectively without admitting the truth of many Freudian and Watsonian theories.

King continued, "Jung and Adler were given quite a bit of attention in Richmond's book, but it so happens that I have always had certain predilections for their theories over against those of Freud and Watson." He ended by raising some questions about the possibility of psychology as an objective science, given that there were at least four different schools of modern psychology, and that even within those schools, there were differences: "For instance, Adler, Jung and Freud have totally different approaches to psychoanalysis, albeit they are within the same school. May we not conclude that we have a long way to go in this whole area of the psychological analysis of personality development?" This paper shows that not only did King study psychology, but he studied enough of it to offer some elementary criticism.

After Morehouse, King decided to enter the ministry, and chose Crozer Theological Seminary to continue his studies. King was not comfortable with a fundamentalist approach to Christianity and the Bible, and felt quite at home with Crozer's liberal bent. It is a particular approach of depth psychology to see the Bible as mythology, rich with archetypes and living symbolism (something we'll explore more in Chapter 8); you can see the same approach in the papers King wrote during that time. He asserted that many things from the Bible must be seen as "merely mythological" and called the stories therein "one of the most logical vehicles of mankind's deepest devotional thoughts and aspirations, couched in language which still retains its original vigour and its moral intensity." He also showed his interest in the psychology of religion during these years, writing one paper called "The Sources of Fundamentalism and Liberalism Considered Historically and Psychologically." In other papers he interpreted events in the Bible from a psychological angle, such as the fall from innocence and the divinity of Jesus. Of the former, he wrote in one paper called "The Place of Reason and Experience in Finding God," "It seems more reasonable to hold that the fall of man is psychological rather than historical."

Finally, King entered Boston University in 1951 to pursue his doctorate in systemic theology, an approach to Christianity which involves collecting and understanding all the relevant passages in the Bible on various topics, then summarizing their teachings in order to know what to believe about each topic. While at BU, King fully embraced the philosophy of Personalism, which asserts that the clue to the ultimate reality is found in personality. Though Personalism is a philosophy, even in that short description, we can see how much it overlaps with psychology.

Professor Edgar S. Brightman was one of King's most profound influences in his study of Personalism. Brightman taught that change is necessary, and it is the nature of personality to grow and develop: "Personalism affirms that human nature in some respects is capable of 'infinite progress.'" Brightman taught, "Human nature is no definite substantial entity but a process and a 'voyage of discovery.'" Personalism also teaches that each person seeks his or her own individual relationship with God, and that relationship is immediate and experiential and does not need to be mediated by a church, a depth psychological approach which echoes in the works of Jung and more recently Lionel Corbett in his seminal work *The Religious Function of the Psyche*. Finally, Personalism teaches that the personal and social aspects of life are intimately and inextricably connected and that an individual develops into an integrated personality only through social interaction with others, another idea echoed everywhere in depth psychology.

King made use of the knowledge he had gained in psychology throughout his career as both minister and civil rights activist. References to psychologists are sprinkled throughout his sermons and speeches. He often referred to Sigmund Freud, considered by many to be the father of depth psychology.

Many of our abnormal fears can be dealt with by the skills of psychiatry, a relatively new discipline pioneered by Sigmund Freud, which investigates the subconscious drives of men and seeks to discover how and why fundamental energies are diverted into neurotic channels. Psychiatry helps us to look candidly at our inner selves and to search out the causes of our failures and fears.

King was strongly influenced by Freud's description of the psyche as consisting of id, ego, and superego, and he referred to these concepts often in his sermons. In a classic example, he would refer to the tension between good and evil in the world as the Freudian tension between the id (the seat of our base physical instincts) and the superego (the seat of our ethics and ideals).

In one of his college papers quoted above, King mentioned his predilection for the work of Alfred Adler, one of Freud's peers in early 20ᵗʰ century Vienna. He mentioned Adler directly in his sermon "The Drum Major Instinct." King defined this instinct as "a desire to be out front, a desire to lead the parade, a desire to be first." He argued that we all have the drum major instinct to some extent.

We all want to be important, to surpass others, to achieve distinction, to lead the parade. Alfred Adler, the great psychoanalyst, contends that this is the dominant impulse. Sigmund Freud used to contend that sex was the dominant impulse, and Adler came with a new argument saying that this quest for recognition, this desire for attention, this desire for distinction is the basic impulse, the basic drive of human life.

From Adler, King seems to have been highly influenced by the power instinct (he was also very intrigued by Nietzsche's "will to power"), as well as Adler's concept of *Gemeinschaftsgefuhl*, or community feeling, which pervades all of King's work.

Another psychologist King referenced is Erich Fromm, a German-born psychologist who moved to the United States in 1934. Fromm was very popular during the 1940's and 1950's, especially well known for his best-selling book, *The Art of Loving*. King made one of his typical references to Fromm when he stated:

Hate is injurious to the hater as well as the hated. Many of the psychiatrists are telling us now that many of the strange things that happen in the subconscious and many of the inner conflicts are rooted in hate and so they are now saying "love or perish." Erich Fromm can write a book like *The Art of Loving* and make it very clear that love is the supreme unifying principle of life.

Fromm was also recognized for his work applying psychological analysis to groups, societies, and nations, something that clearly influenced King in his therapeutic work with his country.

King also referred to one of Fromm's intimates, another German-born U.S. émigré, psychoanalyst Karen Horney. In one sermon he said, "Especially common in our highly competitive society are economic fears, from which, Karen Horney says, come most of the psychological problems of our age." King seems to have taken from both Horney and Fromm the idea that a culture itself can be neurotic and in turn pass that neurosis on to its members, something we'll explore in Chapter 5 when we consider the diagnosis of American society as neurotic, and explore how King attempted to heal that neurosis.

In addition to frequent references to well-known psychoanalysts, King often peppered his sermons and speeches with psychological language. We'll see many more examples of this in the chapters to come, so I'll just offer a few here. He was fond of criticizing psychology's emphasis on adjustment.

There are certain technical words in the vocabulary of every academic discipline which tend to become stereotypes and clichés. Psychologists have a word which is probably used more frequently than any other word in modern psychology. It is the word "maladjusted." This word is the ringing cry of the new child psychology.

But, King maintained, adjustment is overrated, particularly when one is adjusting to an unhealthy system. For that reason, he advocated maladjustment instead. "Well, there are some things in our social system to which I am proud to be maladjusted and to which I suggest that we ought to be maladjusted." His argument here sounds very similar to archetypal psychology's founder James Hillman, a staunch critic of psychology, particularly in his book coauthored with Michael Ventura titled *We've had 100 Years of Psychotherapy and the World's Getting Worse.*

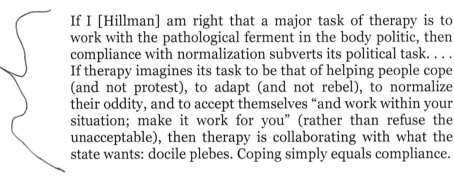

> If I [Hillman] am right that a major task of therapy is to work with the pathological ferment in the body politic, then compliance with normalization subverts its political task. . . . If therapy imagines its task to be that of helping people cope (and not protest), to adapt (and not rebel), to normalize their oddity, and to accept themselves "and work within your situation; make it work for you" (rather than refuse the unacceptable), then therapy is collaborating with what the state wants: docile plebes. Coping simply equals compliance.

Both King and Hillman argued that it is important for the citizen to stay maladapted to dysfunction in the social realm in order to have the energy to transform that dysfunction.

King was well versed in the psychological defense mechanisms such as repression, suppression, sublimation, and rationalization, and he often explained history and current events in light of those terms. King knew that black people were repressing a great deal of hostility over their current treatment, and he knew this repression could be dangerous.

> If his repressed emotions are not released in nonviolent ways, they will seek expression through violence; this is not a threat but a fact of history. So I have not said to my people: "Get rid of your discontent." Rather, I have tried to say that this normal and healthy discontent can be channeled into the creative outlet of nonviolent direct action.

In fact, King saw his nonviolent marches as a crucial way to sublimate that rage into a healthier expression. And when those efforts were not productive, King reasoned that it was natural for black people to use riots as a method to release the rage. After a particularly difficult period of rioting, King explained, "Everyone underestimated the amount of violence and rage Negroes were suppressing and the amount of bigotry the white majority was disguising."

Rationalization was another defense mechanism King found useful to explain human behavior.

With the growth of slavery it became necessary to give some defense for it. It seems to be a fact of life that human beings cannot continue to do wrong without eventually reaching out for some rationalization and to cover up an obvious wrong with the beautiful garments of righteousness. William James, a psychologist, used to talk a great deal about the stream of consciousness. And he said one of the uniquenesses of human nature is that man has the capacity and the ability to temporarily block the stream of consciousness and inject anything in it that he wants to. And so man has the unique and tragic power of justifying the rightness of the wrong. *RATIONALIZATION*

But rationalization of racism was not confined to slavery. King also discussed how white people made use of the defense mechanism to justify segregation: "They rationalized—insisting that the unfortunate Negro, being less than human, deserved and even enjoyed second-class status."

Many more connections could be made here, but they would all serve to illustrate the same points—that King was psychologically aware and astute, and that he freely drew from the language of psychology, particularly from the tradition of depth psychology, in his speeches and sermons. Reverend C. T. Vivian, a man who worked closely with King during the Civil Rights Movement, noted of King, "His depth was the thing that was beyond what we had been accustomed to in the nonviolent activities and actions of which I had formerly been a part. Because Martin understood at a whole depth level that we had not dealt with." King was a man who wanted to practice what he preached, and if what he preached was in large part psychological, what he practiced was also in large part psychological.

King was inclined toward teaching, and we can see in his preaching and in his public speaking how much teaching he actually did, and not just theology, but psychology as well. Another venue for teaching came in the form of an advice column.

King as the Country's Advice Columnist

From August 1957 until December 1958, while he was living in Montgomery and working as pastor of his first church, King wrote a monthly advice column for *Ebony*, a popular magazine targeted to a black audience. In *The Papers of Martin Luther King, Jr., Volume 4* where the columns are collected, the editors note that while it is unclear how the arrangements were made for this column, it may be that Lerone Bennett, Jr., a former Morehouse graduate and associate editor at *Ebony*, was the one to interest King in the column; he definitely facilitated the work by mailing the questions to King in Montgomery. An advertisement for the column appeared in *Ebony's* sister publication, *Jet*, advising readers to send family or religious problems to King, to "let the man that led the Montgomery boycott lead you into happier living." In addition to the advice column, King was planning to write an opinion column for *Ebony* starting in early 1959, but doctors advised him to limit his commitments after a mentally ill black woman stabbed him in the fall of 1958. His December advice column, completed shortly after his convalescence, was to be his last contribution.

Categories of Questions

For seventeen months, King answered a total of eighty-eight questions, five to six a month, sent to him from a variety of readers: black and white, Christian and non-Christian, men and women and children. On average, two or three of those questions would be on race, one or two would be on religion, one or two would be on relationships, and others were on social, philosophical, and political issues. The examples that follow illustrate not only the range of issues upon which King felt comfortable offering advice, but his psychological astuteness and assuredness for a young man of only twenty-eight.

Race

King said nothing new in most of his responses to questions on race, but rather reiterated points he made throughout his life in speeches and sermons all over the world, points such as the importance of forgiving those who discriminate against you, of overcoming a sense of apathy and inferiority in order to take an active part in the struggle against racial injustice, and of the necessity for black self-help and determination.

Several of the questions he was asked addressed the white Christian habit of using the Bible to justify segregation and discrimination. "Does the Bible really say that . . .?" people often asked, and King would assure them that no, it did not.

One interesting question on race was "Why did God make Jesus white, when the majority of peoples in this world are non-white?"

King responded in typical fashion that the color of Jesus' skin made no difference—it was not "His external biological make-up" but "His internal spiritual commitment" that made him significant. "He would have been no more significant if His skin had been black. He is no less significant because His skin was white." King received a follow-up letter from a reader who was "disturbed" by King's assumption that Jesus was white, asking him for the basis of that assumption. King did not reply.

Religion

In addition to the inquiries into the Bible's position on racial issues, King was often asked questions that concerned differences between religions and denominations. A reader who had attended the Methodist Church, the Baptist Church, the Church of Christ, and the Church of God in Christ, and who had talked to Jehovah's Witnesses, wrote about his or her concern that all denominations think they are right, that theirs is the only way to salvation. "Is there a one and only way to God?" King was asked. He answered with an emphatic "NO." God "is bigger than all of our religious denominations" and "the boundless sweep of God's revelation can never be limited to any particular church." Though there isn't uniformity between religions, there should be unity, he opined.

However, King sounded more judgmental and ecumenical when he was asked if Christianity was more valid than their ancestors' African tribal religions. King shared his belief that though God reveals himself in all religions, he doesn't necessarily reveal himself *equally* in all religions. "Christianity," he wrote, "is an expression of the highest revelation of God. It is the synthesis of the best in all religions" and in that sense, it is "more valid than the tribal religions practiced by our African ancestors." Christianity, he further explained, "has incorporated the truths of all other religions and brought them together into a meaningful and coherent system," and Christ, at the center of that religion, "is now and ever shall be the highest revelation of God."

Relationships

As an advice columnist, King fielded questions on relationship problems such as nosy in-laws, errant children, and spousal strife. His typical response suggested three lines of attack: first, rigorous self-analysis to see where one might have contributed to the problem; second, an honest talk with the problematic in-law/child/spouse; and third, if necessary, the intervention of a secular or religious counselor. Each of these will be discussed in the last part of this chapter when we look at King's eight approaches to problem solving.

Social Situation Inquiries

Questions about how to deal with social situations are typical advice column fare, and King received his fair share of these. When the deacon of a church asked a question about the appropriateness of attending cocktail parties, King replied that while it was fine to attend these parties, it was also possible to attend and not drink. He wrote, "This is an individual choice which one must make himself." It is unclear if that choice referred to whether to attend or not attend the party, or whether to drink or not drink while there. Since King was a man who enjoyed his whiskey, it may be fair to infer the latter.

One woman wrote in complaining about the shallowness of her social set, where "the husbands are interested in nothing but Scotch, sports cars and girlie magazines, and the wives do nothing but gossip, drink gin and buy clothes." She wanted to know if King thought she was snobbish for believing there were more important things in life. King did not, and assured her, "You are simply responding to the highest and best in your being. . . . giving your life to better spiritual and creative principles," while at the same time he subtlety admonished her against believing she was intrinsically better than those people around her.

Philosophical Inquiries

King was asked philosophical questions on issues such as the efficacy of nonviolence, passive resistance, and changing prejudices by changing laws, issues he commonly addressed in his speeches and sermons. However, one question allowed him to veer away from oft-addressed themes: it was "Why do people suffer?" He offered three reasons. First, he simply stated, we have all committed sins, consciously or unconsciously. Second, he noted that because of our interconnectedness, sometimes we suffer for the sins of others. Third, he shrugged his shoulders and admitted that sometimes it's just a mystery why we are victims of pain and suffering. Regardless of the reason, he said we must live by the faith "that all suffering has some purpose which the finite mind of man can never comprehend."

Political Inquiries

Many of the political inquires King received dealt with issues of discrimination. One was written by a GI in an army camp in Alabama, embittered by the town's treatment of black GI's who weren't allowed to go anywhere with their white buddies. He wanted to know how to justify fighting for a democracy that treated him like this. King sympathized with him, but told him, "You must believe, however, that conditions will continue to improve" and counseled him to resist bitterness, because otherwise "the new order which is emerging in America will be nothing but a duplication of the old order."

Another reader wrote in wondering why even in towns where it was safe to do so, black people failed to register to vote. King addressed the indifferent and apathetic attitude of many black citizens by first explaining its probable causes. However, regardless of cause, those attitudes "are unfounded and unfortunate," and King challenged black Americans to become part of the solution, rather than furthering the problem, by exercising their political and democratic rights.

Social and Ethical Issues

King was asked questions and gave answers to many of the predominant social and ethical issues of his time. Though some of these issues were addressed in other places in King's writings and public speaking, many of them appear for the first time, and perhaps for the only time, in this short-lived advice column format.

Alcoholism

Progressive scientific and psychological thinking during King's era was starting to disseminate the theory that alcoholism was a physical disease, rather than a moral failing. Two questions written to King allowed him to display his current knowledge in this area. A woman had an alcoholic husband and wanted to know if there was anything she could do to help him. King began by writing, "The person who becomes an alcoholic is victimized with a real sickness. The Yale studies on alcohol reveal that the alcoholic has a disease which is as serious as any other organic disease. Consequently, the alcoholic is in need of sympathy and understanding rather than scorn." He likened alcoholism to tuberculosis, and suggested that the woman try to help him cure his disease. He suggested meeting with their clergyman and joining Alcoholics Anonymous, as well as talking with her husband and convincing him that his drinking was harming himself and his family. Finally, she should tell her husband that he could only be helped if he was willing to help himself. She shared that her husband was physically abusing her; King offered sympathy and yet suggested she stay with him a little longer with the hope of contributing to her husband's "rediscovery" of himself.

In the second letter dealing with alcoholism, King counseled an 18-year-old high school boy whose father was a drunk not to run away to another town in shame over his father's actions, but again, to help direct him to AA and his minister's help. King wrote, "You have youth, health and strength—and I hope love—on your side. So you can afford to be patient with your father and help him out of this abyss that he is too weak to rise from without outside help." While King showed his progressive side in his understanding of the disease model of alcoholism, both of his responses today could justifiably be criticized for fostering co-dependency.

Homosexuality

King was also in line with the current thinking of his time on the issue of homosexuality, which during the 1950's and 1960's was considered a moral failing or psychological disorder resulting from early childhood family dysfunction. It wasn't until the mid-70's when the psychological community took homosexuality off its list of pathologies and replaced it with homophobia instead.

When a boy wrote that he had feelings for other boys, King replied that homosexuality, while not uncommon, "is probably not an innate tendency, but something that has been culturally acquired." He called it a "habit" some adopt for reasons "consciously suppressed or unconsciously repressed." Therefore, he suggested the boy see a good psychiatrist who could lead him back to the past to uncover the experiences and circumstances at the root of his disorder. This is a particularly psychological response from a minister who might have labeled homosexuality a religious sin.

Birth Control

Though the birth control pill was several years away from being introduced in the United States, Planned Parenthood had been around since 1942, and other methods of birth control have existed for as long as women have been having babies. King received a letter from a woman in Harlem who lived in a four-room apartment with her husband, seven children, and another one on the way. She had suggested birth control to her husband, but he told her, "When God thinks we have enough children, He will put a stop to it." Her husband called birth control a sin, and she wanted to know if he was right.

King sided with the woman. He wrote, "It is a serious mistake to suppose that it is a religious act to allow nature to have its way in the sex life," and that natural order was given to us "as something to be guided and controlled." He also noted that social and economic conditions make smaller families desirable and even necessary, and he added that women "must be considered as more than 'breeding machines.'" For these reasons, he deemed birth control "rationally and morally justifiable."

Interracial Marriage

During King's time, there were still laws on the books in many states against interracial marriage. Often the Bible was used as justification for these laws, and a reader wrote in and asked King where such passages could be found. King replied that there were none, and therefore, there was nothing "immoral or irreligious" about such marriages. He noted, "Marriage is at bottom a mutual agreement between two individuals. . . . individuals marry, not races."

A black woman in love with a white man asked if she should go ahead and marry the man over her parents' objections. King's reply again was that individuals marry, not races, and there was nothing morally wrong with interracial marriage. However, he offered a realistic admission that obstacles would be placed in their way by a disapproving society, but he shared that studies revealed that couples who had a thorough understanding of the existing social prejudice could marry and live quite happily.

The Death Penalty

Legally, the death penalty was sanctioned in the United States, but when King was asked if he thought God approved of death for rapists and murderers, he replied that he didn't think God approved of it for any crime. Modern criminology called reformation the purpose of imprisonment rather than punishment, he noted, and the death penalty did not allow for the former, and was the harshest form of the latter. Moreover, King believed God was not a resentful God, but was concerned with improving people by bringing them to conversion, a process the death penalty could truncate.

Gambling

King received one letter from a woman concerned about her husband who bet on horses. His justification—it was legally right. Her argument—it was morally wrong. King agreed with both of them. His argued that gambling was morally wrong "based on the principle of taking from society without giving anything in return. It is really getting something for nothing." He also pointed to the breakdown in the structure of social life and in the decaying moral principles of society where gambling is present.

Nuclear Weapons

Of course, as an unrelenting pacifist, King spoke out strongly against nuclear weapons development, testing, or usage of any kind, and his answers to two questions on the subject are emphatic on this point. Not only that, but he expressed in both letters that "the principal objective of all nations must be the total abolition of war, and a definite move toward disarmament."

Rock and Roll Music

The 1950's were the decade marking the boom in popularity of rock and roll music. A 17-year-old musician who belonged to the church wrote in and asked King, "I play gospel music and I play rock 'n' roll. Is it a sin to play rock 'n' roll music for a living?" King's response was surprisingly conservative for a man who could be so liberal in his beliefs. He wrote that the two types of music are "totally incompatible," and that "the profound sacred and spiritual meaning of the great music of the church must never be mixed with the transitory quality of rock and roll music. The former serves to lift men's souls to higher levels of reality, and therefore to God; the latter so often plunges men's minds into degrading and immoral depths." He advised the young person to choose gospel, and ended by chiding him to "never seek to mix the two."

Premarital Sex

On the subject of premarital sex, King was not as rigid or moralistic. In the two letters he received from young women who felt pressure from men to have premarital sex, he did not tell them never to give in, though he did encourage them to hold to their principles. To one he wrote that the problems created by premarital sex were greater than the problems created by premarital virginity. He felt that "the suspicion, fears, and guilt feelings" brought on by premarital sex were contributing to the breakdown of the family, and he repeated the oft-stated idea that if a man really loves and respects you, he'll wait.

In an interesting twist on his answer, when a 24-year-old woman shared that she had a problem finding nice young men who wouldn't push her for sex, he began by telling her, "One of the first things that you should do in an attempt to get at your problem is to go through a process of self examination. Are you sure that you have a radiating personality, a pleasant disposition, and that feminine charm which every man admires?" If she fell short in any area, King told her she must seek to improve on them. His reason for this suggestion? Maybe sex had nothing to do with it and she couldn't find a boyfriend because she lacked attractive qualities in herself. However, he ended by reiterating his earlier response that if a man truly loved her, he wouldn't push for sex, assuring her that "every well thinking man admires a woman who has high moral standards on the question of sex."

Extramarital Sex

King addressed the issue of extramarital sex in his response to three letters, all written by women. In the first, a woman who was married to a handsome minister wrote that this caused all sorts of problems because there were women in the congregation whose "interests are not entirely spiritual." She wanted to know what to do to discourage them. I quote King's response in full because it is indicative of his moral feelings on infidelity, particularly a minister's infidelity, and because it is interesting to juxtapose this with his own infidelities.

> Your husband has the responsibility to minister to the spiritual needs of every member of his congregation. In order to do this he must be sure at all times that his personal life is on the highest moral and spiritual plane. If he remains on this high level of spiritual and moral dignity, even the most aggressive women will have to respect him. Almost every minister has the problem of confronting women in his congregation whose interests are not entirely spiritual. This he is not responsible for. But if he carries himself in a manner representative of the highest mandates of Christian living, his very person will discourage their approaches.

A second question came from a woman whose husband was requesting nights out without her, but held a double standard that wives did not have the same right. King said that if the intention of the night was to enjoy friends of the same sex and socialize, then both husband and wife were entitled to that. However, "If a night out means participating in activities and affairs that cannot be known by your mate, then it is something that neither husband nor wife should request."

Finally, a woman whose husband wouldn't give up his mistress asked what to do, since she didn't believe in divorce but also was not willing to share her man. King wrote, "Your unwillingness to share your husband is perfectly natural and normal. No person wants to share his or her mate with another." He suggested she get her husband to see a clergyman or marriage counselor.

Divorce

Divorce was less common during King's time than it is today, of course, and many religions condemned it as a sin. King again took a more liberal position. He shared his feelings that "religion, while remaining true to absolute moral standards, should forever help individuals adjust to the changing problem[s] of life." The Christian Church "must continue to take a strong stand on the problem of divorce which is plaguing the American family, while at the same time continuing to give guidance to those individuals who, for various reasons, find it almost impossible to live together." He did not consider it immoral for a woman reader to have divorced her first husband nor to want to marry a second; he simply advised her "to profit by the experiences and mistakes of your former marriage."

King's Eight Psychological Approaches to Problem Solving

In addition to expressing his opinions and beliefs on a wide category of specific problems in the personal, social, and political domains, King's answers in his column also reveal his general psychological approach to problem solving. The eighty-eight answers he provided during this period reveal eight basic approaches for solving personal problems. Interestingly, he used all eight of these himself when helping the country to solve her problems during the Civil Rights Movement.

The Importance of a Rational Approach to Problem Solving

As we'll explore in more detail in the next chapter, King's general approach to the world and its problems was through his tough-minded thinking side rather than his soft-hearted feeling side. King did offer sympathy and/or understanding to several of his readers, and at times, praised them for the way they were approaching their problems, but for the most part, the tone of his letters was not empathic or heart-felt, but rather to-the-point and rational.

In the most startling example, a 28-year-old woman wrote in who was lonely and worried and afraid after a horrible car accident a year prior had killed her 5-year-old son and left her husband hospitalized for months. King did not show any compassion or sympathy, but began his response by telling her that she felt lonely and afraid because "you have not succeeded in getting the tragedy which befell your family out of your mind." He attributed her worries to "an over absorption in self." First, he advised her to rise above her misfortune by realizing that it could have been worse. Second, he told her to find "proper avenues of escape from self pity" like hobbies, friendships, or religious worship. While the tone of all of his letters was cool, this one is uncharacteristically cold; one wonders why he didn't take the time to open the letter by commiserating over the loss of her young child and her husband's terrible injuries.

Though King understood the nature of the passions, he always returned his readers to rationality for the solution to their problems. A widow in her mid-fifties wanted to know if she was foolish, as her friends said, to marry a 28-year-old man. He responded that the gap between them left little possibility for compatibility, either physically or emotionally. He acknowledged her love for the man, "but love must always be tempered with reason. Love devoid of rational and practical considerations can become a wild and fanatical emotional that can only lead to psychological disintegration."

In another response, he called again for the importance of rationality in making decisions about love. A man described how he was in love with a young woman unsuited for him, while there was another girl he didn't love but who was better for him. Was romantic love too slippery of a foundation to build a future on, he asked? King could not agree that romantic love was merely transitory, and noted that at best, it can be "an enduring love which grows with the years." However, he felt it was too risky to base a marriage entirely on romantic love, which may just be a "temporary emotional feeling." He advised the young man to pursue the woman he was not in love with, and hope that he would grow to love her.

His belief in rationality led him to suggest a three-stepped methodical approach to solving most problems: rigorous self-analysis, talking through problems, and when those failed, seeking medical or religious help. Because he so commonly recommended all three in that order, we will discuss them here in the same.

The Primacy of Self-Analysis

The first step King almost always recommended in the face of any interpersonal problem was to undergo rigorous self-analysis. The problem often came from something people themselves were doing, so they should look within first.

A woman shared that her husband was a great pillar of the church, but when he came home, he completely changed, becoming a tyrant who seemed to hate her and their kids. King suggested that the woman "analyze the whole situation and see if there is anything within your personality that arouses this tyrannical response from your husband." Another time a man shared, "I have been married for 21 years and they have all been hell." What can a man do to make a marriage successful, he asked. King responded, "In advising anyone on marital problems I usually begin by urging each person to do an honest job of self analysis." The man should first ask himself if he had done anything to cause his wife to react the way she did. When a woman wrote in saying her husband mocked her in front of company and made fun of her family, King advised her to see if there was anything she did to deserve it. "Sometimes," he told her, "individuals embarrass other individuals in public in an attempt to pay them back for being humiliated in private." In all of these cases, King also advised a heart-to-heart with the spouse as well.

At times, his call for self-analysis could border on insensitivity or could be simply unrealistic. King advised the woman mentioned above whose husband was having an affair with someone in their housing project to analyze the woman and compare herself to her to see where she might be lacking. His suggestion?

You might study her and see what she does for your husband

that you might not be doing. Do you spend too much time with the children and the house and not pay attention to him? Are you careful with your grooming? Do you nag? Do you make him feel important . . . like somebody? This process of introspection might help you to hit upon the things that are responsible for your husband's other affair.

In another letter, a child shared that she was in pain because her mother favored all her half brothers and sisters who were light-skinned. The girl wanted to know what to do to be loved too. Instead of acknowledging the pain of the situation, or even admitting that there might be some objective reality to the mother's possible internalized racism, King focused only on what the girl might have done to deserve the disfavor, counseling her toward self-analysis. He added, "You must honestly ask yourself the question, whether the problem has arisen because of an inferiority complex that you have developed as a result of your complexion." He warned her about developing bitterness over her color that would drive people away from her. "Maintain a wholesome attitude at all times and a radiant personality. These qualities, I am convinced, will awaken within those around you a responding attitude of kindness." In this case, he didn't even suggest his typical next move: talking through your feelings with the source of the conflict.

The Importance of Dialogue

King's traditional second step to rational problem-solving involved sitting down with the person and revealing how much you and others were hurting as a result of his or her actions. For instance, with the woman above whose husband was a pillar of the church but a tyrant at home, King suggested that she sit her husband down and patiently talk with him, "showing him the unhappiness and disharmony that he is bringing within the whole family." To the 18-year-old boy with the alcoholic father, King suggested that the boy talk to him during one of his sober moments and "tell him how hurt you are of his acts. It may well be that this frank expression will be the one thing that shocks your father back to reality."

In other cases, King added a new suggestion: confront the offending persons with how much they are hurting themselves and their own reputation as well. In the letter from the woman whose husband mocked her and her family in public, King advised that she share her own hurt and embarrassment, but also to "point out to him that he is not only hurting you, but in a real sense he is hurting himself. He will begin to show up before people in a bad light." For the woman who had an alcoholic husband, King suggested that their heart-to-heart include trying to convince the husband of the damage he was doing to himself in addition to her and their family.

Combining Secular and Religious Therapies

Finally, if self-analysis and frank dialogue failed, King suggested a third route: therapy. Sometimes he advised people to turn to their ministers, but more often than not, he suggested a combination of a religious and a secular therapist (either a medical doctor or a psychologist). For instance, a woman who had a child out of wedlock feared she would pay for the mistake for the rest of her life, losing esteem in the eyes of her family and community. King counseled her that she must find her solution "in the domains of psychology and religion" so she would avoid being overwhelmed with guilt.

One reader wanted to know how to stop worrying so much. King suggested that worry comes from several sources, such as feelings of inadequacy, repressed emotions, illusions, and subconscious fears. The person needed first to identify the sources of his or her worry, which cannot be done alone, but need be done with a counselor. He also suggested turning to religion, for "one of the things that a positive and healthy religious faith gives an individual is a sense of inner equilibrium which removes all basic worries." Religion allows a person to "transcend every worry situation with power and faith." He concluded, "With this combination of medical advice and healthy religion, I am sure that you can solve your problems."

Always Seek the Root of The Problem

Therapists and ministers were important because they could help a person get to the root of the problem, right down to its very source. A man wrote in saying that the harder he worked, the further in debt he got. King told him, "In order to deal with your problem it is necessary for you to get to the root of it." He offered some general causes for why a person gets in debt, and then offered solutions for those causes, but what was most important was to get at the root cause of the problem first.

When a man who was separated from his wife for nine years

complained that he wasn't meeting any nice women, King offered two possible causes of the problem. Perhaps he wasn't going out enough, or wasn't active enough in community and church affairs. Or perhaps he had a deficient personality trait and it wasn't the fault of the women in his community. "In any case," King wrote, "you can easily improve the situation if you find the cause for it."

In another letter, a black person confessed that he disliked all Jewish people. Again, King said the man "must get at the roots" of his dislike for Jewish people in order to transform his feelings. And that could be done by coming to know some Jewish people personally, another problem-solving technique that King often offered.

The Importance of Knowing the Other

One woman wrote in that her new husband and her daughter did not get along. It had come to the point where one of them must go, and she wanted to know if King thought she should divorce her husband. King thought not, and cogently explained why. "People fail to get along with each other because they fear each other. They fear each other because they don't know each other. They don't know each other because they have not properly communicated with each other." Therefore, the daughter and husband should be brought together to talk, to honestly discuss their differences and confess their mistakes. This would heal their broken relationship, King thought.

Knowing each other would make all the difference in healing many interpersonal, interracial, or interreligious problems. To the man who disliked Jewish people, King again noted that the roots of many prejudices come from prejudging someone rather than coming to know them. King suggested that the man "seek real personal fellowship with Jews," that "through this type of personal fellowship, you will come to know them and love them and thereby transcend the bounds of bigotry." He reiterated what he told the mother above: "Men hate each other because they fear each other; they fear each other because they don't know each other; they don't know each other because they are so often separated from each other."

Coming to know each other would naturally facilitate coming to understand each other, he thought. When a 17-year-old girl expressed that she didn't like her mother and father, that she didn't understand them or feel understood by them, King told her to try harder to understand them. "An integrated home makes for an integrated personality," he wrote. Through a heart-to-heart, she should be able to get to the real cause of the misunderstanding, and heal their relationship. He gave similar advice to a couple wondering if they should get married even though they were of different faiths. King counseled that if one of them could not be persuaded to change his or her faith, "both of you should be willing to learn as much as possible about the other's faith."

Never Run Away From Problems

Even in the face of the most difficult problems, King advocated not running away from or avoiding conflict, but staying in the midst of strife and suffering through it. There were two basic reasons behind his thinking. First, staying to face a problem would make you stronger; he believed that if you ran away from specific problems, you would never learn to face and surmount any general problems. He stated this clearly to the 18-year-old boy whose dad was an alcoholic and who had lost friends as a result. When he asked King if it was okay to run away, King responded, "Running away is not the answer because this may start you on a course of running as soon as a problem which seems insurmountable confronts you." He assured the boy that he would find problems everywhere, "maybe not so potent as this one, but nevertheless problems." Staying around to solve this problem would build a muscle that would make solving each succeeding one that much easier.

He gave similar advice to a 15-year-old boy from North Carolina who wanted to know if he should go up to the North after high school where he would have greater opportunities, or stay in the South and be called names. King told him that going North would not guarantee that he would not be called names, that in fact everywhere he went he would find name-callers, so he should not run away but learn to face them.

The second reason he advocated staying to face a problem was his belief that it could be good for the problem itself. If that problem is a person, like the alcoholic husband and father above, staying could help to heal the person or the relationship. A woman who had conflict with her pastor and was being insulted by him asked if she should simply ignore him or leave the church. King thought it was a mistake to leave the church, and called it her "Christian duty" to seek reconciliation with him.

If the problem was a social issue, staying and fighting could help to improve the issue as well. For instance, a preacher in a small town in Mississippi felt like he couldn't take the segregation and discrimination of the Jim Crow laws any longer, but he feared that if he spoke out, he might be killed or run out of town. King wrote that he understood the predicament, and that the preacher had three choices: to leave Mississippi, to accept the status quo of the Jim Crow laws, or to stand up against them "and suffer the consequences." King suggested the third. He stated that as a Christian minister and as a symbol of "the new Negro," the man had the responsibility to stand up against the laws of the city despite the consequences. "The fear of physical death and being run out of town should not be your primary concern. Your primary concern should be a devotion to truth, justice, and freedom." King acknowledged that this would be difficult, but it was a necessarily sacrifice to secure freedom and transform the problem of discrimination.

Concentrating on Higher Virtues

Finally, when people were in the midst of problems that felt out of their control, King suggested that they turn their vision to higher virtues. When a person asked how to overcome a bad temper, King laid out the steps to transforming any moral weakness. First, you must recognize it and honestly admit it. Then, you should concentrate on a higher virtue: "You expel a lower vice by concentrating on a higher virtue. . . A destructive passion is harnessed by directing that same passion into constructive channels." Finally, he advised submitting the will to the power of God, and realizing "the need for depending on a higher power."

To the woman who had a child out of wedlock and feared she may pay for the mistake for the rest of her life, King advised her to seek secular and spiritual help, then gave her a final piece of advice. She must turn her vision toward the future, he wrote, concentrating on noble pursuits and the heights of life she wished to reach, rather than focusing on self-pity regarding her fall. "With this wholesome attitude," he told her, "you will be able to stand up amid all of the criticisms that persons in your town will direct toward you. In other words, you can so outlive your past mistake that even the most ardent critic will develop a warm respect for you."

To the woman who had lost her 5-year-old son in the horrible car accident, King counseled her to find "proper avenues of escape from self pity" like a love of music, a sense of purpose or cause beyond herself, genuine friendships, and regular religious worship. Whenever people were in the depths of despair, or pulled down under the crushing weight of worldly concerns, King advised them to lift their eyes toward more noble sights. In an uncharacteristically poetic response for the advice column venue, King replied to the woman who complained about the shallowness of her social set, "Man is more than a dog to be satisfied by the bones of sensory pleasure and showy materialism: He is a being of spirit, born for the stars and created for eternity."

Conclusion

Though King's advice column responses are not without their psychological weaknesses at times, it still remains rather amazing that a man of only twenty-eight would have such aplomb and feel such authority to advise on such a wide variety of issues both secular and spiritual. Even more amazing is how far he had come in two years, from a newly married young man and father who was just beginning his first real job in one city in America's black belt, to a man with enough gravitas to accept questions and offer answers to the entire United States of America.

His work as an advice columnist offers us unique insight into King's psychological, spiritual, philosophical, and cultural beliefs. It also offers us deeper insight into King's belief in the therapeutic nature of the ministry, the importance he placed on tending the whole of the soul, the earthly as well as the spiritual dimension.

Not only could ministers serve a therapeutic role, but also an educational one: each advice column question afforded King a teachable moment. Toward the end of his life, he lamented that he never had a chance to become a professor and do some teaching, but as this book will demonstrate throughout, King was always teaching while preaching and healing.

Professor and historian Lewis V. Baldwin noted of King:

> His notion of sermonizing involved the proclamation of God's word in relationship to a myriad of human concerns, and with the idea that every sermon should have as its purpose the head-on constructive meeting of some spiritual, social, cultural, or personal problem that puzzles the mind, bears upon the conscience, and interferes with the complete flow of life.

Seen in this way, King's eighty-eight advice column responses contain both teaching and preaching; they are little sermons, each covering personal, social, cultural, political, and philosophical problems, varying only from his church sermons in their brevity.

In the next chapter we'll explore four of King's full-length sermons that were primarily psychological in nature.

4 PREACHINGS:

FOUR OF KING'S MOST
PSYCHOLOGICAL SERMONS

As we saw in the last two chapters and will continue to see throughout this book, King often combined the roles of minister and therapist. This can be seen not only in his advice columns, but in his sermons as well. Taken as a whole, King's sermons reveal a minister who was more concerned with the lives of his parishioners here on earth rather than their afterlives in heaven; a minister who was more concerned with improving souls here rather than gathering them for there; a minister who sought to bring as many souls to a deeper relationship with themselves and others as he sought to bring to a deeper relationship with God. If such a division could be made without being too artificial, many of his sermons are two-thirds psychological, one-third theological; if the references to God were removed, the sermons could be delivered with equal applicability to clients in group therapy as to congregants in church.

King's ability to integrate the role of the therapist and the minister is just one of the many ways his life and message embodied integration. We see it within the social realm in the integration of black and white people, and later in his life, within the economic realm with his growing emphasis on the integration of the rich and the poor. We see it in the religious realm in the integration of the temporal and the eternal, of this life and the next. We see it within the political realm in the integration of capitalism and communism into his preferred system, democratic socialism. And we see it within the psychological realm in the integration of the personality.

Psychologists use different words to describe the integration of the personality, such as *individuation*, *self-actualization*, or *self-realization*, and their definitions vary to a degree, but in general, most would agree that one goal of human development is to bring together the split or opposing parts of the personality into one unified whole that is greater, or wiser, or stronger, or truer, than the sum of its parts. When the psyche is free from having to resolve its own oppositions, from having to do battle with itself, tremendous energy becomes available to pour into more fulfilling and meaningful channels. This is the integrated personality.

It's not hard to find sermons of King's that focus on personality integration; in fact, the hard part is how to select just a few. For this chapter I have chosen four sermons that I believe are integral illustrations of King's view of the psyche, that demonstrate his understanding of psychological principles, and that show his concern with imparting those psychological principles to his parishioners for their development, healing, and transformation. His sermon "A Tough Mind and a Tender Heart" will serve as a starting point for understanding King's dualistic view of the psyche, and his belief in the importance of synthesizing the opposites within. "Unfulfilled Dreams" continues this theme and contains a clear description of King's belief in the tension between good and evil that lies within the human personality, as well as the difficulty inherent in overcoming evil. The last two sermons, "Overcoming an Inferiority Complex" and "Conquering Self-Centeredness," come from his four-part series entitled "Problems of Personality Integration" delivered in 1957 and also contain psychological themes that he would reiterate and rework throughout his life.

Before we begin, a word about the organization of each section. I begin by summarizing the sermon, and then place it within a psychological context by comparing it to theories of the depth psychologists with whom King was familiar. Then, I examine to what extent King himself was able to practice what he preached, or in other words, how integrated his own personality was. It is here that I am on speculative ground. I was not King's therapist, I was not privy to his innermost thoughts or internal struggles, and in fact I did not know him personally at all. Moreover, I have mixed feelings about psychobiographies where the writer attempts to analyze a person who is long deceased by piecing together information left behind; part of me finds it fascinating, like a good mystery where the question is not "who done it" but "why did they do it the way they did it," while another part of me finds it intrusive, even disrespectful somehow to attribute motives and feelings to persons who can no longer defend or explain themselves. Finally, I am aware of just how subjective psychoanalysis can be even when the subject is in the room, let alone in the grave. Therefore, in my analysis of King in this chapter, I've come to peace by only using what is public—the words he said about himself, and the actions he took in the world—leaving it to people who knew him better, or who are comfortable with the speculation and subjectivity inherent in psychobiography, to deepen, broaden, and/or correct my tentative and limited analysis.

"A Tough Mind and a Tender Heart"
The Sermon

In 1963 King published fifteen of his sermons in the book *Strength to Love*, adapting them only slightly for the reader rather than the listener. From that book I take the text of "A Tough Mind and a Tender Heart." In this sermon, King lays out in the first paragraph the entire philosophical premise: "The strong man holds in a living blend strongly marked opposites." However, very few men achieve a balance of those opposites: "The idealists are not usually realistic, and the realists are not usually idealistic. The militant are not generally known to be passive, nor the passive to be militant. Seldom are the humble self-assertive, or the self-assertive humble." But, King asserts, "Life at its best is a creative synthesis of opposites in fruitful harmony." He quotes one of his favorite philosophers, Georg Hegel, that truth is not found in thesis or antithesis, but in the synthesis reconciling the two.

King then turns to Jesus, who also recognized this need for blending opposites. He quotes Matthew 10:16: "Be ye therefore wise as serpents, and harmless as doves." King blends this saying with his own: "We must combine the toughness of the serpent and the softness of the dove, a tough mind and a tender heart."

King defines the tough mind as one "characterized by incisive thinking, realistic appraisal, and decisive judgment. . . . [it] is sharp and penetrating, breaking through the crust of legends and myths and sifting the true from the false. . . . [it] is astute and discerning"; the person with the tough mind "has a strong, austere quality that makes for firmness of purpose and solidity of commitment." Such tough minds are rare, King argues. Thinking is difficult, and easy answers are preferable. Softmindedness is one of the basic causes of racism, as people would rather prejudge someone than make up their own minds. With soft minds, we are amazingly gullible, and he offers the following examples: the success of advertising, the propaganda of the written word as it may appear in the press, the presence of dictators and politicians who capitalize on their softminded constituencies to move forward their agendas, our willingness to believe in superstition, and those religious people who reject science "with a dogmatic passion." King ends by writing, "The shape of the world today does not permit us the luxury of softmindedness. A nation or a civilization that continues to produce softminded men purchases its own spiritual death on an installment plan."

But it is not enough to have a tough mind, King continues. A tough mind without a tender heart is cold, detached, and passionless. Hardhearted people never truly love other people, but use them to serve their own needs, treating them as depersonalized objects. They are isolated islands, detached from "the mainland of humanity." They never really see other people, and they lack the most basic feelings of compassion and friendliness. Thus, he reiterates his basic point, "To have serpent-like qualities devoid of dovelike qualities is to be passionless, mean, and selfish. To have dovelike without serpent-like qualities is to be sentimental, anemic, and aimless. We must combine strongly marked antitheses."

He applies this theory to black participants in the fight for freedom and justice. If they are too softminded, he argues, they will simply "acquiesce and resign themselves to segregation," but if they are too hardhearted, they will "combat the opponent with physical violence and corroding hatred." He suggests the third way—nonviolent resistance—which combines the tough mind and the tender heart and avoids both dull complacency and bitter hatred.

Finally, King ends his sermon by giving an example of the greatest toughminded and tenderhearted one of all—God. God is both austere and gentle. He can punish and forgive. He can control and offer grace. He can demand justice and give mercy and love. King concludes, "When days grow dark and nights grow dreary, we can be thankful that our God combines in his nature a creative synthesis of love and justice which will lead us through life's dark valleys and into sunlit pathways of hope and fulfillment."

Psychological Theory

Before placing this sermon in psychological context, it is appropriate to discuss it from a philosophical one instead, since King credits a philosopher first for his basic theory. In the work of Hegel, King found a philosophy he would return to again and again: truth is not found in thesis or antithesis, but in a synthesis that reconciles the two. Synthesis is not found in either/or, but in both/and. For example, King did not believe in white power or black power, but in the shared power of humanity; he did not believe that the truth could be found in communism or capitalism, but in a creative synthesis of the best of both political systems. King believed there was a partial truth, a partial good, in each opposite, and when those truths and goods were brought together, a powerful synthesis of higher truth, of higher good, would be found.

Psychologically, this idea finds its most complete expression in the work of C. G. Jung. Jung focused on the dual nature of the psyche, believing that the psyche was fundamentally oppositional. Like Hegel, Jung thought truth did not lie at either end of the opposites; in fact, he stated that neurosis was often the result of bouncing back and forth between the two seemingly irreconcilable poles. A psychologically healthy person would live in a state where the opposites are in harmonious relationship with each other. Harmony does not necessarily come through compromise, but in a creative synthesis of the opposites which creates a third and new possibility. Jung often found this third possibility occurring in the form of a symbol that unites the opposites.

King used such a uniting symbol in his sermon. The two opposites were symbolized by the serpent, representing toughness, and the dove, representing softness. The serpent and the dove cannot literally be reconciled, nor can the serpent or dove compromise their nature to become more like the other. Rather, a third possibility arises that unites the two, and that uniting symbol for King is God, who holds both opposites in harmonious balance. Nonviolent resistance is also offered as a third way and as a uniting symbol, for it is neither softminded like acquiescence, or toughhearted like violence, nor is it a compromise between the two.

Jung believed opposition was inherent in the psyche, and one of his most popular contributions to the field, his theory of psychological types, reflects this belief. He defined three different sets of oppositions: introverted/extraverted, intuitive/sensate, and thinking/feeling. He made it clear that these types are not fixed or exclusive, but rather, there is usually one side that dominates a person's actions or attitudes toward oneself, other people, and the world. Jung called the dominant type the "the superior function" and the type that remains recessed and sometimes difficult for the person to access "the inferior function." We move toward personality integration when we are able to draw upon the inferior function, thus enriching our lives through broadening our range of possibilities.

Two of Jung's opposites—the thinking and feeling functions—find their parallel in King's tough mind and tender heart polarities. King struggled in his life with synthesizing those opposites in himself.

Applying the Sermon and the Psychology to King

In reading King's autobiographical statements, it is obvious that his thinking function was dominant in his childhood, adolescence, and early adulthood; this is seen most clearly when examining his approach to religion. Jung's thinking and feeling functions relate to how we make decisions: objectively or subjectively, with the mind or with the heart. Remember we discussed in Chapter 1 that King decided to join the church at five, not because he "believed" nor had any feeling of God, but because he wanted to keep up with his older sister. At thirteen, he questioned the bodily resurrection of Jesus; it simply made no rational sense to him. His studies in college made him even more skeptical of the fundamentalism of religion. "My studies had made me skeptical, and I could not see how many of the facts of science could be squared with religion."

Not only did he approach religion with a tough mind, but he eschewed the tender-heartedness of it. He revolted against the emotionalism of religion, "the shouting and stamping. I didn't understand it, and it embarrassed me." He also knew that most black ministers were uneducated and were not trained in seminaries, and he "wondered whether it [religion] could serve as a vehicle to modern thinking, whether religion could be intellectually respectable as well as emotionally satisfying." Though he always had a deep urge to serve humanity, he began college by thinking he would do so as a doctor or lawyer, both professions where he could capitalize on the strength of his tough mind.

However, the turning point in choosing his profession came when he took at class on the Bible where it was stripped of its literalism and came alive symbolically. "I came to see that behind the legends and myths of the Bible were many profound truths which one could not escape." This gave him a new way of thinking about the Bible, a third way where the stories were not seen as either literal truths or literal lies, but as symbolic truths. He also came across learned men who were both ministers and professors, and he came to believe that he wouldn't have to leave his tough mind—his dominant thinking function—behind as a minister.

As explored in Chapter 1, King did not note many emotional experiences in the church until the infamous "kitchen table incident" where he felt for the first time the presence, companionship, and support of God. This experience may have been the awakening of his feeling function when it came to religion; it is certainly the emotional experience that he recounted most frequently and most passionately. Though in his younger days he had criticized the emotionalism of ministers at the pulpit, as he developed his style he became more and more emotionally expressive, able to move audiences to great emotional heights by the passion and feeling in his voice. Though his sermons would always contain intellectual references that made clear his learned mind, he found a way to balance those with poetic phrases emphatically expressed, awakening and stimulating both the heads and the hearts of his listeners.

The subjects of his sermons and speeches also reflect his growing ability to balance his thinking and feeling, his head and his heart, and are reflected in two of his most common themes: justice and love. He would wax philosophical about the nature of justice, discussing it from a historical or legal or political point of view, bringing an audience to intellectual agreement about its importance, but he could just as easily bring an audience to tears by making them *feel* what injustice feels like, feel in their bones that injustice is wrong, and feel in their bodies that they must fight against it. This was true with love as well. King could express his love for others and bring an audience to a felt experience of love, but he would also discuss love intellectually, teaching his audiences about the distinctions between different types of love, making them *think* about love differently, think that they may be able to find a way to love their enemies by changing their thoughts.

In summary, though the thinking function was dominant in King's early life, he came to balance it as he grew older with the feeling function. In fact, sometimes he even led with the feeling function, as was the case when he finally decided to speak up aggressively against the Vietnam War. He was always intellectually against the war, as he was intellectually against violence in general, but it wasn't until he saw a picture of a Vietnamese mother holding her dead baby who had been killed by American napalm that his feelings irrevocably moved him to protest against the war with all his might. Certainly one reason King was such a powerful speaker was his ability in a single speech or sermon to reach into the hearts of the feelers and address the minds of the thinkers; one reason why King was such a powerful healer was his ability in any given speech to open the minds of the feelers and open the hearts of the thinkers. Only a man who holds those two opposites in harmonious balance within could do as much.

"Unfulfilled Dreams"
The Sermon

"Unfulfilled Dreams" is a sermon King gave a month before his death, in March of 1968. Though it is particularly poignant when set in this context, it is important to understand that King was always working and reworking his sermons; because of the sheer volume of public speaking he did each year, it would be impossible for him to generate a new sermon or speech from scratch every time. This particular sermon is a reworking of "Shattered Dreams," which appears in King's 1963 volume of sermons, *Strength to Love*. In the preface to that volume, King writes that "Shattered Dreams" was one of several sermons written while "visiting" Georgia jails. While the differences between the two speeches are interesting in and of themselves, it is the 1968 rendition of the sermon and its theme of unfulfilled dreams that shows King at his psychological best, particularly in his clear definition of the struggle between our good and evil natures.

King begins by placing his sermon in biblical context. In the eighth chapter of First Kings, there's a little-known passage where King David has the dream of building a great temple for God. He starts to build it, but is unable to finish. Yet God said to David, "Whereas it was in thine heart to build a house unto my name, thou didst well that it was within thine heart."

King takes the biblical story and moves it closer to home, into the lives of his congregation. Many of us start out to build a temple, "temples of character, temples of justice, temples of peace," yet so often those temples are unfinished. King calls this "one of the great agonies of life," to know that we are trying to finish what is unfinishable. He calls life "a continual story of shattered dreams," and he provides several examples: Gandhi's shattered dream of a united Hindu and Moslem nation, Woodrow Wilson's unfulfilled dream (during his lifetime) of a League of Nations, the apostle Paul's unfulfilled dream of going to Spain, and the unfulfilled dream of slaves yearning for freedom. But King reminds his listeners that

God is always there, reassuring them that it is well that the dream is within their hearts.

Then King shifts the sermon, explaining that anyone who sets out to build a temple "must face the fact that there is a tension at the heart of the universe between good and evil." In his typical intellectual style, he gives several examples of this historically: Hinduism calls it the struggle between illusion and reality; Platonic philosophy calls it the tension between body and soul; Zoroastrianism calls it the tension between the god of light and the god of darkness; Judaism and Christianity call it the tension between God and Satan; and Sigmund Freud calls it the tension between the id and the superego.

King terms this struggle "a civil war" that manifests in our own souls as well.

> I don't care who you are, I don't care where you live, there is a civil war going on in your life. And every time you set out to be good, there's something pulling on you, telling you to be evil . . . Every time you set out to love, something keeps pulling on you, trying to get you to hate. Every time you set out to be kind and say nice things about people, something is pulling on you to be jealous and envious and to spread evil gossip about them.

King calls this civil war within us a kind of schizophrenia, the presence of a Mr. Hyde and a Dr. Jekyll within our very souls. He ends this point by saying, "And whenever we set out to dream our dreams and to build our temples, we must be honest enough to recognize it."

After bringing that civil war right into the very hearts of his parishioners, King moves back to what he calls the basic point of the text. "In the final analysis, God does not judge us by the separate incidents or the separate mistakes that we make, but by the total bent of our lives." God knows that his children are weak and frail, and all he requires is that our hearts are right. King assures his congregation, "Salvation isn't reaching the destination of absolute morality, but it's being in the process and on the right road." No one is all good but God, but if we are on the right road, God has the power to make us recipients of his grace.

King puts the question to his congregation: "Is your heart right?" And if it's not, he tells them to fix it right away, so that God can say about each of them, "He may not have reached the highest height, he may not have realized all his dreams, but he tried. . . . He tried to be a good man. He tried to be a just man. He tried to be an honest man. His heart was in the right place." King then offers his personal testimony, telling them that he is not a saint, but "I'm a sinner like all of God's children. But I want to be a good man." He hears God's voice saying to him that he is accepted and blessed, because he tries.

He concludes by telling his congregation that they must have "a strong boat of faith" because the winds will blow and there will be storms of disappointment and the feeling of agony and anguish; the only way to survive is by having God as an anchor. With God by our side, we need never fear, he tells them, and we will never be alone.

Psychological Theory

More than any other psychological or philosophical theory, the dual nature of the human soul was of primary importance to King. He came to believe that the world and each soul in it was divided into human and divine realms. While he saw us as the children of God, always pulled up toward our better angels, he also recognized us as creatures of the earth, pulled downward into our baser natures. This was the fundamental struggle of humanity, which he placed into the language of the struggle between good and evil.

In this sense, the temple in King's sermon is a symbol for the psyche itself. While we can work on perfecting our nature—and indeed, it is well that it is within our hearts to want to perfect ourselves—King believed that it was of prime importance that we recognize the psychic reality of our split natures, of our propensity for both good and evil. Here, King was on solid ground with the depth psychologists he studied, such as Erich Fromm.

> Man *is* neither good nor evil. If one believes in the goodness of man as the only potentiality, one will be forced into rosy falsification of the facts, or end up in bitter disillusionment. If one believes in the other extreme, one will end up as a cynic and be blind to the many possibilities for good in others and in oneself. A realistic view sees both possibilities as real potentialities, and studies the conditions for the development of either of them.

In a similar vein, Jung wrote, "One can no longer avoid the

realization that evil, without man's ever having chosen it, is lodged in human nature itself, then it bestrides the psychological stage as the equal and opposite partner of good." In fact, Jung termed the self "the unfathomable union of good and evil." King believed this, stating this idea many times: "Within the best of us, there is some evil, and within the worst of us, there is some good."

For King, simply recognizing this fact was not enough. When King saw dualities, as discussed in "A Tough Mind and a Tender Heart," he taught that we should take the best of one side and the best of the other, and bring them together in some sort of synthesis which would be an improvement on both. However, this practice could not apply here. King preached that there was some good in every evil man[5], and some evil in every good man, but he could not preach that man should try to take the best of his good side and the best of his evil side and bring them together into some synthesis. Here was one set of dualities where King thought it important to try to overcome one side with the other. In fact, this was the one duality where he preached of "higher" and "lower," holding them in hierarchical relationship, rather than side by side, holding them as equally valid.

However, the Jungian theory of dualities still holds here, that when there are irreconcilable dualities, a third thing must be found, and that thing is often a symbol. And, as it often was for King, the third thing is God. While we should try to do everything possible on earth to overcome our evil nature, it is finally only in God that our good and evil sides can be reconciled. As King points out, for God, it is only important that you *try* to overcome your evil nature, for God realizes that nobody is all good except for himself.

Jung would disagree with King about this point, for he believed that God, or what he called "the God-image," was not perfect itself, but like man was striving toward perfection: the Bible (particularly the Old Testament) serves as a record of that struggle (see Jung's *Answer to Job* for this argument). For Jung, this was the fundamental truth of the biblical verse that man is made in God's image—he reasoned that if man is made in God's image, and man can never be perfect but can only strive for perfection, then God,

---

[5] I am mindful of the gendered nature of this pronoun, but will use it because King, Jung, and Fromm all used it, though of course they were referring to women as well.

too, is not yet perfect, but is striving. Setting aside this disagreement, what's fundamental to both King and Jung's thinking is that humanity can never reach perfection. Indeed, when Jung talked about individuation as a psychological goal, he was quick to make two points: first, that individuation is a process, and indeed, is the most difficult process there is, and second, that individuation does not mean overcoming the baser side of one's humanity, but rather, "that a person becomes conscious in what respects he or she is both a unique human being and, at the same time, no more than a common man or woman." This is reflected in King's sermon by the creative temple we set out to build that will never be complete; we too will never complete the struggle with our darker natures.

Applying the Sermon and the Psychology to King

King shared in his sermon that he was no saint himself, but that he *tried* to be a good man. What he didn't share in that sermon was just how guilty he felt when he failed. Perhaps no one knew this side of him better than his wife, who wrote, "His conscience was a formidable thing that kept him on the path he thought was right. If he ever did something a little wrong, or committed a selfish act, his conscience fairly devoured him."

> My husband was what psychologists might call a guilt-ridden man. He was so conscious of his awesome responsibilities that he literally set himself the task of never making an error in the affairs of the Movement. He would say, "I can't afford to make a mistake," though he know that as a human being he was bound to.

Though King faced public criticism on a daily basis, Coretta said of him, "He criticized himself more severely than anyone else ever did."

King sometimes spoke about this side of himself as well, his relentless self-examination.

> I subject myself to self-purification and to endless self-analysis; I question and soul-search constantly into myself to be as certain as I can that I am fulfilling the true meaning of my work, that I am maintaining my sense of purpose, that I am holding fast to my ideals, that I am guiding my people in the right direction.

Where did this intense self-criticism and guilt come from? Coretta had her own ideas about this.

> He felt that having been born into what was a middle-class African-American family was a privilege he had not earned, just as he felt the many honors heaped on him in the later years were not his alone. He would constantly examine himself to determine if he was becoming corrupted, if he was accepting honors too easily. He was very sensitive about having people do things for him because of his position. He was extremely grateful for any help he got. He was a truly humble man and never felt he was adequate to his positions. That is why he worried so much, worked so hard, studied constantly, long after he had become a world figure.

King's good friend and advisor Stanley Levison agreed.

> Martin could be described as an intensely guilt-ridden man. The most essential element in the feelings of guilt that he had was that he didn't feel he deserved the kind of tribute that he got . . . . when you don't feel you're worthy of it and you're an honest, principled man, it tortures you. And it could be said that he was tortured by the great appreciation that the public showed for him. If he had been less humble, he could have lived with this kind of acclaim, but because he was genuinely a man of humility, he really couldn't live with it.

As the gap between the public fame and the private humility grew larger, King confessed to his friend and mentor J. Pius Barbour, "I am conscious of two Martin Luther Kings. I am a wonder to myself. . . . I am mystified at my own career. The Martin Luther King that the people talk about seems to be somebody foreign to me." He told Barbour there was "a kind of dualism in my life" and that "Martin Luther King the famous man was a kind of stranger to him."

Not only did King recognize the stranger in himself, but he also recognized the sinner. The area where his sinful nature is most obvious and well known is in his frequent extramarital affairs. One could speculate about whether King's overwhelming sense of guilt and propensity for self-criticism caused him to act out sexually, or whether acting out sexually caused the guilt and gave him reason for self-criticism; regardless, King seems to have been caught in a cycle of sin and guilt, exacerbated by the very real fear and threats that he would be exposed publicly.

King biographer David J. Garrow has documented King's affairs in the book *The FBI and Martin Luther King, Jr.* and in *Bearing the Cross: Martin Luther King, Jr., and the Southern Christian Leadership Conference.* In brief, Garrow states that King had multiple affairs with women, some of them apparently one-night stands and some of them long-standing relationships, and that these affairs were public knowledge among King's intimate friends; there are even hints of orgies, or "sexual parties." The FBI, who originally wire-tapped King to prove his Communist affiliations, was able to record King's affairs; at one point they sent him an anonymous tape of those liaisons along with a letter threatening to expose him and urging him to avoid this by committing suicide. It was Coretta who first listened to the tape and read the letter, which called King "a great liability for all us Negroes" and said "Satan could not do more. What incredible evilness. Your end is approaching. You are done. There is but one way out for you. You better take it before your filthy, abnormal fraudulent self is bared to the nation."

Garrow reports that King's initial response was to see the tapes as God's way of warning him he wasn't living up to the role history had cast upon him. He told a friend that he had sinned, but he would do better in the future, but according to Garrow and to King's acquaintances, he continued to carry on extramarital relationships, including and up to the night of his death.[6]

Even though King knew he was being wire-tapped and spied upon, even though the threat of exposure of his infidelities was very real, even as his staff expressed their concern that his reputation was on the line, he continued to carry on extramarital affairs. It is difficult to hear him talk about the Dr. Jekyll and Mr. Hyde who

---

[6] See Garrow, *Bearing the Cross*, pages 373-376. Georgia Davis Powers, a senator from Kentucky, wrote a book called *I Shared the Dream* where she acknowledges being one woman he was intimate with toward the end of his life; he was in her hotel room the night before his death, and she witnessed his body on the balcony immediately following his assassination.

reside within us all without thinking of those within him as well. It makes sense psychologically that he would turn to God's grace and forgiveness as the way to reconcile his own dual nature.

One of King's sermons entitled "The Prodigal Son," delivered in 1966, perhaps illustrates his own understanding and interpretation of his very real struggle.

> Sex is sacred. It's beautiful, it's holy. [But] if one becomes a slave to sex, you can never satisfy it. And then the long road of promiscuity comes along. And then you discover what hell is. Hell is God giving a man what he thought he wanted. When you get it, you discover you don't want it any longer, and you move on and you get something else. Whenever you become a slave to a drive, you can never satisfy it. It's a strange mixture in all of us, isn't it? You'll do what's right most of the time, but every now and then you'll do some wrong. You'll be faithful to that and those that you should be faithful to most of the time. But every now and then you'll be unfaithful to those you should be faithful to. Do you know that there's a bit of a coward in the bravest of us, and a bit of a hero in the meanest of us? There is much good in the worst of us, and so much bad in the best of us.

But like the story of the prodigal son, in the end, he assures us (himself?) that the father will welcome the straying son home and forgive him.

He returned often to this theme of the dual nature of the psyche. In one sermon, he told his congregation, "Each of us is two selves. And the great burden of life is to always try to keep that higher self in command. Don't let the lower self take over . . . . Every now and then you'll be unfaithful to those that you should be faithful to." It is unclear whether or how King tried to keep his lower self in check, whether he tried to resist sexual temptation or whether eventually he just reconciled himself to his drive; what is clear is the general and overwhelming guilt he carried with him, for as he told his congregation, "Guilt will accompany us when we sin, for God's unbroken hold on us is something that will never permit us to feel right when we do wrong, or to feel natural when we do the unnatural."

After King heard the FBI tapes, he reportedly said, "What I do is only between me and my God," and in the end, it was only with

God that King would have to make peace.[7] Clearly he believed what he preached—perfection was impossible, as everyone, including himself, was a sinner—and he found comfort that at the end of his life, God would not judge him by the separate mistakes he made, but by the total bent of his life. King told his congregation, "I want to hear a voice saying to me one day, 'I take you in and I bless you, because you try. It is well that it was within thine heart.'"

"Overcoming an Inferiority Complex"
The Sermon

The sermon "Overcoming an Inferiority Complex" was the first of four in a series King titled "Problems of Personality Integration"; it was delivered in the summer of 1957. Here, King relates the biblical story of Zacchaeus, a man who suffered from an inferiority complex because he was so small. Not feeling accepted by society, he tried to gain attention by becoming a tax collector, making big money by being something untrue to his nature. Many people, says King, suffer from feelings of inferiority like Zacchaeus for things ranging from physical handicaps, to ill-health, to lack of social charm or good looks, to "love failures and because of moral failures."

Despite the reasons for the inferiority complex, King notes that some ways of overcoming the feeling of inferiority are not constructive, like Zacchaeus' method of becoming something he was not. Some people flee to fantasy or daydreams, trying to escape the world. Others turn to alcohol, trying to drown out the complex. But King says both these methods are dangerous because they lead to a

---

[7] What about Coretta? How did she respond to the tapes? To what extent did she know of his extramarital affairs? Did King seek her forgiveness, and did she grant it? Garrow quotes Coretta in saying, "During our whole marriage we never had one single serious discussion about either of us being involved with another person. . . . If I ever had any suspicions . . . I never would have even mentioned them to Martin. I just wouldn't have burdened him with anything so trivial. . . All that other business just didn't have a place in the very high-level relationship we enjoyed." Interestingly, Georgia Davis Powers said something very similar: "Others have speculated about Dr. King's relationships with women. I have no knowledge of affairs he may have had with other women; that was not what we talked about when we were together. I only know that our relationship began as a close friendship between two people sharing the same dream, working for the same goals, and it crossed the line into intimacy."

split personality. "Individuals become so accustomed and absorbed in running away from the conditions of life, in trying to escape their actual selves, that their personalities actually become so thin that they split and the real self recedes into the background."

There are other ways people deal unconstructively with inferiority complexes. Some act like the fox in Aesop's fable and call everything they don't have and can't reach "sour grapes." Some belittle other people, living "a life of criticism and a life of negativism." Others use what King called the "smoke-screen" method, attempting to overcome their sense of inferiority by acting superior, boasting and bragging all the time.

King then turns to focus on the healthy ways of overcoming the complex. The first way is through "the principle of self-acceptance." Conflict comes, he tells them, when "individuals find a sort of impassable gulf between their actual selves and their desired selves." In this case, he advises they pray to God for the ability to accept themselves, just as they are, "with all limitations and with all of the endowments that come as the results of our being born in this world." He tells again the story from his Morehouse days when he was taking a statistics class, and he had the classmate who was gifted in mathematical skills and could do well in one hour what King struggled to do in three. King shares, "I had to just come to the point of accepting myself and my dull tools and doing it the best that I could, and this is the thing that every individual must do."

Second, after accepting their limitations, people must remember that "anything that you do for the upbuilding of humanity is significant no matter how small you think it is. Don't consider your work insignificant. Consider it of cosmic significance." Not everyone can do big things, but people can do little things in a big way, he tells them; not everyone can do the extraordinary, but people can do the ordinary in an extraordinary manner. "No matter how small you consider it, you can dignify anything," he said before he shared the story of his favorite shoe-shiner in Montgomery who "can do more with just shining shoes than most people can do with their Ph.D.'s. He can get more music out of a rag shining shoes than Louie Armstrong can get out of a trumpet. And I just love to see him shine shoes. He has dignified shoeshining."

His third constructive method of overcoming inferiority is to master "substitutionary compensation," whereby you take your inadequate points and transform them into something adequate, even "into something meaningful and something constructive." He uses the example of an unattractive girl who can compensate by developing wit and charm and a kind of soul beauty, or the shy young man who directs his energy "into the channel of great scientific research and great artistic development."

That leads to King's fourth method, which is to overcome inferiority "by absorbing yourself in some cause, in some principle, in some ideal greater than yourself." Here, he uses the example of Abraham Lincoln, a failure in the business world, a man who lost his great love, a man defeated more often than not in politics, but a man who became interested in the slavery issue and gave his life to the cause. "And because of his being embedded in this cause, in giving himself to this cause and losing himself into this cause, he became a great man."

Finally, the last method is to "develop an abiding religious faith because there is something about religion that gives you a sense of belonging." He quotes Jung who wrote, "Of all of the hundreds and thousands of patients that have come to me for treatment and counsel over the past few years, I think I can truly say that all of them past the middle of life had conditions which could be cured by the proper religious faith." In a society where "it's so easy to feel that we are sort of depersonalized cogs in a vast industrial machine," religion says that all individuals count and have significance because there is a God who created them and who cares for them.

This is especially significant "for the race problem and for every Negro who stands in America." It is easy for them to feel inferior because of the tragic history of slavery, oppression, and injustice. He mentions several great social psychologists—Gordon Allport, Gardner Murphy, and Kenneth Clark—all of whom wrote on how segregation generates inferiority complexes among black people. But religion offers "the assurance that you belong and that you count and that you are somebody because God loves you." Religion provides meaning, dignity, self-respect, and a sense of belonging. So he closes his sermon by encouraging his congregation to "go out of this church with a new faith in yourself, with a new self-confidence, with a new sense of dignity, knowing that there is a God in this universe who loves all his children."

Psychological Theory

It was in the early 20th century when psychologist Alfred Adler posited the ubiquity of inferior feelings and popularized the "inferiority complex." For Adler, the desire for power was an even more important instinctual drive than Freud's drive for sex, and he believed that feelings of inferiority develop when a person is thwarted in gaining power in some way. This is a natural feeling in children who feel inferior in power to the adults and older children they see in their lives. Indeed, Adler believed that to be human is to struggle against feelings of inferiority throughout the entirety of our lives. In agreement with Adler, King called the feeling of inferiority "one of the first and basic conditions of life."

Adler believed that these feelings of inferiority, often unconscious, and the subsequent defense mechanisms we build up to depotentiate them played a dominant role in determining our behavior. King must have agreed with Adler regarding the power of inferiority feelings, as he opened his sermon by calling the complex "one of the most stagnating and strangulating and crushing conditions of the human personality," one that "distorts the personality and plunges it into the abyss of inner conflicts."

Adler called the defense mechanisms "safeguarding devices" because they keep the ego safe from being crushed or debilitated or overwhelmed by the effects of inferiority.

> Individuals can use safeguarding devices in attempts both to excuse themselves from failure and depreciate others. Safeguarding devices include symptoms, depreciation, accusations, self-accusations, guilt, and various forms of distancing. Symptoms such as anxiety, phobias, and depression, can all be used as excuses for avoiding the tasks of life and transferring responsibility to others. In this way, individuals can use their symptoms to shield themselves from potential or actual failure in these tasks.

King discussed many of these same safeguards in his sermon, including distancing (in the form of alcoholism), fantasy, sour grapes, depreciation, accusation, and reaction-formation (when a person adopts the exact opposite attitude as the one held unconsciously; i.e., when someone who feels inferior acts superior).

There are healthy defense mechanisms for dealing with inferiority feelings, according to Adler, and sublimation is one of them. King mentions sublimation under his "constructive" or healthy ways of overcoming inferiority as well, saying, "You can sublimate and take these inadequacies and somehow transform them into something meaningful and something constructive." Sublimating feelings of inferiority means taking the negative feelings and pushing them down, transmuting them into a socially acceptable form; for example, when King's shy young man directs his shyness into the socially acceptable form of the lone research scientist. Another healthy defense mechanism for Adler is compensation, which King termed "substitutionary compensation"; for example, when King's homely girl compensates by developing wit and charm as a healthy response to her perceived inferiority.

In the healthy forms of defenses, what Adler called a "minus situation" is turned into a "plus situation," thus curing the complex. Feelings of inferiority can be useful in the sense that they encourage us to strive toward self-realization and development. In this way, they push us on toward our own goal of perfection and wholeness, and aid in the whole point of King's sermon—"personality integration." King offered other ways to turn the minus into a plus, including absorption in a cause or principle, and the dedication of ourselves wholeheartedly to our work with the belief that it is significant and dignified.

The other pathway Adler suggested to curing the complex is through positive social interaction. He thought that psychological disturbances were caused by two main factors: inferiority feelings, and/or a lack of community feeling. Developing a strong social network and strengthening the sense of community belonging could go a long way to lessening feelings of inferiority. King offered this cure as well, telling his parishioners to consider working for the good of humanity, to devote themselves to a social cause, and to attach themselves to a religion that gives them a sense of belonging in the community and in the wider universe.

Finally, Adler and King shared the same belief that while some feelings of inferiority derive from personal handicaps or shortcomings, many of them derive from societal influences. Adler asserted that any kind of social discrimination such as classism, racism, or sexism could exacerbate inferiority feelings. King spoke of this briefly in his sermon, of the crippling effects of racism and its unjust byproducts of segregation and discrimination, and how these make it easy for black people "to feel that we don't count, that we are not significant, that we are less than [as we] stand every day before a system which says that to us."

This is a theme he would continue to develop in the decade

following this sermon. In his 1967 book *Where Do We Go From Here: Chaos or Community?*, he spent several chapters elaborating the theme of how a racist society makes its black citizens feel inferior. This small passage provides just a flavor of his later thinking on the subject:

> And so being a Negro in America is not a comfortable existence. It means being a part of the company of the bruised, the battered, the scarred and the defeated. Being a Negro in America means trying to smile when you want to cry. It means trying to hold on to physical life amid psychological death. It means the pain of watching your children grow up with clouds of inferiority in their mental skies.

In fact, examining the latter book in light of Adlerian therapy shows how adept King was as a cultural therapist. Adler's therapeutic model can be summarized, in part, by the following elements: empathy, interpretation, encouragement, action, and the development of community feeling. King provided all of these in his book, and in his public speaking engagements in both secular and religious environments. First, he gave empathy to black people for their situation, both their past through the institution of slavery, and their present through institutionalized racism, discrimination, segregation, and oppression. Not only did he empathize with his fellow black Americans, but he called on white Americans to do the same. "It is impossible for white Americans to grasp the depths and dimensions of the Negro's dilemma without understanding what it means to be a Negro in America. Of course it is not easy to perform this act of empathy," he told them, "yet, if the present chasm of hostility, fear and distrust is to be bridged, the white man must begin to walk in the pathways of his black brothers and feel some of the pain and hurt that throb without letup in their daily lives."

Part of the way he conveyed his empathy was through Adler's second therapeutic move: interpretation. King was masterful at interpreting the black psyche and situation, and conveying that interpretation to white and black people alike. He carefully explained where the inferiority complex came from, how it developed, and what some of its painful repercussions were. Then, he took the next step in Adlerian therapy; he provided encouragement that the inferiority complex could be overcome. For instance, he talked about how even during the darkness, the anger, and the anguish of slavery, their ancestors clung to faith in God. When the Civil Rights Movement began having successes of its own, he used those successes to encourage his people. In fact, he called courage "the Negro's most potent weapon in achieving self-respect," and he encouraged them to develop "this spirit, this drive, this rugged sense of somebodiness" as the first and most important step to take in dealing with long-ingrained feelings of inferiority.

Along with developing a new sense of somebodiness, King encouraged black Americans to take the next step Adler deemed critical to healing: action. In the case of the inferiority complex, action means doing things differently than they have been done before, in order to turn a minus situation into a plus situation. King challenged black Americans "to unite around powerful action programs to eradicate the last vestiges of racial injustice." He warned them that they were misled if they thought that the problem would work itself out, that "structures of evil do not crumble by passive waiting." King combined taking action with Adler's call to develop stronger community feelings, as much of the action was taken *as* a community on *behalf* of the community. King encouraged black Americans to "work passionately for group identity. . . The kind of group consciousness that Negroes need in order to participate more meaningfully at all levels of the life of our nation."

In summary, King closely followed all aspects of Adler's work on the inferiority complex—he understood the developmental factors that caused it, he knew the destructive defenses that would build up around it and the constructive defenses that would mediate its power, and he practiced the therapeutic technique necessary to help facilitate the cure.

Applying the Sermon and the Psychology to King

We now turn to ask to what extent did King himself struggle with feelings of inferiority, and how did he deal with those? The answer appears to be that he struggled very little, mostly due to a very healthy childhood, which allowed him to struggle against and overcome feelings of inferiority. As Adler wrote, inferiority feelings are normal in a child, and the influence of the family and the siblings is crucial in helping children overcome them.

Most of what we know about King's interpretation of his childhood comes from his college essay "An Autobiography of

Religious Development," written in 1950. There King paints a picture of a rather idyllic childhood where he was born into a "very congenial home situation," using the word "intimate" over and over again to describe his relationship with his siblings, with his parents, with his grandmother and other relatives who lived with them, and between his parents themselves. Physically, he was "an extraordinary healthy child" and mentally, he points out that his I.Q. stood "somewhat above the average."

Adler, like many other psychologists, considered the influence of the mother the primary factor in the child's development. By King's account, his mother was wonderful. He described her as always "behind the scene setting forth those motherly cares, the lack of which leaves a missing link in life." In front of the scenes was his father, whom King called "a real father" who always put his family first and provided everything they needed to live a comfortable existence.

King certainly had others besides his family who helped him to thrive. From the beginning, he was enmeshed in community, a good and kind community with his father's church as the focal point. In this community, King was "exposed to the best educational conditions in my childhood," and he was able to achieve great success in school, skipping grades and graduating from high school at age fifteen.

Adler wrote that if parents could help instill in children a satisfactory way of handling the three tasks of life—work, community, and love—then they would be inoculated against feelings of inferiority and would in fact develop the courage and ability to continue to grow and develop and make a contribution to society. All three of these tasks were inculcated in King from the time he was young; he saw both his father and his mother making a difference in their community through the work they both did in the church—and in the case of his father, in the political arena as well—and as far as love goes, King noted of his childhood, "I grew up in a family where love was central and where lovely relationships were ever present."

One place where it would have been natural for King to struggle with inferiority, however, is in the social and civic realm, because even the most optimal family and community conditions can't keep a child from experiencing racism outside its domain. Even there, as we discussed in Chapter 1, King encountered relatively little racism, and when he did, his parents seemed to have inoculated him so well that he didn't suffer from any feelings of his own inferiority. When he was six and his white childhood playmate's father no longer allowed the two children to play together, King asked his mother what had happened. She explained the facts of slavery, discrimination and segregation, and then she assured King, "You are as good as anyone." His father too reacted with dignity, pride, and firm resolution to acts of racism, and King learned from him that rugged sense of somebodiness he felt was so important for black people to develop. King described momentarily turning to the reactions of anger and hatred when he faced racism himself as a young man, but his parents and his religion helped him deal with those feelings by emphasizing the importance of love and forgiveness.

Another place we might speculate King would struggle with feelings of inferiority is in the academic world. Because he was moved at an accelerated pace through his education, he entered college at the age of fifteen not as prepared academically or seasoned intellectually as his peers. This academic inferiority conceivably could account for his widespread plagiarism of papers and entire chunks of his dissertation; however, he was a good student, even a gifted one, and he was able to pass his exams with high marks, so the plagiarism is curious because it appears academically unnecessary. Michael Eric Dyson explored King's plagiarism from many angles, and then hones in on the explanation that it was likely a small measure of intellectual inferiority writ large with the pressure of being a black student at a primarily white college. Dyson wrote "The most highly gifted black student could harbor insecurities about his talents in the white world that insisted on his inferiority, even in a relatively benign environment like Boston University, which had a reputation for nurturing bright black students."

Dyson discussed the concept of "stereotype threat," a term created by Stanford University psychologist Claude Steele and his colleagues to denote the threat minority students feel about being seen through the lens of a stereotype, or the fear of falling into one. King appears to have labored under this threat. While in graduate school, he was described as being "terribly tense, unable to escape the fact that he was a Negro in a mostly white world. He was painfully aware of how whites stereotyped the Negro as lazy and messy, always laughing, always loud and late." King described how he compensated for that stereotype.

> If I were a minute late to class, I was almost morbidly conscious of it and sure that everyone noticed it. Rather than be thought of as always laughing, I'm afraid I was grimly serious for a time. I had a tendency to overdress, to keep my room spotless, my shoes perfectly shined and my clothes immaculately pressed.

Thus, it becomes less a matter of King's felt sense of his own inferiority, and more that he personalized the cultural stereotype of black inferiority that may have led him to overachieve through his egregious plagiarism.

As an adult, King did practice what he preached in his sermon regarding what people should do to overcome feelings of inferiority: he accepted his limitations, he did his work with a sense of importance and dignity, he absorbed himself and gave his life over to a great cause, and he knew himself to be a beloved child of God with a strong sense of belonging in the community and in the universe. While King was not immune from psychological weaknesses, we can safely say the inferiority complex was not primary among them, though he was sensitive to subverting stereotypes of racial inferiority. He would struggle much more with the subject matter of the next sermon: self-centeredness.

"Conquering Self-Centeredness"
The Sermon

This sermon was the fourth and final one in the "Problems of Personality Integration" series. Delivering it on a squelching hot day in a church that had no air-conditioning, King promised not to preach too long, just long enough "to suggest certain ways to conquer self-centeredness and at least place the subject before you. So that you can go out and add the meat and try, in some way, to make it meaningful and practical in your everyday lives."

As often happened in King's sermons, he lays out the entire premise—the central problem and its solution—in the very beginning of the sermon, after opening with some text from the Bible. In this case, the text came from Jesus, who said, "He who finds his life shall lose it; he who loses his life for my sake, shall find it." King then states the problem.

> An individual has not begun to live until he can rise above

the narrow horizons of his particular individualistic concerns to the broader concerns of all humanity. And this is one of the big problems of life; that so many people never quite get to the point of rising above self. And so they end up the tragic victims of self-centeredness. They end up the victims of distorted and disrupted personality.

King compares these people to children who have never outgrown their natural early developmental stage of egocentricity. Showing his understanding of child psychology, he makes reference to psychologist Dr. William Henry Burnham, who taught that during the first six or seven years of development, egocentricity is inevitable. But at some point, King notes, we mature. This maturity is marked by the ability to love people for their own sake, to live for a cause or something outside of oneself, and to have higher loyalties.

After stating the problem, King then points out the effects, which he termed "tragic." Self-centered people are frustrated, disillusioned, and unhappy, never able to get enough of the admiration they need, mostly because their self-centeredness makes them unappealing to others. Self-centered people are touchy and sensitive, too easily victims of defeat and disappointment. They are hypersensitive to criticism. At worst, their self-centeredness can rise "to ominous proportions [leading] to a tragic sense of persecution," as they come to feel that the whole world and its occupants are against them.

Next, King offers some suggestions for how to overcome self-centeredness. First, he points to the importance of discovering "some cause and some purpose, some loyalty outside of yourself" and giving your life to it. The best way to overcome the ego is not to suppress it, but to channel it into meaningfulness, to project the ego outside of the ego. The ego can't be trampled down, King says, because "all human beings have a desire to belong and to feel significant and important." He quotes Ralph Waldo Emerson, "O, see how the masses of men worry themselves into nameless graves, while here and there, some great unselfish soul forgets himself into immortality." You cannot be absorbed in your self when you are absorbed in something beyond your self, King argues.

The second way to overcome self-centeredness is "by having the proper inner attitude toward your position" which is to realize that you are where you are in life because somebody helped you get there. You can't be arrogant or supercilious when you acknowledge the contributions of others and recognize the forces of history that helped shape the stage for your performance.

Finally, the proper religious faith will help overcome self-centeredness. The genius of a great religion, King tells his congregation, is that it "gives man a sense of belonging and on the other hand, it gives him a sense of dependence on something higher." God could say "I am that I am," but humans must say, "I am, because of." He quotes from the song "Amazing Grace" and says that we must realize we are dependent for everything on the grace of God. He summarizes his sermon with these words:

> He who seeks to find his ego will lose it. But he who loses his ego in some great cause, some great purpose, some great ideal, some great loyalty, he who discovers, somehow, that he stands where he stands because of the forces of history and because of other individuals; he who discovers that he stands where he stands because of the grace of God, finds himself. He loses himself in that something but later finds himself. And this is the way, it seems to me, to the integrated personality.

Psychological Theory

King's preaching on that hot summer day follows Jung's concept of "the relativization of the ego." Jung believed that the development of the ego is important because it is the very self-awareness that makes us individual human beings. However, Jung thought the ego is only one part of what makes up the larger Self which we can designate with a capital "S" to distinguish it from the smaller self of the ego. The larger Self, if it can be defined at all, is the archetype of wholeness, whereby we know ourselves as part of the larger universe, much larger than our own awareness. The Self includes such relationships as ours with nature, with God, and with our fellow humans, past and present: in other words, our interconnectivity with all that is. Therefore, one of the marks of mature individuals is the relativization of the ego, whereby they come to seem themselves as a small piece of a more whole and more universal Self. When individuals are able to relativize their ego and live inside of the larger wholeness and potential of the Self, they move toward an integrated personality; Jung termed this the process of individuation.

King's preaching and Jung's teaching follow along remarkably similar lines. First of all, neither negated the importance of the ego, particularly in early childhood development. However, both noted that if the ego is the only part of the personality to develop, inflation could occur, causing a person to become self-centered, egotistical, and narcissistic. Both were in agreement about ways to develop the Self, which is to relativize your own ego and attach yourself to a larger, more universal vision, to see yourself as part of a larger whole. For King, this meant "to extend the ego into objectively meaningful channels," giving yourself to "something outside of yourself." Both Jung and King used the imagery of the ego as a small circle inside of the larger circle of the Self, with King noting that self-centered people "just move around in their little circles," and are only "bounded all around by themselves."

Both King and Jung also realized the importance of human relationships to the relativization of the ego, particularly the realization of our dependence upon others. Jung called relationships "an indispensable condition, for without the conscious acknowledgment and acceptance of our fellowship with those around us there can be no synthesis of personality . . . The inner consolidation of the individual . . . emphatically includes our fellow man."

For both Jung and King, the relationship to the Self also meant a relationship with God, which Jung at times called "the god-image" to be inclusive of all religious systems and other senses of spiritual connection that come outside of organized religion. King believed that "the proper religious faith" provided the individual with the balance and perspective to view his ego as part of the great "something beyond in which he lives and moves and even moves and gains his being." Humans are not significant when they put their own egos at center, but become significant and centered when they give themselves over in relationship with God or their god-image.

Finally, both King and Jung asserted that in order to become a whole human being, an integrated personality, it is important to lose the ego in order to find the Self. This loss is not literal, only a relativizing of the egoic circle into the larger circle of wholeness. Both pointed to the many dangers of living life at the level of the ego, not the least of which is a lack of fulfillment, meaning, and connection with other humans and the whole of the natural and spiritual world.

Applying the Sermon and the Psychology to King

King made it very clear in this sermon and in others that he was not immune to the problem of self-centeredness. As early as 1957, when his name and notoriety were still confined to his successes in the Montgomery Bus Boycott, King shared with his congregation that "one of the problems that I have to face and even fight every day is this problem of self-centeredness, this tendency that can so easily come to my life now that I'm something special, that I'm something important."

It is particularly poignant to read these lines knowing that this problem was just beginning for King, that it would in fact widen in scope and deepen in intensity.

> Living over the past year, I can hardly go into any city or any town in this nation where I'm not lavished with hospitality by peoples of all races and of all creeds. I can hardly go anywhere to speak in this nation where hundreds and thousands of people are not turned away because of lack of space. And then after speaking, I often have to be rushed out to get away from the crowd rushing for autographs. I can hardly walk the street in any city of this nation where I'm not confronted with people running up the street, "Isn't this Reverend King of Alabama?"

Given this attention, King noted he could easily develop the dangerous tendency to believe that he was someone special, someone ingenious and important, and to become arrogant as a result.

But King worked on his self-centeredness the same way he preached that his congregation should work on theirs. First, he embodied the definition of a man who had given himself to a cause and a purpose. Long before the Montgomery Bus Boycott, long before there was such a thing as the Civil Rights Movement, we've seen that King committed his life to serving humanity, to following that "inescapable urge to serve society." As explored in the first chapter, King followed that calling to extremes most humans are incapable of understanding, let alone emulating, until he was able to say of himself:

> You have to give yourself entirely. Then, once you make up your mind that you *are* giving yourself, then you are

prepared to do anything that serves the Cause and advances the Movement. I have reached that point. I have no option anymore about what I will do. I have given myself fully.

King not only gave himself to a cause, he also devoted himself to a principle, a principle he was willing to die for—nonviolence.

If every Negro in the United States turns to violence, I will choose to be that one lone voice preaching that this is the wrong way. Maybe this sounded like arrogance. But it was not intended that way. It was simply my way of saying that I would rather be a man of conviction than a man of conformity. Occasionally in life one develops a conviction so precious and meaningful that he will stand on it 'til the end. This is what I have found in nonviolence.

Secondly, King practiced what he preached with regard to self-centeredness by realizing his dependence on others. He told his congregation that he turned to God to help him see "that where I stand today, I stand because others helped me to stand there." He relativized his own ego in the Civil Rights Movement by praying to God to help him

to see myself in my true perspective. Help me, O God, to see that I'm just a symbol of a movement. Help me to see that I'm the victim of what the Germans call a Zeitgeist and that something was getting ready to happen in history; history was ready for it. And that a boycott would have taken place in Montgomery, Alabama if I had never come to Alabama. Help me to realize that I'm where I am because of the forces of history and because of the fifty thousand Negroes of Alabama who will never get their names in the papers and in the headline. O God, help me to see that where I stand today, I stand because others helped me to stand there and because the forces of history projected me there. And this moment would have come in history even if M. L. King had never been born. And when we come to see that, we stand with a humility. This is the prayer I pray to God every day, "Lord help me to see M. L. King as M. L. King in his true perspective." Because if I don't see that, I will become the biggest fool in America.

The third way King taught others to manage their own self-centeredness, and managed his own, was to realize his dependence on God and on his grace. King recognized all he had been given by God in his relatively easy youth. He also realized it could have gone a different way. He spoke of this in his sermon by sharing an insight he had upon visiting some prisoners one day. As he walked away from the prisoners, "I couldn't walk out with arrogance. I couldn't walk out with the feeling that I'm not like these men." Instead, he walked out of the prison with a "ringing in my heart saying, 'But for the grace of God, you would be there.'" "When you see that point," he told his congregation, "you cannot be arrogant. But you walk through life with a humility that takes away the self-centeredness that makes you a disintegrated personality."

It's not surprising that King struggled with keeping his own ego relativized, for he was both human and, because of his symbolic status in the movement, considered by some divine. People including those who knew King intimately and those who only had peripheral contact with him in the movement have differing judgments and assessments regarding how well he was able to conquer his own self-centeredness—there are those who think his ego was completely annihilated, and on the other end of the spectrum, those who think his ego was inflated to that of a god. However, King himself never claimed victory in the struggle or mastery over the problem, only claimed that it *was* a struggle, only claimed that it *was* a problem. King would surely agree with Jung that the process of relativizing the ego and integrating the larger Self is the work of a lifetime, the most difficult work we will ever do and one that few ever truly accomplish except in rare, grace-filled moments.

Conclusion

In the last chapter, we examined the breadth of King's psychological knowledge through the "mini-sermons" contained in his advice column responses, and this chapter sought to examine the depth of his knowledge by looking at some of his longer sermons. In each of these sermons, the psychology he teaches and preaches is well-grounded in depth psychological principles and practices, and we see King striving to apply those very principles and practices to his own life, and to the process of integrating his own personality, to varying degrees of success.

From tending to the souls of his readers in his advice column to the souls of his parishioners in his church, we move in the next chapter to examine how King used psychology to tend to the souls of the citizens of his country, all the while with the same goal: the integration of the personality.

5

THERAPY:

AMERICA ON THE COUCH

This chapter makes an imaginative leap in casting Martin Luther King, Jr. in the role of a therapist working with America as his client. Though therapeutic processes were designed in the consulting room in the dyadic relationship of therapist and client, I want to suggest here that they can work just as well when the dyad is that of an individual therapist and a group of people, or even an entire country. They also work when the therapist is not an individual but a committed group of individuals working together with the goal of healing and transformation. Though King is the subject of this book and therefore the focus of this chapter, of course we know that he did not act alone, nor would he have been as effective if he did act alone. King's power to transform the culture came from the willingness of others to work with him in the transformation, as well as the willingness of the culture itself to *be* transformed, for it is a psychological truism that no "body" (be it an individual or a group) changes without wanting to change on some level.

Before we begin examining how King "treated" America, we must first understand his diagnosis of her problem.

Diagnosing America

In general, diagnosis is problematic in therapy; the idea of taking very complex human beings and giving them a label that reduces them to their pathology, as if they were *nothing but* bipolar, schizophrenic, anorexic, etc., is troubling to many a therapist and client alike. However, diagnostic labels do function as useful lenses through which to examine an individual, or in the case of this chapter, a country. So when we explore America as neurotic in this chapter, I do not mean that as a statement of her essence, as if she were *nothing but* neurotic, for America is a complex country full of multiple functions and dysfunctions, and others could make the argument for a different diagnosis such as addictive, narcissistic, or ADHD, all labels that can also apply.

The fact that King found America's soul to be troubled goes without saying, for there would be no need to redeem the country unless it was fallen somehow. As Richard H. King highlights, however, King chose interesting language for a minister. "Increasingly, the vocabulary King used to describe such transformations of the self was largely psychological or medical rather than religious. Analogous to his concern with the therapeutic effects of action was a diagnosis of American society in terms of health and sickness as much as right and wrong." In other words, King referred to America less as a "sinful" nation as he did to a "sick" nation, and the diagnoses he used for her sickness were primarily psychological in nature.[8]

King labeled America with three basic diagnoses. Often, he referred to the schizophrenic nature of the cultural psyche. He stated, "America has been something of a schizophrenic personality, tragically divided against herself. On the one hand we have proudly professed the great principles of democracy, but on the other hand we have sadly practiced the very opposite of those principles." King also referred to America as neurotic, telling his staff, "We live in a sick, neurotic nation," and the Movement was based on "the hope that we can move this sick nation away from at least a level of its sickness." He expressed fear that America would move from neurotic to psychotic:

> If America would come to herself and return to her true home, "one nation, indivisible, with liberty and justice of all," she would give the democratic creed a new authentic ring, enkindle the imagination of mankind and fire the souls of men. If she fails, she will be victimized with the ultimate social psychosis that can only lead to national suicide.

Of King's three psychological diagnoses, neurotic is the one we will use for this chapter. Psychotic is a diagnostic stretch of the imagination, and King used it rarely and only in the context of warning the country what it was in danger of becoming, not what it

---

[8] The most common medical metaphor King used compared America to a cancer patient, with himself as a doctor performing surgery to remove the tumor.

was. He used schizophrenic often, but always in the simplistic context of a split or a division within a personality. Schizophrenia is a much more complicated diagnosis, and we won't use it here for two reasons: first, while America clearly has a split psyche, most of the other symptoms of schizophrenia don't apply, and second, the split in the personality King referred to belongs to the neurotic, as we'll see below. [9]

To make the argument for America as neurotic, we'll draw on psychologist Karen Horney's classic text *The Neurotic Personality Of Our Time,* published in 1937. King referred to this book in at least one sermon, calling it one of the bestsellers of his day, suggesting he had read it or was at least familiar with it. While the book is primarily concerned with the individual neurotic, Horney argued that conditions can exist in a culture which could make many of its citizens neurotic; King took it one step further and asserted that the *cultural personality as a whole* could be neurotic.

In brief, Horney defined neurotic personalities as those who have a gap between their *idealized self* (the self they think they should be and therefore convince themselves they are) and their *actual self* (the self they exhibit for others to see), which keeps them from being their *real self,* the integrated personality they could become without the neurotic gap between their idealized and actual selves. The task of the therapist is to help neurotics become aware of the idealized self, to show them the costs of maintaining such a self, and to help them relinquish the idealized self in favor of the more real self and the fuller relationships that self could engage in. This can be no mere intellectual understanding; it is not enough for neurotics to intellectually *know* there is a gap, but rather, they must be made to *feel* the gap if any real change is to take place.

Unlike Freud, who thought that neuroses arose from frustrated instinctual drives, primarily sexual, Horney argued that neuroses come from disturbed relationships and can be improved when those relationships improve. Though she didn't think it would be easy, she was more optimistic about the lessening or a "curing" of a neurosis than other psychologists before her.

In the remainder of this chapter, let's further explore her definition of a neurotic and see how that definition applies to the

---

[9] Take our two party political system as an example. The Republican elephant and the Democratic donkey—we aren't even the same animal.

United States. Then we can understand King's greatest therapeutic contribution to the United States during the Civil Rights Movement: the lessening of her neurosis around the issue of race.

Defining Neurosis

Horney defined neurosis as *"a disturbance in one's relation to self and to others."* In the case of America during the Civil Rights Movement, the main disturbed relationship was between black and white Americans, a rent that historically began with the act of enslavement. Despite the Civil War, the Emancipation Proclamation, and the Thirteenth Amendment, the relationship remained deeply disturbed.

Horney made an important distinction between a conflict and a neurosis. Basic conflicts are a normal part of life for everyone. What distinguishes neurotic conflict from basic conflict is that neurotic conflicts are typically unconscious and repressed, and the neurotic resists unearthing them because they have a disruptive power. As quick proof of the neurosis of America with regard to race, we need look no further than the Civil War, a battle fought in large part because the relatively more conscious North met with such resistance from the relatively more unconscious South over the injustice of slavery that only a hugely disruptive force such as a five year war could unearth it—and even then, history shows that the South capitulated in large part only because it could no longer resist physically, not because it became conscious of its repression and oppression psychologically.

Because of their disruptive potential, Horney asserted that neurotics go to any length to deny the existence of a conflict. In the South, in particular, there were a whole series of denials around slavery. Kenneth Stampp examined these in detail in his seminal book about the psychology of slavery, *The Peculiar Institution.* To summarize some of the denials and the defenses around slavery, southerners and supporters of slavery told themselves that white people were not physically able to do that kind of labor in the southern environment; they argued that Africans had racial traits which suited them for bondage; they characterized black people as barbarians who needed to be disciplined and controlled; they reassured themselves with the reminder that they had not invented bondage but were simply participants in a long lineage of cultures built on slavery; they asserted that most slaves were quite content with servitude, and in fact, their living conditions in the United

States were superior to those they had left behind in Africa; and they comforted themselves with the religious justification that they had saved Africans from their pagan religion and their sure eternal damnation by introducing them to Christianity and its salvation. These justifications were necessary psychological defense mechanisms to allow the injustices of slavery to persist.

Though the institution of slavery was eventually abolished by law, that law did little to repair the neurotic disturbance in relationships between black and white people, and a new neurotic institution was created: segregation. As with slavery, many white people went to great lengths to deny the basic conflict inherent in segregation, arguing that black people did not want to eat, or learn, or ride in public transportation, or use public accommodations, or stay in a motel, or live in the same neighborhood, or participate in recreation with white people any more than white people wanted to do these things with black people.

White people also used other forms of denial and rationalization: they told themselves segregation was the law of God, and that black people were dirty and thus racial mixing was unhealthy for white people. They told themselves that separate could be equal and in fact wrote it into the law in the 1896 Supreme Court case, Plessy v. Ferguson. Horney stated you can spot a neurotic conflict by its inconsistency: in America, from the time-period of slavery through the Civil Rights Movement, the most obvious inconsistency and the clearest evidence of her neurotic personality lay in her professed belief that "all men are created equal" while treating black citizens as anything but.

The Genesis of a Neurosis

If neurosis doesn't come from the frustration of an instinctual drive, as Freud thought, then what is its genesis? Horney traced neurosis back to childhood. If a child grows up and doesn't feel a sense of belonging, or worse, grows up in an openly hostile environment, that child will feel a "profound insecurity and vague apprehensiveness" that will develop into what she called *basic anxiety,* the feeling "of being isolated and helpless in a world conceived as potentially hostile."

> Harassed by these disturbing conditions, the child gropes for ways to keep going, ways to cope with this menacing world. Despite his own weakness and fears he unconsciously shapes

his tactics to meet the particular forces operating in his environment. In doing so, he develops not only *ad hoc* strategies but lasting character trends which become part of his personality. I have called these "neurotic trends."

She delineated three trends in the neurotic personality: compliance, where the primary feeling is helplessness and the neurotic copes with that helplessness by *moving towards* people; aggression, where the primary feeling is hostility and the neurotic copes by *moving against* people; and detachment, where the primary feeling is isolation and the neurotic copes by *moving away* from people. Neurotics usually have more than one trend, but one of them is typically overemphasized.

Painting the genesis of this country[10] in the broadest of strokes, it is easy to see how the United States developed its neurosis, and to spot some of the neurotic trends within it. To begin with, we could argue that the original colonizers who came here were already neurotic themselves. They had experienced England as an oppressive parent, hostile to their needs for freedom and self-expression. They didn't feel they belonged in that country, and longed for a place where they could feel at home. They felt menaced and were full of basic anxiety, and as a result exhibited the neurotic trait of detachment by *moving away* from mother England to the United States.

Once here, they faced more hostility in the form of harsh conditions for survival, and their insecurity and sense of isolation was not alleviated, as they had hoped, but instead increased. At first they *moved towards* Native Americans for support in their helplessness in the new country, but eventually became aggressive and *moved against* them to take their land. That aggression was also a *moving against* nature in their attempts to tame the wilderness. When mother England reached back for a relationship with them (albeit an unhealthy, controlling relationship), they *moved against* her in the battle for independence, again exhibiting the trends of detachment and aggression.

---

[10] By "the genesis of this country," I mean this colonized "white" country which began with the arrival of the Puritans in Massachusetts who brought with them the conditions for establishing a neurotic new world.

The Idealized Self

For neurotics, when safety is paramount and their real selves are threatened, they become alienated from that real self, experiencing it as inadequate and powerless. Needing a new sense of identity, they form an idealized image which is always stronger, more powerful, more glorious, and more perfect then they themselves could ever be. Some neurotics become unconsciously identified with the idealized image, thinking it is truly who they are, while others become consciously identified with the idealization, believing this is who they *should* be or who they *could* be. Regardless, Horney noted, "Conscious or unconscious, the [idealized] image is always in large degree removed from reality, though the influence it exerts on the person's life is very real indeed. What is more, it is always flattering in character."

In the case of the Puritans, they brought to America the idealized image of themselves as God's chosen people, set apart to build *a city upon a hill*. There, all the eyes of the world would watch them create a utopian society, God's people in God's kingdom on earth. They were incessant in their drive to create the perfect society, and as a result, they created a culture just as hostile and oppressive and menacing as the one they left behind. The neurotic can't stand the gap between idealization and realization, Horney stated, and incessantly attempts "to bridge the gap and whip himself into perfection." One need only to think of Nathaniel Hawthorne's *The Scarlet Letter* to see a very real, though fictional depiction of this phenomenon among the early Puritans: remember Hester Prynne banished to jail and then to the edge of the woods, forced to live apart from the community for her imperfection though the sin of adultery; remember fellow adulterer Reverend Dimmesdale flagellating himself in the closet, trying to whip himself into perfection while simultaneously punishing himself for his failure to uphold his ideal.

The idealized image of the neurotic eventually turns into the idealized self. This happens when the actual self is too painful to hold, so neurotics shift their energies into realizing their idealized selves. To maintain the ideal, the neurotic turns to several strategies: the search for glory, the compulsion for perfection, the drive toward neurotic ambition, and the need for vindictive triumph. All these drives are compulsive, and when following them the neurotic becomes insatiable, easily frustrated and over-reactive to setbacks, and full of arrogance and pride. Of the latter, Horney wrote, "The development of pride is the logical outcome, the climax and consolidation of the process initiated with the search for glory." She noted, "As soon as we go off on the search for glory we stop being concerned about the truth of ourselves. *Neurotic pride, in all its forms, is false pride.*" This false and elevated pride leads the neurotic "into the fantastic, into the realm of *unlimited possibilities.*"

There are two manifestations of those fantastic, unlimited possibilities of America's idealized self that I want to briefly touch on here.[11] The first is the two documents that came out of 1776 and 1787—the Declaration of Independence and the Constitution of the United States. Here the idealized self of America was placed on parchment paper for the entire world to see. In the former document, the country declared, "We hold these Truths to be self-evident, that all Men are created equal, that they are endowed by their Creator with certain unalienable Rights, that among these are Life, Liberty and the Pursuit of Happiness." In the latter document, the country declared its commitment to "form a more perfect Union, establish Justice, insure domestic Tranquility, provide for the common defence, promote the general Welfare, and secure the Blessings of Liberty to ourselves and our Posterity." Put the two opening statements of the country's two most important documents together, and a definition of America's idealized self emerges: it is the perfection of the principles of equality, life, liberty, happiness, unity, justice, tranquility, and general welfare for now and forever more.

We can see a second manifestation of America's unlimited and fantastic idealized self in the Manifest Destiny Doctrine of 1840. Historian Michael T. Lubragge defined the doctrine and explained how America rationalized such a sense of destiny.

> It [America] had a future that was destined by God to expand its borders, with no limit to area or country. All the traveling and expansion were part of the spirit of Manifest

---

[11] I am aware that I'm attempting to do in just a few pages what could be done in an entire book, and though that book interests me, my purpose here is simply to show that it's *reasonable* to imagine America as neurotic and driven by neurotic pride, and then to move on to the real question this chapter poses: how did King apply therapeutic techniques to transform the disturbed soul of America?

Destiny, a belief that it was God's will that Americans spread over the entire continent, and to control and populate the country as they see fit. Many expansionists conceived God as having the power to sustain and guide human destiny. . . . For example, the idea that the Puritan notion of establishing a "city on a hill" was eventually secularized into Manifest Destiny—a sort of materialistic, religious, utopian destiny.

Historian Robert W. Johanssen wrote that white people in the United States then "had a reputation that they were in awe of nothing and nothing could stand in their way. The word was boundlessness—there were no bounds, no limits to what an individual, society, and the nation itself could achieve." This description matches Horney's assessment that neurotics live in the realm of unlimited possibilities. Johanssen also recognized the basic anxiety present in the American psyche at the time.

> In many ways, this was also an age of paradox because there were anxieties and apprehensions. An erosion of values seemed to be threatened by the changes that took place. The changes were so vast, so important, so penetrating and so much a part of people's lives, that individuals had a hard time adjusting to them. The kind of changes that were taking place during this period of time, in turn, bred a kind of anxiety, restlessness, concern, and apprehension on the part of individuals whose lives were changing.

To summarize our diagnosis of America so far, the basic anxiety that the Puritans brought with them from the Old World fueled the formation of the New World, and during the early childhood years of the country, led to the creation of the idealized self and the concomitant suppression of the real self. America's idealized self can be seen in its documents of the 18th century and its grandiose philosophy of the 19th century, and continues to manifest in false pride to this day.

It is important to note here that the idealized self of the neurotic is never wholly fictitious. Horney called the idealized self

> an imaginative creation interwoven with and determined by very realistic factors. It usually contains traces of the person's genuine ideals. While the grandiose achievements

are illusory, the potentialities underlying them are often real. More relevant, it is born of very real inner necessities, it fulfills very real functions, and it has a very real influence on its creator.

Part of the function of the idealized self is to instill a sense of identity and unity among its parts. In the case of this country, the idealized self lives in its very name, "the United States of America" and lives in her motto, "E pluribus Unum"—out of the many, one. Yet unity is an idealized image that America has never lived up to in reality.

One of the clearest places where America's neurosis has been visible is in the disunity of its black and white citizens, a disunity that started with slavery and continued through segregation. This disunity is also illustrative of the wide gap between her idealized self and her actual self, because no country professing the values of equality, life, liberty, happiness, unity, justice, tranquility, and general welfare for now and forever more can possibly justify slavery and segregation except by the strongest system of unconscious, neurotic defenses. So we turn now to the Civil War in brief and the Civil Rights Movement in more detail, viewing them as attempts to end the unconsciousness, to cure the neurosis, and to cause America to close the gap between her ideal and real self.

The Civil War

Abraham Lincoln understood the symbolic nature of the Civil War; America was fighting over the gap between her idealized self and her real self. He knew the country conceived eighty-seven years earlier was not living up to its great propositions; he called the country "a house divided" and asserted, "'A house divided against itself cannot stand.' I believe this Government cannot endure permanently half slave and half free." Lincoln followed Horney's steps for curing a neurosis: first he helped the country intellectually understand the divided self. Then, he helped her *feel* the gap by witnessing the horrors of a war where that divided self was made visible.

After the Civil War, Lincoln reminded the nation that the dead had hallowed the ground with their sacrifice, and encouraged the living to resolve "that these dead shall not have died in vain, that this nation under God shall have a new birth of freedom, and that government of the people, by the people, for the people shall not perish from the earth." These deaths would not be in vain if they led to the rebirth of the *authentic* America, an America that could live up to and make real its ideals. The Emancipation Proclamation declared an end to the gap, and declared once again on paper America's commitments to her ideals.

However, slavery as an institution was quickly replaced with segregation as an institution, and injustice and inequality still existed in both the letter and the spirit of the law. Liberty and equality suffered blows again, and in actual deed, America was still not living out her creed during the 20th century.[12]

The Birth of the Civil Rights Movement

The Civil War did emancipate the slaves, but it did not destroy the neurotic relationship between America's black and white citizens; the disturbance simply went underground briefly and then surfaced in the form of legal segregation and discrimination and continued racial and economic injustice. These were an extension of the neurotic trends that America had already developed and displayed: aggressiveness and detachment.

While aggressiveness by white owners against black slaves was ended by abolition, it remained against black citizens in other ways: in physical aggression like lynchings and beatings that went mostly unpunished or at least unpunished commensurate with the crime; in the denial of the right to vote; and in intimidation and harassment. Detachment was achieved through segregation, creating separate worlds where the two races would not have to interact with each other at all, except in the relationship of employer/employee, which in itself can be seen as an aggressive relationship. And because white people made all the segregation laws and enforced them, they were aggressive *in their detachment*, holding all the power and withholding any authentic relationship.

In 1990, Shelby Steele's best-selling book *The Content of Our Character: A New Vision of Race in America* explored the long relationship between power and race.

---

[12] I'm not denying that abolishing slavery was a huge step forward for America, but I am arguing that replacing it with segregation and other forms of racial and economic injustice is like telling a patient that your class 5 cancer is now only class 3—the point being, you still have cancer.

The distinction of race has always been used in American life to sanction each race's pursuit of power in relation to the other. The allure of race as a human delineation is the very shallowness of the delineation it makes. Onto this shallowness—mere skin and hair—men can project a false depth, a system of dismal attributions, a series of malevolent or ignoble stereotypes that skin and hair lack the substance to contradict. These dark projections then rationalize the pursuit of power. Your difference from me makes you bad, and your badness justifies, even demands, my pursuit of power over you—the oldest formula for aggression known to man. Whenever much importance is given to race, power is the primary motive.

Power, in turn, is often an unconscious defense against fear. Horney argued that we cannot underestimate the power of fear in creating neurotic defenses. These defenses maintain the status quo and protect the fragile real self that the idealized self shelters. Slavery was the status quo for over two hundred years, and when that was violently dismantled, the white psyche feared the loss of any further power, so it asserted that power in all new forms of injustice.

King was well aware of the psychology of fear and its connection to power and race:

> Racial segregation is buttressed by such irrational fears as loss of preferred economic privilege, altered social status, intermarriage, and adjustment to new situations. Through sleepless nights and haggard days, numerous white people struggled pitifully to combat these fears. By following the path of escape, some [the detached type] seek to ignore questions of race relations, and to close their minds to the issues involved. Others [the aggressive type], placing their faith in legal maneuvers, counsel massive resistance. Still others [more aggressive still] hope to drown their fears by engaging in acts of meanness and violence toward their Negro brethren. But how futile are all those remedies! Instead of eliminating fear, they instill deeper and more pathological fears.

We will return to the relationship between power and fear, and discuss the complicated way King provoked, placated, and manipulated white America's fears during the Civil Rights Movement. First, however, it is important to orient King's rise to leadership in a particular time in history. King stepped onto the scene in 1955, the year after the Supreme Court decision outlawing segregation in public schools. There was real hope in the air after Brown v. Board of Education, hope that the decision, in the words of a *Washington Post* editorial, would "bring to an end a painful disparity between American principles and American practices. It will help to refurbish American prestige in a world which looks to this land for moral inspiration and restore the faith of Americans themselves in their own great values and traditions." As historian Dr. Arthur Schlesinger declared, "The Supreme Court has finally reconciled the Constitution with the preamble of the Declaration of Independence."

Both of these statements show that faith was alive during 1954 and 1955, faith that false pride would give way to real pride as the country closed the gap between her ideal and her actual self and became authentically the *United States* of America. But when many recalcitrant Southern schools obstinately refused to desegregate, despair set in again.

King and the Idealized Self

It was at this moment when King set foot on the scene, answering Horney's call for a therapist to illuminate the discrepancy between the idealized self and the actual self that would lead to the birth of the real self. King was keenly aware of this discrepancy since he was a young boy; in fact, he entered—and won—an oratorical contest when he was fourteen-years-old with a speech called "The Negro and the Constitution." In that speech, we see the themes that would occupy him his entire life. He talked about slavery, calling it "a strange paradox in a nation founded on the principles that all men are created free and equal." He talked about The Emancipation Proclamation, and how "the nation in 1865 took a new stand—freedom for all people." But he also pointed out, "Black America still wears chains. The finest Negro is at the mercy of the meanest white man." And he argued, we cannot have "an enlightened democracy" when one group lives in ignorance, ill health, and poverty. He called upon the spirit of Lincoln and Jesus Christ to "cast down the last barrier to perfect freedom."

In his first speech before the bus boycotters in Montgomery

twelve years later, he returned to his boyhood ideas. He declared that they protested because of their love for democracy and a "deep-seated belief that democracy transformed from thin paper to thick action is the greatest form of government on earth." For the next twelve years of his life until his assassination, that love for democracy would inform all the actions he took on behalf of the paper ideals of his country, and even when he was weary, he would carry on, explaining that he could not rest until he "had achieved the ideals of our democracy."

It was this love of his country that moved Jesse Jackson to call King "the greatest American patriot of the twentieth century." He loved the idealized image America had created for herself, and in *Search for the Beloved Community: The Thinking of Martin Luther King, Jr.,* professors Kenneth L. Smith and Ira G. Zepp assert that King quoted the Declaration of Independence and the Bill of Rights more than any other document other than the Bible.

But as a lover of America, and one in a committed relationship with her, he insisted upon the right to question her and hold her to her ideals. He told that crowd in Montgomery, "There is never a time in our American democracy that we must ever think we're wrong when we protest. We reserve that right." As America's therapist, he loved her even though he recognized that her idealized and actual selves were very far apart. White America, he said,

> has been torn between selves—a self in which she proudly professed the great principles of democracy and a self in which she sadly practiced the antithesis of democracy. This tragic duality has produced a strange indecisiveness and ambivalence toward the Negro, causing America to take a step backward simultaneously with every step forward on the question of racial justice.

Here, in his role as a cultural therapist, King did something theologian and philosopher Martin Buber argued was important to genuine healing—"real meeting." Buber wrote that when you meet someone, you must "accept and confirm him as he now is." But that's only the first step. Next, he counseled, "I must take the other person in his dynamic existence, in his specific potentiality . . . for in the present lies hidden what he *can become*. His potentiality makes itself felt to me as that which I would most confirm." In simplest terms, what King did was hold a real meeting with America. In that meeting, he confirmed her for who she was right at the moment (her actual self), but then he confirmed *in* her that which he most wanted to see—her potential to close the gap and make real her noble ideals.

As events in the 1950's coalesced into the Civil Rights Movement, King saw that Movement as the vehicle to restore the country to her original dream. He spoke in lofty terms of what the Movement would achieve. His 1963 text "Letter from Birmingham City Jail" provides one example.

> We will reach the goal of freedom in Birmingham and all over the nation, because the goal of America is freedom. Abused and scorned though we may be, our destiny is tied up with America's destiny. Before the pilgrims landed at Plymouth, we were here. Before the pen of Jefferson etched the majestic words of the Declaration of Independence across the pages of history, we were here. For more than two centuries our forebears labored in this country without wages; they made cotton king; they built the homes of their masters while suffering gross injustice and shameful humiliation—and yet out of a bottomless vitality they continued to thrive and develop. If the inexpressible cruelties of slavery could not stop us, the opposition we now face will surely fail. We will win our freedom because the sacred heritage of our nation and the eternal will of God are embodied in our echoing demands.

Professor Maurice Friedman argued that a therapist, in attempting to help to facilitate a patient's cure, "may have to wrestle *with* the patient, *for* the patient, and *against* the patient. He is not only concerned with the person he is at the moment, but also with his becoming what he or she is called to become." Here we see King as the country's therapist willing to wrestle *with* America, *for* America, and *against* America to make her see what she was at the moment, and to become what she was called to become. For this he was willing to do more than just wrestle—as we explored in Chapter 1, he was willing, ultimately, to die. The above portion of the letter makes clear why he was willing to do this: he saw himself and the Movement as an instrument of "the sacred heritage" of America and "the eternal will of God."

King spoke often to America of her professed sacred ideals, but let's remember Horney's admonition, that it's not enough for neurotics to have an intellectual understanding of the gap between ideals and actuality, but they must be made to *feel* the gap, particularly its irrationality. King knew this, knew that talk was cheap and that many other powerful leaders, both black and white, had said and were saying the same words, yet progress was still too slow in terms of legal and societal transformation. King's particular brilliance was the systemic way he made America *feel* the gap, to experience the rage, the anger, the hostility, the hatred, and the violence that were all irrational given what was warranted by the occasion.[13]

King, as an unwavering advocate of nonviolence, could not and would not literally wrestle with America, but instead, used the method of nonviolent resistance, primarily in the forms of boycotts, marches, sit-ins, civil disobedience, and mass demonstrations. I want to concentrate primarily on the marches, because through them he gained most of his major victories, and through them he demonstrated his psychological acuity by outwardly dramatizing the inner situation of the country's psyche. As he said, "I'm still convinced that there is nothing more powerful to dramatize a social evil than the tramp, tramp of marching feet." To understand why the marches were the most powerful way of dramatizing America's neurosis, we need to peer a little deeper into King's understanding of the psychology of the times.

The Entrenchment of the White Ego

First, King was deeply aware of how just how terrified white America was to change. Horney listed several common fears that plague neurotics. To begin with, they are afraid of having their equilibrium disturbed. Any change in routine can facilitate this, and neurotics will do anything to avoid such changes. They have a fear of exposure, either to themselves or to others, exposure of the less-than-perfect selves they need to believe they are. They have a deep fear of disregard, humiliation, and ridicule that would cause further injury to their self-esteem. They suffer from "terror of the unknown,

---

[13] By means of quick example—children marching peacefully for equality being bitten by dogs and plastered to walls by high-powered water hoses by police, those officers charged with protecting *all* citizens from harm—how could one not *feel* the irrationality of this response?

of having to relinquish safety devices and satisfactions hitherto gained."

Neurotics desperately need to maintain the status quo since they created and maintain that status quo to give them power over their anxiety. They will even put up with some degree of suffering to stave off what they think would be unbearable suffering if they were forced to change. Thomas Jefferson spoke to this in the Declaration of Independence when he wrote, "All experience hath shewn, that mankind are more disposed to suffer, while evils are sufferable, than to right themselves by abolishing the forms to which they are accustomed."

C. G. Jung thought this was a law of the psyche as well, that it was predisposed to the maintenance of the status quo, and would only be roused to change by some strong motivation.

> Clearly, no one develops his personality because somebody tells him that it would be useful or advisable to do so. . . . Without necessity nothing budges, the human personality least of all. It is tremendously conservative, not to say torpid. Only acute necessity is able to rouse it. The developing personality obeys no caprice, no command, no insight, only brut necessity; it needs the motivating force of inner or outer fatalities.

In Montgomery, in face of a bus boycott that lasted over a year—something that no one initially anticipated—King learned this important yet painful lesson about the stubborn entrenchment of the ego. He stated humbly,

> I soon saw that I was the victim of unwarranted pessimism because I had started out with an unwarranted optimism. I had gone to the meeting with a great illusion. I had believed that the privileged would give up their privileges on request. This experience, however, taught me a lesson. I came to see that no one gives up his privileges without strong resistance.

In a colorful analogy, he said, "Now it might be true that old man segregation is on its deathbed. But history has proven that social systems have a great last-minute breathing power. And the guardians of the status-quo are always on hand with their oxygen tents to keep the old order alive." King took to heart the words of one of his favorite philosophers, Reinhold Niebuhr, who wrote, "America will not admit the Negro to equal rights if it is not forced to do so."

All this philosophy and psychology floated around in King's head, and names such as Niebuhr and Jefferson joined with Jesus and Thoreau and Gandhi and attached to something he read in college, and there in Montgomery, his strategy crystallized as he was called into action. Cultural critic Gerard Early described that strategy.

> King had been greatly influenced by Gunnar Myrdal's massive 1944 sociological study of race relations, *An American Dilemma.* King was a sociology major at Morehouse, which he attended from 1944 to 1948, and doubtless read at least a portion of this work. The book made clear for King the strategy that other African-American leaders played out with less success. If the problem in America was the disjuncture between the American creed of freedom and equality and the existence of blacks as a disenfranchised, pariah group, then the solution was to make the country uncomfortable, embarrassed, downright guilty, explosively tense, about this disjuncture and the hypocrisy it implied until whites were moved or forced to make the country live up to its creed by including blacks as full-fledged citizens.

To make the country "uncomfortable, embarrassed, downright guilty," the Movement would create "explosively tense" situations and allow them to play out. There was a war going on between black and white America, but to some degree, it was going on too comfortably, too unconsciously. King aimed to make it fully conscious so that America could not avoid seeing it, and then feeling it, with the eventual goal of healing it.

The New Civil War

Jung used war imagery to describe neurosis: "Neurosis is an inner cleavage—the state of being at war with oneself." In order to cure a neurosis, the war would have to be fought. But, he also states "since no war was ever won on the defensive, one must, in order to terminate hostilities, open negotiations with the enemy and see what his terms really are. Such is the intention of the doctor who volunteers to act as a mediator." If the country was neurotic and at war with itself, King did as Jung suggested and volunteered himself as its mediator, willing to place himself on the front line in order to open negotiations with the enemy.

King used the language and imagery of war as well. Of the Birmingham campaign he said, "We did not hesitate to call our movement an army. It was a special army, with no supplies but its sincerity, no uniform but its determination, no arsenal except its faith, no currency but its conscience. It was an army that would move but not maul. It was an army that would sing but not slay." He described the people who attended the March on Washington as

> an army without guns, but not without strength. It was an army into which no one had to be drafted. It was white, and Negro, and of all ages. It had adherents of every faith, members of every class, every profession, every political party, united by a single ideal. It was a fighting army, but no one could mistake that its most powerful weapon was love.

And this is what distinguished the war for Civil Rights from the Civil War in King's mind; this would be a war where one side went on the offensive with no weapon but love, with no weapon but nonviolent resistance, with no weapon but redemptive suffering. This, primarily, was to be a psychological war, with no captives, but converts instead.

King learned the potential of these three weapons—love, nonviolence, and redemptive suffering—from his study of Mahatmas Gandhi, who in turn had used them for the first time in history to successfully wage war against the British in India earlier in the century. For King, they were not just the only practical weapons available to a minority fighting against a majority, but they were superior psychological weapons as well. If neurosis was caused by a disturbance in human relationships brought about by hostility and anxiety, then it is only logical that adding more hostility and anxiety in the forms of hatred and violence would serve to disturb the relationship even more, doing nothing to cure the neurosis. If white America was defending the status quo out of fear of losing power, then violence and hatred against them would both justify and increase that fear, leading to an aggressive reassertion of power. King argued that "violence only serves to harden the resistance of the white reactionary." He knew he had to soften resistance, not harden it.

King correctly assessed that while white America as a whole had developed trends toward aggression and detachment in dealing with the country's neurosis, black America as a whole had developed trends toward compliance and detachment. The strategy was to switch the terms of the battle in every way. In order to fight and win the war, black people would need opportunities to meet with white people as allies on the battlefield, overcoming their trend toward detachment, and engage with white people in aggressive, though nonviolent, confrontation, overcoming their trend toward compliance. Black people had primarily been on the defensive in the country; precipitating a crisis meant that they would go on the offensive. During the battle, King would counsel, "Please don't be too soft. We have the offensive . . . . In a crisis we must have a sense of drama." And King was a masterful director of that drama, which, in psychological terms, began by lifting the curtain and calling the cultural unconscious out from the shadows and onto the stage.

Bringing the Tension to the Surface

Socrates taught that it was necessary to create tension to stimulate growth: King knew he did not need to create tension between black and white Americans, but instead he needed to allow the already underlying tension to surface. He said, "The injustice was there under the surface and as long as it stayed below the surface, nobody was concerned about it. You had to bring it out in the open." Whenever King was criticized for entering a community and creating tension, he would explain, "We who engage in nonviolent direct action are not the creators of tension. We merely bring to the surface the hidden tension that is already alive. We bring it out in the open where it can be seen and dealt with." He often defended himself by using the medical analogy of cancer: if a physician uncovered cancer in a patient, no one would accuse the physician of causing it, but would instead laud him for bringing it to the attention of the patient in time to facilitate its cure.

Once, when King was accused of "disturbing the peace," he made a distinction between negative peace and true peace.

> You have had a sort of negative peace in which the Negro too often accepted his state of subordination. But this is not true peace. True peace is not merely the absence of tension; it is the presence of justice. The tension we see in Montgomery

today is the necessary tension that comes when the oppressed rise up and start to move forward to a permanent, positive peace.

Through dramatic crisis, he sought to root out negative forces and replace them with positive ones, creating through his nonviolent war a more perfect peace.

Psychologist James Hillman wrote, "Consciousness is really nothing more than maintaining conversation, and unconsciousness is really nothing more than letting things fall out of conversation, no longer talking about something." Through the marches, demonstrations, and protests waged in different cities all over the nation, King sought to keep racism and injustice in the forefront of the nation's consciousness, and he made shrewd use of the media to maintain the conversation by keeping it on the front page of the nation's news. Because here is something else King understood psychologically—the power of visual imagery to impress injustice upon the conscience and sear affect into the soul.

The Importance of Seeing

Jung described psychology as "concerned with the act of seeing." In his opinion, "only the tiniest fraction of the population learns anything from reflection; everything else consists in the suggestive power of ocular evidence." Without something remaining in our field of vision, we

> conveniently sink into the sea of forgetfulness, and that state of chronic woolly-mindedness returns which we describe as "normality." In shocking contrast to this is the fact that nothing has finally disappeared and nothing has been made good. The evil, the guilt, the profound unease of conscience, the dark foreboding, are there before our eyes, if only we would see.

King knew this as well, knew that seeing would lead to believing with the tough mind, and to feeling with the tender heart, and this combination could ultimately lead to psychological and social transformation. King often turned to the symbol of sight and the image of vision when speaking of symptoms and cure. For example, he described the Movement as one that did not ask for "an eye for an eye but one that summoned men to seek to open the eyes of blind prejudice."

King knew firsthand how visually witnessing an injustice could awaken a slumbering soul to feeling—he had viscerally experienced this throughout his life. One of his earliest memories occurred around the age of five during the Great Depression when he saw people standing in breadlines. Of that memory, he wrote, "I can see the effects of this early childhood experience on my anti-capitalistic feelings." Growing up he had seen police brutality, and worse: "I remember seeing the Klan actually beat a Negro. I had passed spots where Negroes had been savagely lynched. All of these things did something to my growing personality." When he worked summers in his late teens at a plant that hired both black and white employees, he spoke of the experience: "Here I saw economic injustice firsthand, and realized that the poor white was exploited just as much as the Negro. Through these early experiences I grew up deeply conscious of the varieties of injustice in our society." Later in life, he spoke fondly of a trip to India he and his wife had taken, but he also shared more depressing moments as well. "How can one avoid being depressed when he sees with his own eyes millions of people going to bed hungry at night? How can one avoid being depressed when he sees with his own eyes millions of people sleeping on the sidewalk at night?" Everything he felt, he felt as a result of what he saw; his sensitivities were developed through his sense of sight. This insight led him to realize and then to capitalize upon the importance of *seeing* in the battle for the soul of America.

We must acknowledge here the portion of King's success that came from leading the Movement so soon after the invention of television. More than a fortuitous synchronicity, it was the seal on the deal for the cause of civil rights. Literary critic Henry Louis Gates called television "the ritual arena for the drama of race." And King did know how to work in that arena, staging large-scale battles for the small screen.

Civil rights scholar and sociologist Aldon D. Morris described the powerful partnership of man, Movement, and media.

> The tactic of mass nonviolent direct action that disrupted entire communities and forced white racists violently to attack black citizens under the glare of television forced America to take notice. Public opinion had to come to grips with the wrenching reality that black people were treated like subjects of a vicious totalitarian state in a country

claiming to be the leader of the free world. King was acutely aware of the role the media played in revealing the day-to-day oppression of black people. He was also aware that he possessed a charismatic personality that attracted the media and thus focused the eyes of the world on the obstacles faced by the movement.

Indeed, how could anyone forget those media images of the police brutality under Birmingham police chief Bull Conner, when television and all the newspapers in America and all over the world "carried pictures of prostrate women, and policemen bending over them with raised clubs; of children marching up to the bared fangs of police dogs; of the terrible force of pressure hoses sweeping bodies into the streets." These images showed the world that Southern racism was more entrenched and more vitriolic than they realized—or America had admitted. Often, it was the national and international media coverage that forced the White House to act; for example, the next day after the most violent days of demonstrations in Birmingham, two key members of the Attorney General's office came to the city and helped facilitate a meeting between the Movement and the white businessmen, and President Kennedy devoted the entire opening statement of his planned press conference to the situation.

If Birmingham is an example of how negative imagery helped to awaken the conscience of a nation and its government, the March on Washington later that year offers an example of the power of positive imagery. A quarter of a million people of all races descended upon Washington for the march, but King knew all eyes were predominately on the black ones. He declared the importance of what they saw.

> Millions of white Americans, for the first time, had a clear, long look at Negroes engaged in a serious occupation. For the first time millions listened to the informed and thoughtful words of Negro spokesmen, from all walks of life. The stereotype of the Negro suffered a heavy blow. This was evident in some of the comments, which reflected surprise at the dignity, the organization, and even the wearing apparel and friendly spirit of the participants. If the press had expected something akin to a minstrel show, or a brawl, or a comic display of odd clothes and bad manners, they were

disappointed. . . . As television beamed the image of this extraordinary gathering across the border oceans, everyone who believed in man's capacity to better himself had a moment of inspiration and confidence in the future of the human race. And every dedicated American could be proud that a dynamic experience of democracy in the nation's capital had been made visible to the world.

Writer Alice Walker described what it was like as a young black girl to watch the March on television. "Like a good omen for the future, the face of Dr. Martin Luther King, Jr. was the first black face I saw on our new television screen. And, as in a fairy tale, my soul was stirred by the meaning for me of his mission. . . . and I fell in love with the sober and determined face of the Movement." As she listened to King deliver his "I Have a Dream" speech, she remembers, "I felt my soul rising from the sheer force of Martin King's eloquent goodness." It was the advent of television that allowed for this, and the Movement never failed to enlist the media as a core part of its war strategy, raising consciousness through the power of both positive and negative imagery.

Awakening the Conscience, Stirring the Soul

For Alice Walker, her soul was stirred and awakened by seeing the Civil Rights Movement unfold on television before her, and like thousands of others, the images led her to join the Movement. What stirred for Walker and millions of black Americans was a sense of pride, purpose, and power, and those emotions led many to participate in ways great and small. Of course a number of white people were activated to participate as well, but even many of those who didn't participate had their consciences awakened by feelings such as sympathy and shame.

One participant in the Movement noted this strategy. "You just have to uncover the unrecognized sympathy in the white man for the Negro's humiliation." This was one reason King gave for filling the jails during the Movement: "This courageous willingness to go to jail may well be the thing to awaken the dozing conscience of many of our white brothers." Again, using the language of awakening, he wrote, "Maybe it will take this type of self-suffering on the part of numerous Negroes to finally expose the moral defense of our white brothers who happen to be misguided and thusly awaken the dozing conscience of our community."

However, keeping in mind Horney's stress on the importance of *feeling* in the curing of a neurosis, King's intention was to awaken a stronger feeling than sympathy: that of shame. I call it a stronger emotion for this reason: people feeling sympathy for victims can keep those victims at a distance, one step removed, treating them like objects on the screen to feel sorry for. However, people feeling shame awaken to the fact that *they* are the subject, *they* are the victimizer, and they cannot remove themselves at all from the scene. It is true that the majority of white people did not act shamefully during the Civil Rights Movement, but it is also true that the vast majority of people acting shamefully *were* white. In the same way that white people had projected their own dark shadows onto black people for centuries, they were confronted now with the dark side of the white psyche in themselves and in others.

One aspect of the shadow that white people had projected onto black people was barbarianism and physical depravity. But how could they continue the projection after Selma? Here they saw black citizens doing nothing but marching nonviolently across a bridge singing songs of freedom, asking for what was legally theirs—the right to vote—when the police, the *white* police, a symbol of American civic law and order, viciously gassed and clubbed at random those peaceful protesters, including women, children, and ministers, chasing them through town on their horses through a cloud of gas, and sending seventy to eighty of them to the hospital for wounds ranging from broken teeth to gashes in the head to fractured ribs. How could they help but withdraw their projections and see that barbarianism and physical depravity were within their race as well?[14] As King said simply, if white Americans have any conscience, they are ashamed.

In fact, King said of the whole Movement, "More white people learned more about the shame of America, and finally faced some aspects of it, during the years of nonviolent protest than during the century before." Again, much of this was due to the power of television and the media to broadcast images immediately around the world, a power not available during slavery and after emancipation when white America behaved shamefully as well.

---

[14] ABC interrupted their broadcast of the movie about the Holocaust, *Judgment at Nuremberg,* to show footage of the brutality, awakening millions of Americans to the fact that vitriolic hatred based on race was *their* country's problem too.

However, even if there had been television during slavery, it is doubtful the media could have captured this sort of shameful footage, for several reasons. First, much of the brutality of slavery took place "behind closed doors," on private plantations where the media would not have access, whereas the Civil Rights Movement purposely took place in public spaces where the media was welcome, even invited. Second, during slavery black people were for the most part on the defensive, never knowing when brutality would strike, whereas black people during the Civil Rights Movement were on the offensive, carefully planning out campaigns well aware that violence was likely to occur, and making sure the press was there to witness it. Third, during slavery a white owner could justify beating a slave because the slave was his private property to do with as he wished, and regardless of the truth, he could say the slave deserved it, whereas during the Civil Rights Movement, these were free black citizens who were brutalized for doing nothing more than marching across a bridge, sitting down at a lunch counter, or riding a bus, and all of America knew it.

It was also the manner in which black Americans conducted themselves while protesting during this time period that produced so much shame in white Americans. They protested in solidarity, usually wore their best clothes and always donned their best behavior, gathered in churches before and after their protests, prayed and sang spirituals and other songs, refrained from verbal or physical retaliation no matter how provoked, and accepted the repercussions of their actions by submitting to arrest and to jail. King said of this kind of behavior, "This amazing unity, this profound self-respect, this willingness to suffer, and this refusal to hit back will soon cause the oppressor to become ashamed of his own methods." This was another reason why King unequivocally insisted on nonviolence—because violence would leave white Americans "less ashamed of their prejudices toward Negroes."

In his book *Violence: Reflections on a National Epidemic*, James Gilligan argued that violence stems from shame, though the violent one may outwardly manifest the opposite of shame: pride. Pride, as discussed earlier in this chapter, is one of the qualities of neurotic personalities, who seek to cover their shame with the false coat of the idealized self. In front of the whole world, America took off its coat, rolled up its sleeves, and threw punches, and everyone knew a country that could do that while professing to be devoted to life, liberty, equality, and justice was little more than a sham. White

America got its pride kicked out from underneath it, while in another one of the psychological reversals that occurred during this time, black America had its shame removed and replaced with hard-won pride.

The unwarranted shame black Americans felt since slavery has been well documented in psychological literature, so just two examples here. In the 1968 book *Black Rage*, psychiatrists William H. Grier and Price M. Cobbs wrote of the endless circle of shame, humiliation, and lack of self-esteem black individuals suffered from which led to all manners of social dysfunction in the black community. In the classic 1979 study *The Nature of Prejudice*, psychologist Gordon W. Allport discussed the unfortunate but almost inevitable self-hatred and shame which arise from internalizing the oppressor's judgments and opinions about one's racial group.

King did much to reverse black shame. First of all, he was a black man that the black community was proud of, a well-educated doctor of philosophy, a minister, a Nobel Prize winner, an author, a man who comported himself with dignity and had the ear of dignitaries. They listened to him when he said, "We must appreciate our great heritage. We must be proud of our race. We must not be ashamed of being black. We must believe with all our hearts that black is as beautiful as any other color." He taught them a sense of self-worth, and, in the gendered language of the day, a sense of manhood.

> One must not overlook the positive value in calling the Negro to a new sense of manhood, to a deep feeling of racial pride and to an audacious appreciation of his heritage. The Negro must be grasped by a new realization of his dignity and worth. He must stand up amid a system that still oppresses him and develop an unassailable and majestic sense of his own value. He must no longer be ashamed of being black. The job of arousing manhood within a people that have been taught for so many centuries that they are nobody is not easy.

Alice Walker wrote that the Movement awakened black people to "the possibilities of life" and to their own possibilities, restoring a slumbering sense of dignity. In the language of King's sermon discussed in the last chapter, participating in "the Cause" allowed black people to overcome their inferiority complex. For white people, it showed them that the moral depravity they had projected onto black people also belonged to them. Sociologist and King scholar Michael Eric Dyson wrote, "Through his dramatic efforts to contrast black dignity and white brutality sharply, King forced the nation to confront questions that it could no longer dismiss."

If white America lay down on the couch and put its newly conscious questions into words, it might have asked, "Who is the real dark one now? Who is the light? What is the source of our pride, of our shame? What are we so afraid of? How did we move so far away from our ideals? Who are we really? Who are *they* really?" This is the work of therapy, whether it is the confrontation of ego and shadow in the psyche of one individual or one nation. James Hillman wrote, "Therapeutic work cannot avoid meeting the shadow. An aim of Jungian therapy is a mutual accommodation of the two brothers, ego and shadow, and a relativization of their previous antagonistic attitudes, lightening the dark and darkening the light." There needed to be a role reversal: black people needed to be seen *en masse* carrying the good qualities that were previously encoded as white, and white people needed to be seen *en masse* acting out the bad qualities that were previously projected onto black people. Black people needed to gain moral and ethical superiority; white people needed to lose it. Black people needed to feel pride; white people needed to feel shame. Black people needed to feel their innocence; white people needed to feel their guilt.

As Dyson noted, "The white soul slumped to repressed guilt for repressing blacks. Ironically, many whites often drowned their guilt by wading deeper in the fiery lake of hate. The sadistic habit of attempting to escape shame by repeating the act that causes it is one that King, a fellow Southerner and Christian, completely understood."

The Power of Guilt

King believed that the arousal of shame would lead to a sense of guilt, and guilt would be a motivating factor in transforming the cultural soul. He offered his analysis of the Southern white psyche as haunted "by a deep sense of guilt for what it has done to the Negro—guilt for patronizing him, degrading him, brutalizing him, depersonalizing him, thingifying him: guilt for lying to itself. This is the source of the schizophrenia that the South will suffer until it goes through its crisis of conscience." King knew that feeling their guilt would lead some white people toward further negative behavior to drown the feeling, but he trusted that it would ultimately lead them as a whole to assuage the feeling through atonement.

It is important to make a distinction here between individual and collective guilt. Most white people were not guilty of major sins against black people. Most did not subjugate, mistreat, oppress, harass, lynch, rape, or otherwise abuse black people, but instead, most simply ignored them (remember Horney's neurotic trends, aggression and detachment). Ignoring someone, unless it is through overt discrimination, is not a crime. However, Jung offered us a definition of psychological guilt. "The psychological use of the word 'guilt' should not be confused with guilt in the legal or moral sense. Psychologically, it connotes the irrational presence of a subjective feeling (or conviction) of guilt, or an objective imputation of, or imputed share in, guilt." For example, though a white woman in the North has not done anything legally wrong by not wanting black people to live in her neighborhood, she may still feel subjectively guilty, for she knows that this is not "neighborly," a value she upholds in theory. This brings us back again to the definition of neurosis. The woman in our example suffers from neurosis when she sees the gap between her ideal self and her actual self.

Additionally, Jung's statement makes clear that we don't have to commit the crime ourselves in order to feel an "imputed share" in the guilt. Therefore, that same woman who feels subjective guilt over her discriminatory feelings may also feel guilt when she watches a white man in the faraway South brutalize a black man, though she did not commit the brutality herself. As Jung further explained, "Psychological collective guilt is a *tragic fate*. It hits everybody, just and unjust alike, everybody who was anywhere near the place where the terrible thing happened." Jung did note that this sort of collective guilt is unfair and in some ways irrational, but that makes it no less psychologically real.

To move past the feeling of collective guilt, Jung thought it important to publicly acknowledge the "moral inferiority" that led to the unethical acts without minimizing them or rationalizing the behavior. Collectives that can own their guilt without defense or denial can begin to absolve their guilt. But he also cautioned against the victims mercilessly judging the perpetrators' actions without acknowledging their own propensity for wrong-doing. In the classic teaching aphorism from Jesus, if we are going to point out the sliver in our brother's eye, we best do so by also acknowledging the log in our own.

King took this lesson to heart and taught it to others. Though his primary responsibility as a cultural therapist was to help white Americans confront their own shadow, he was not above pointing a finger at black people as well, starting with himself. As discussed in the last chapter, King was a man who suffered from his own shame and guilt, and he shared some of his struggle in public and private. Talking about *his* struggles with *his* shadow gave him the moral authority to speak to the *black* struggle with the *black* shadow. As a minister, he preached to his black congregants about their shadow in his sermons; as an advice columnist he wrote about it in *Ebony* magazine; and as a Civil Rights Leader, he spoke about it publicly on occasion.

King named part of the black shadow "stagnant passivity and deadening complacency," traits of Horney's compliant personality type. Though he understood the psychological roots of those traits, he had little patience for their expression. In his call to arms to black people and the black church, he riled them out of their complacency with his speeches and out of their passivity with opportunities for action. In this way, the black community began to see its own unity, efficacy, and power, allowing it to withdraw those projections from the white community.

King expected himself and his people to do what he was asking America at large to do: own your guilt and stop projecting it onto others. He knew there was psychological truth in what Jung wrote:

> When we are conscious of our guilt we are in a more favourable position—we can at least hope to change and improve ourselves. As we know, anything that remains in the unconscious is incorrigible; psychological corrections can be made only in consciousness. Consciousness of guilt can therefore act as a powerful moral stimulus. In every treatment of neurosis the discovery of the shadow is indispensable, otherwise nothing changes.

King felt the same way about shame, that it could be a stimulus for transformation in its role as a powerful awakener of the conscience.

Reconstructing the Real Self
Returning to Horney's treatment of the neurosis, the final step

for the therapist is to help the client to relinquish the idealized self in favor of a more authentic way of being. This is crucial: a therapist cannot simply *deconstruct* the idealized self, but must help the client *reconstruct* the real self. To leave a client swimming in the sea of shame guzzling gallons of guilt will not cause the neurosis to lessen—it will simply cause the client to drown. However, guilt can be a catalytic drive for change.

King provided this opportunity for white America to change in several ways. First, he invited them into the Movement with open arms, white citizens and white churches alike, stating that "consciences must be enlisted in our movement. . . . not merely racial groups." Second, he gave white America a to-do list, usually a very specific, concrete one, and when it did those things on the list, he was quick to recognize and praise its progress. For example, when the Civil Rights Act passed in 1964, King praised President Johnson and the "strong white allies" who joined together with black people to create a "'coalition of conscience' which awoke a hitherto somnolent Congress." He understood how important it was to the morale of black people that they win victories, but he understood it was equally important to the morale of white people to have the opportunity to redress the injustices that made them feel shame and guilt.

Steele's *The Content of Our Character* contains a thesis that is useful to apply here. His book's premise is that innocence is power, and that "the racial struggle in America has always been primarily a struggle for innocence." During the Civil Rights Movement, "blacks used the innocence that grew out of their long subjugation to seize more power, while whites lost some of their innocence and so lost a degree of power over blacks." King talked a great deal about white guilt, of course, but he didn't talk about black innocence per se. However, his demands that black participants in the Movement uphold stellar standards of conduct, remain free from violence or even retaliation to violence, and accept the legal repercussions of civil disobedience are means of maintaining black innocence.

Steele argued that historically, black people have handled racism in two ways: bargaining ("granting white society its innocence in exchange for entry into the mainstream") or challenging ("holding that innocence hostage until their demand for entry—or other concessions—was met"). "A bargainer says, *I already believe you are innocent (good, fair-minded) and have faith that you will prove it.* A challenger says, *If you are innocent, then prove it.* Bargainers *give* in hope of receiving; challengers *withhold* until they receive."

King was a bargainer, according to Steele. He used black innocence, but unlike other leaders, it was *genuine* innocence in contrast to *presumed* innocence. The difference is that the former "must be earned through sacrifice while the latter is unearned and only veils the quest for privilege. And there was much sacrifice in the early civil rights movement. . . . A price was paid in terror and lost life, and from this sacrifice came a hard-earned innocence and a credible moral power." Steele labeled nonviolent passive resistance a bargainer's strategy, and violence a challenger's strategy. He argued that the Movement was successful

> because of its belief in the capacity of whites to be moral. It did not so much demand that whites change as offer them relentlessly the opportunity to live by their own morality—to attain a true innocence based on the sacrifice of their racial privilege, rather than a false innocence based on presumed racial superiority.

But all that fell apart in the mid 1960's when the Black Power Movement emerged with its demands for racial as well as moral power without genuine innocence. Steele argued, "Now suddenly the movement itself was using race as a means to power and thereby affirming the very union of race and power it was born to redress. In the end, black power can claim no higher moral standing than white power." King, according to Steele, knew this better than anyone.

> King understood that racial power subverts moral power, and he pushed the principles of fairness and equality rather than black power because he believed those principles would bring blacks their most complete liberation. He sacrificed race for morality, and his innocence was made genuine by that sacrifice. What made King the most powerful and extraordinary black leader of this century was not his race but his morality.

Steele understood why so many black people were lured into the Black Power Movement: "The sacrifices that moral power demands are difficult to sustain, and it was inevitable that blacks would tire of these sacrifices and seek a more earthly power."[15] Steele argued that by the mid 1960's, "white guilt became so palpable you could see it on people." The Black Power Movement sought to capitalize on that guilt by grabbing for more power, whereas King's philosophy was to use that guilt to illuminate the only "road back to innocence—through actions and policies that would bring redemption." A genuine admission of guilt followed by atonement through actions and policies would lead white American to "the redemption of innocence, [and] the reestablishment of good feeling about oneself." Not only that: it could establish good feelings of respect for black Americans and a sense of equality through shared power, whereas the Black Power Movement would only establish fear of black Americans and continue the power struggle.

In the end, Black Power itself can be interpreted as a neurotic response to the anxiety and hostility stirred up by the Civil Rights Movement, exhibiting its own neurotic trend toward aggression and its own idealized self summarized in the blanket statement "Black is Beautiful." King was courageous in his willingness to criticize the Black Power Movement, especially as it gained popularity and proved itself a competitor movement, antithetical to almost everything he held dear.

> In the final analysis the weakness of Black Power is its failure to see that the black man needs the white man and the white man needs the black man. However much we may try to romanticize the slogan, there is no separate black path to power and fulfillment that does not intersect white paths, and there is no separate white path to power and fulfillment, short of social disaster, that does not share that power with black aspirations for freedom and human dignity. We are bound together in a single garment of destiny. The language, the cultural patterns, the music, the material prosperity and

---

[15] King understood all of this as well: his fifty page analysis of the lure of the Black Power Movement in the book *Where Do We Go From Here: Chaos or Community* is brilliant and shows King at his psychological best. Still, he concluded, "But even though I can understand it psychologically, I must say [that] black supremacy is as dangerous as white supremacy. . . . God is not interested merely in the freedom of black men and brown men and yellow men. God is interested in the freedom of the whole human race."

even the food of America are an amalgam of black and white.

For King, black *was* beautiful—but so was white, and brown, and yellow, and red—King saw everyone as God's children, precious in his/His sight. He knew Black Power was neurotic, because though it stressed that black people should love themselves, its rhetoric included hatred and hostility toward white people which King opposed on moral, religious, and psychological grounds.

King would agree with the words of author James Baldwin: "In short, we, the black and the white, deeply need each other here if we are really to become a nation—if we are really, that is, to achieve our identity, our maturity, as men and women. To create one nation has proved to be a hideously difficult task." It *was* a hideously difficult task, for as King knew, all Americans, black and white included, were living "in a sick, neurotic nation," and neuroses were never easy to cure. And still he and the Movement marched on.

Conclusion

King's greatest success in working with the soul of the nation came in the war he led against racism. In the war that wages within the neurotic, Horney noted that the most comprehensive conflict of all is

> between his pride system and his real self, between his drive to perfect his idealized self and his desire to develop his given potentials as a human being. A gradual line-up of forces occurs, the central inner conflict comes into focus, and it is the foremost task of the analyst in the ensuing time to see to it that it stays in sharp focus because the patient himself is liable to lose sight of it.

King helped incite this conflict, this new civil war called the Civil Rights Movement. He made sure America *knew* the gap between her actual and her idealized self, and he made her *feel* the gap by calling forward all her sublimated rage, hostility, and hatred in full force on a battlefield seen on screens around the world. He kept the conflict right in front of America's eyes, never letting her grow complacent or fall back into the slumber of unconsciousness. He called the country his beloved, and called upon her to live up to her God-given potential. He showed America her shame and her guilt, and then he showed her the way back to genuine innocence through redemption and atonement and actions consistent with her ideals.

King helped guide America through what Horney termed the "most turbulent period of analysis" which varies in degree and duration depending upon "the violence of the inner battle. Its intensity is commensurate with the basic importance of the issue at stake." This describes the 1950's and 1960's that King helped to define, an intense and turbulent period, violent inside and outside, where the war against racism was not won but many individual and important battles were, and where the most important issues of all were at stake: how can we live together in beauty, love one another in harmony, and actualize our real selves as individuals and as a nation? As its therapist, King did not *cure* the country, nor did he save its soul, but he helped to lessen its neurosis around race by closing some of the overt gaps, while he infused the country with the dream of its own integration.

6

MYTHOLOGY:

EXPLORING THE KING MYSTIQUE

In the beginning of this book I raised the question, Why King? Why did this man rise above the masses and become a living example of C. G. Jung's great personality? The subsequent chapters of this book have been attempts to flesh out the answer to that question, exploring the role King's psychological astuteness played in his power and popularity, and the efficacy of his therapeutic work with the nation. In this chapter and the ones to follow, we turn to mythology as an answer from another angle, looking at how Martin Luther King, Jr. took on mythological stature during his life, and how the myth-making continued—and was distorted—after his death.

Since the time of Sigmund Freud, mythology and psychology have been intimately entwined. Some consider the Oedipal complex, based on the myth of King Oedipus, to be Freud's most important contribution to psychology besides his work on dreams (and since he interpreted so many dreams through the lens of the Oedipal complex, some argue it is Freud's central contribution). Jung continued the work of his former mentor, often turning to mythology to illuminate psychological matters; particularly notable was his analysis of Hitler and Nazi Germany based on the Norse myth of Wotan. These two pioneers of depth psychology laid the foundation in the first half of the twentieth century for interpreting mythology psychologically and interpreting psychology mythologically.

In the second half of the twentieth century, this foundation was expanded upon by the work of two important men: Joseph Campbell and James Hillman. Joseph Campbell was the great cross-cultural mythologist who made explicit the connection between mythology and psychology: he saw mythology as ancient psychology and psychology as modern mythology. James Hillman, founder of the field of archetypal psychology, devoted much of his career to the connections between mythology and psychology. In one of his seminal books *Healing Fiction*, Hillman argued that if we want to understand a person's psychology, we can find clues in the myths he or she embodies, consciously or unconsciously. The same applies to groups or to countries; that is, if we want to understand the psychology of a country, we look to the myths it embodies both consciously and unconsciously, and to those "great personalities" it uses to carry those myths forward.

We already began some of that exploration in the last chapter when we looked at the Puritan myth of the utopian "city on the hill" and the American myth of "the United States" of America. In the next several chapters, we turn our focus on it more directly. What's most important here is not simply to explore *what* myths King embodied, though that's interesting and we will spend some time there. What's more important to the theme of this book—and ultimately, I would argue, to history itself—is to explore the more psychological *hows* and *whys*. How did King come to carry these myths for the country? How much awareness did he have of the myths projected onto him, and then, how consciously was he able to manipulate them or use them to manage his mystique? How did the myths surrounding King come to change over time, and why? What is the danger of turning a person into a myth, the dangers to both the person and to the collective? And the broader questions: why do people make myths out of men and women to begin with? Why do myths have so much power over us?

In order to begin this exploration, it is important to share some basic understanding of the concepts we'll be using. There are four that are primary here: myths, archetypes, complexes, and projection.

Myths

Contrary to popular usage, the term "myth" does not mean a lie. This is how we commonly use it—when we see headlines like "5 Myths About Weight Loss" or "10 Myths About Teen Suicide," we expect to see the lies or misunderstandings enumerated, then corrected.

In contrast, the proper definition of a myth is not a lie, but a story. The story might be true or might not be true; its literal veracity is not the point. The point is that myths, in their classic meaning, are stories meant to convey universal or symbolic or psychological truths. The word "story" itself is linked etymologically with "storehouse," so myths are storehouses, cultural treasuries wherein lie the wisdom and values of the culture that originated the myth, often writ large into fantastic stories.

Let's use the example of the myth of Santa Claus. In the United States, he's one of our most fantastic stories writ large; a fat, jolly old white man with a beard, dressed in a red suit and black boots, who leaves his house at the North Pole once a year on a sleigh driven by reindeer and delivers presents made by elves to all children who have been more nice than naughty. This meets our definition of a myth; it is a fantastic story writ large, part of the cultural treasury of the United States, and meant to convey the spirit of generosity, and to instill in children the psychological value of good behavior. The adult culture in the United States understands that this myth is meant to teach symbolic truth, while the youth culture, particularly the youngest of the youth, believe in the myth quite literally. Thus, myths may be literal truths for one culture and symbolic truths for another culture. And like all good mythological figures, Santa Claus has a broad, if not universal appeal. The United States did not create him, but rather, adapted him from myths from other cultures: aspects of him can be seen in the Dutch *Sinterklass*, the German *Kris Kringle*, the Italian *Saint Nicholas*, the English *Father Christmas*, or the Spanish *Papa Noel*. Other cultures like Japan and Puerto Rico have adopted him, testimony to his legendary appeal.

Archetypes

Myths are of great interest to psychology, especially the branch of depth psychology, because they are thought to be expressions of the universal language of the soul, expressing human needs, desires, fears, aspirations, and values. The term "archetypal" is used to describe the universal dimension of myths. Myths are considered to be containers that carry archetypes, or universal patterns. For example, Joseph Campbell popularized the monomyth of the hero's journey in his first book, *Hero With a Thousand Faces*, illustrating how the hero's journey occurs in every culture in every time period throughout history. If the hero's journey is a container, each culture fills that container with different specific contents: it's Perseus doing battle with Medusa; it's David up against Goliath; it's Osiris struggling against Seth, it's Luke Skywalker fighting the dark side in Darth Vader. The particular expression of the myth will differ, but the hero and the battle between good and evil are universal and thus the individual stories will share many common elements or features.

Though some people believe in their myths literally, the way children believe in Santa Claus, for other people, their appeal is their archetypal dimension: Santa Claus is an archetype of the spirit of generosity and optimism, and in the long, dark days of winter, he is a welcome visitor. Myths tap into some universal life force and are tremendous carriers of energy. For example, just think of the lengths parents go to in order to preserve the myth of Santa Claus: every Christmas season, post offices are flooded with letters parents have their children write to Santa; every Christmas Eve, millions of parents put on Santa suits or stuff the stockings late at night, or leave out cookies for Mr. Claus; and it's hard to imagine a child in the United States who has not had his or her picture taken on Santa's lap at the local mall. This myth is perpetuated year after year, generation after generation, because of its archetypal power. In the same way movies, which are popular carriers of myth today, play over and over again the archetypal stories of love, revenge, sacrifice, temptation, etc.

If movies are our biggest secular carriers of myths today, religion has been and still is the primary spiritual carrier of myths. Some people see the myths of their religion as symbolic stories, while others believe in the myths of their own religion literally. In fact, entire religious denominations have been cleaved around this philosophical divide, with the fundamentalists of every faith holding to literal interpretations, and the liberals holding to symbolic ones. Of course, even fundamentalists are able to see the myths of *other* religions as symbolic, so while Christians may literally believe in the virgin birth of Jesus, they'll dismiss as a fanciful story the birth of Dionysus from the thigh of Zeus.

Martin Luther King, Jr.'s Understanding of Myths and Archetypes

King was raised in the black Baptist tradition that held to the fundamentalist, literal interpretation of the Bible and its myths. This, after all, was his family and his culture's understanding of the Bible, and would have been the taken-for-granted worldview that dominated King's childhood. However, as we discussed earlier, at the age of twelve King shocked his Sunday School class by denying the bodily resurrection of Jesus, and from that point on, he struggled mightily with his love for the church versus his disbelief in its fundamentalist teachings.

In college, King was able to articulate his views without feeling like a heretic. In one paper he wrote that many things in the Bible must be seen as "merely mythological," calling the Bible an "allegory" which must be read in "literary, not scientific or philosophical, language." He made a distinction between finding it "true," which would make it "full of errors, contradictions, and obvious impossibilities" and finding it "truth," which makes it "one of the most logical vehicles of mankind's deepest devotional thoughts and aspirations, couched in language which still retains its original vigour and its moral intensity." In other words, he saw the Bible as a beautiful and powerful carrier of myths.

He also showed his interest in the psychology of religion during those years, writing one paper called "The Sources of Fundamentalism and Liberalism Considered Historically and Psychologically." In other papers he interpreted events such as the fall from innocence and the divinity of Jesus from a psychological angle. Of the former, he wrote in one paper called "The Place of Reason and Experience in Finding God" that "it seems more reasonable to hold that the fall of man is psychological rather than historical" (read "archetypal rather than literal") and of the latter, he wrote that it is important not to see Jesus as possessing some metaphysical substance that makes him divine, because then we'll believe we can never obtain what he obtained. Instead, King argued that the "true significance of the divinity of Christ lies in the fact that his achievement is prophetic and promissory for every other true son of man who is willing to submit his will to the will and spirit of God. Christ was to be only the prototype of one among many brothers." Here, King used the word "prototype" interchangeably with "archetype," pointing to Christ's universal dimension as a man who submits his will to God. Because he is archetypal, all of us can be Christs as well, in the same way that any number of parents can be Santa Claus on Christmas Eve.

King did not view Jesus as the literal metaphysical incarnation of the divine and did not see his "substantial unity with God." Instead, King found Jesus' mystery and power, his divinity, in "his filial consciousness and in his unique dependence upon God." Jesus was the supreme revelation of God because of his devotion to God and trust in God. King saw Jesus as a man who had "at last realized his true divine calling: That of becoming a true son of man by becoming a true son of God," having "completely opened his life to the influence of the divine spirit."

King's understanding of Jesus as archetypally divine versus literally divine is crucial to understanding the next few chapters of this book. King argued that not only was it inadequate and erroneous to believe that Jesus had some "inherent metaphysical substance within him" that made him one with God, but it was "actually harmful and detrimental" to do so. Why would this be? King reasoned that if we believe Jesus is the one and only true son of God, we could use that belief as an excuse to not live up to our Christ-like potential, saying to ourselves, "Well, it was easier for Jesus because he was a God. I'm just a human." He wanted to see Jesus as a model, as a prototype or archetype that all of humanity could strive to emulate. He believed that "this divine quality or this unity with God was not something thrust upon Jesus from above, but it was a definite achievement through the process of moral struggle and self-abnegation." For King, the true power of Jesus was that he was able to reach divinity through his own struggles and through cultivating selflessness, and that meant that King—and every other human being—could do the same.

I call this understanding crucial because it will keep us in the following chapters from viewing King as a man who elevated himself to literal god-like proportions. In the next chapter, we'll look at how King embodied the archetypal deliverer, the prophet, and the martyr-savior, and because King was working in the Christian tradition, we'll look at Biblical figures for comparison. King saw himself as a deliverer *like* Moses, as a prophet *like* Amos and Jeremiah, and as a martyr-savior *like* Jesus, but he likewise believed that *all* of humanity had the capacity to be deliverers, prophets, and martyr-saviors, because those were archetypal roles. King associated himself with those myths because he knew they were powerful carriers of archetypal truths that would resonate with the culture he was working within, but because he did not believe in those myths literally, he did not believe he was the literal incarnation of those mythological figures. It sets a very different tone for a man to say "I *am* Jesus" rather than saying "I am *like* Jesus, and you are too, and so are we all."

The Power of Archetypes

Though comparing Jesus Christ and Santa Claus may seem irreverent to some, they do share in common the fact that they are both powerful archetypes, conveyers of spirit and wisdom and values. In fact, I'm confident that almost any child, without adult correction, would classify Santa Claus as a god due to his power and magic. James Hillman wrote that archetypes "form the structures of our consciousness with such force and such possession that we might, as we have in the past, call them Gods." He noted, "But one thing is absolutely essential to the notion of archetypes: their emotional possessive effect, their bedazzlement of consciousness so that it becomes blind to its own stance. . . . An archetype is best comparable to a god."

Indeed, this is a characteristic of archetypes: when we are in their presence, we are possessed, bedazzled, empowered, and awed. They stir us emotionally, often bypassing the rational mind and moving straight to our hearts and souls. Think of the movie "ET" for a moment. "ET" is an archetypal story of feeling alien and longing to return home; people were and are still awed by that movie, and though they know it is not rationally true, it remains emotionally stirring nonetheless. In addition, archetypes are powerful because they fill us with energy, almost as if we have plugged into a secret power source in the universe. Anyone who has ever had the archetypal experience called "falling in love" is aware of the strange way the experience can move in and take over our rational minds, making us feel possessed by some blinding ecstatic energy, like we're walking on sunshine, like we're on cloud nine. Anyone who has watched a football coach pump up a team of players with the warrior energy in the locker room before a game understands the energy that comes with archetypal possession.

Archetypes work us up; they change our behavior; they empower us and sometimes overpower us. In the presence of an archetype, we may become spellbound, and others who are not possessed by the same archetype may find our behavior strange and inexplicable (and thus, the statement, "I don't see what you see in her," even though we know our newly beloved is an angel). Borrowing an analogy from C. G. Jung, archetypes are like deep currents worn in the riverbeds of the human psyche. When we have an experience that tosses us into the water, it is easy to get swept away by the current.

Complexes and Projection

Being possessed or swept away by an archetype may lead to what psychology calls a "complex." Complexes usually develop as a result of childhood exposure or experiences; for example, a child who is the family scapegoat may develop a martyr complex, or a child who has to protect and defend a weaker sibling may develop a hero complex. Complexes are often present in a child's early predilections for games and role-playing; for example, a little girl who always wants to play the part of the princess in need of rescue by the prince may manifest a Cinderella complex as a woman.

Regardless of their genesis, the hold of a complex on an adult is usually quite powerful, especially if and when we are unaware or unconscious about the mythic pattern we are living. Then the archetypes become susceptible to "projection," a defense mechanism by which we take something that lives in us, usually unconsciously, and project it onto others. For example, a woman with a Cinderella complex may project Prince Charming onto every new man she meets. While in the beginning he may still be perfect enough to hold the projection, inevitably he will disappoint her, and she'll be the victim of her own myth, left to wonder why the men she meets are so imperfect instead of realizing she is the creator of the situation through the power of her projections. She will seek out men in her life that psychologists call "projection-carriers," those willing—again, usually unconsciously—to carry the projections of another. People often carry the projections of others because it matches a complex of their own: for example, when a woman with a Cinderella complex meets a man with a savior complex, you can expect there will be a powerful explosion of archetypal energy and projections galore.

King as a Projection-Carrier

Any time you see a person rise up from the fray and take on immense power in the public eye, you can be sure you're in the presence of a projection-carrier. Think of Marilyn Monroe's rise to fame; she became an archetypal Venus, carrying the projection of the goddess of love and sexuality. In the same way, Martin Luther King, Jr.'s sudden rise to fame and his still iconic stature suggests that he, too, carried and still carries the projections of the masses. Lerone Bennett, Jr. recognized this as early as 1964 in his essay "When the Man and the Hour are Met." Bennett wrote,

> The adulation which King received in 1957 [during the Montgomery Bus Boycott] cannot be explained entirely by King's acts. It must be explained, at least in part, by what men and women saw in King. For some fifty years, Negroes

had been expecting a leader. Now, as King's image rose on the horizon, Negroes of all ranks and creeds pooled their psychic energy and projected it onto King, anxiously asking themselves, anxiously asking King, with every gesture, every glance: "Art thou he who should come or should we seek another?"

A leader is an archetypal role, and as Bennett points out, black people were expecting a leader and projected the energy of that role onto King with overwhelming enthusiasm even though he was only a 28-year-old man, a young father and a newly minted preacher. King obviously had what Jung called a "hook" to hang the projection on, because he took up the mantle of leadership immediately. Even his last name, King, seemed prescient for the mythic role he was perhaps born to play.

Lincoln's astute analysis also serves to remind us that the projections King carried for the black psyche differed in part from those he carried for the white psyche. As we explored in the last chapter, the white American psyche needed more of a minister who could forgive its collective sins and absolve it of its guilt; King was uniquely qualified to do that. The black American psyche needed a leader who would take it from segregation to integration, from separate and unequal to together and equal. The black psyche projected this powerful leadership role onto King, and King in turn empowered the black psyche to take its rightful place as full citizens at the country's table.

We continue to circle around this question of "why King?" and this is a good place to add another angle, another theoretical lens, this time from the discipline of self psychology, that will help us understand King's power as a projection-carrier. In self psychology, the term "selfobject" refers to another person who is necessary to us to define our nascent sense of self and hold it for us until we can hold it for ourselves. A selfobject "can act like scaffolding for the developing personality" until we are able to fully support ourselves and our own needs. These selfobject needs are considered universal and structured into our very nature, and therefore can be seen as archetypal as well. In his book *The Religious Function of the Psyche*, psychologist Lionel Corbett details different types of selfobject needs; we can see how King met four of them for black Americans.

The first is the need for a mirror. Corbett defined mirror needs as including "those for affirmation and confirmation of our value, for emotional attunement and resonance, to be the gleam in somebody's eye, to be approved of, seen, wanted, appreciated and accepted." Certainly King made black people feel this way. He held them to be immensely valuable, reminding them that their source of value was inherently theirs as children of God. He made them feel like theirs was a unique and powerful role in history, that they were the promised people whose calling it was to transform the world. He also made them proud of their culture. He told them, "We must appreciate our great heritage. We must be proud of our race. We must not be ashamed of being black. We must believe with all our hearts that black is as beautiful as any other color."

A second need is for someone to idealize. According to Corbett, this selfobject meets "the need for alliance with, or to be psychologically a part of, a figure who carries high status and importance, who is respected, admired, wise, protective and strong." Again, King met this need for black people. At a time when very few black ministers had advanced degrees, they were proud of the "Doctor" in front of King's name, even called him "Reverend Doctor King." He was the second African-American to win the Nobel Peace Prize; his name was recognized all over the globe; and he had the ear of important world leaders, including two Presidents of the United States. He was a powerful man, and when people marched with him, they were powerful too. He was their King, and many people referred to him that way. As an extreme example, one black man, after he heard of King's assassination, ran out and killed his white neighbor in retaliation, crying "my King is dead."

A third selfobject need is for twinship or kinship. In Corbett's description, "These involve the need for sameness with others, and the sense of being understood by someone 'like me.'" Black people looked at King and saw kin, saw a brother or a son, saw someone fundamentally like them who thus could understand them. "They used to love to call him 'My boy' or 'My son.' They worshipped him," R. D. Nesbitt, one of King's congregants said. Not only was he family, but he gave them a *larger* family, a larger community of people who were also like them and with whom they could participate in a noble struggle. Corbett wrote, "To be in a community of people of shared beliefs and attitudes in which one belongs. . . is supporting and enhancing to the self."

And finally, King gave them opportunity to meet their efficacy needs. In Corbett's definition, this is the need "to feel that we can have an effect on the other person and that we are able to evoke what we need from him." For black citizens used to feeling powerless, this was an extremely crucial need. Take the right to vote, for example. In Selma, if you were black and tried to register to vote, you would be denied on some technicality almost every time. Thus, you were denied your efficacy needs in two ways: by not being able to effect the voter registrar into giving you the right to vote, and then, by not being able to effect change in the political world through the power of that vote. King showed them how to effect change in the world, and with every success, helped meet their efficacy needs. And even when they did not achieve immediate success, simply marching and getting a response from the police could meet the need for efficacy, which offers one psychological explanation for why going to jail was a positive, powerful, self-affirming experience for so many people.

It is of little wonder then that King was such an important person to the black community, as he met at least four of their selfobject needs, leading them into a fuller relationship with both themselves and the world. In fact, Corbett pointed out that "to the extent that the Self cannot embody because of lack of environmental responsiveness, the [person] is not fully ensouled"; thus, in helping to meet their selfobject needs, one of King's functions was to bring the black soul more fully into embodiment and expression. Corbett argued that selfobject needs are numinous and speak to the soul "because they are aspects of the Self which are intended to bring about what is depicted archetypally as the *coniunctio.*" *Coniunctio* is the Latin term for conjunction, for union and communion, for integration, and it is an archetypal need.

This need for *coniunctio* occurred on two different levels during the Civil Rights Movement: the communion with the Self, as black people were able to reclaim their previously disowned and disempowered psyches, and also the communion with the white community, which had been separated from the black community via legal and social segregation. For many in the black community, King served a god-like healing function, sewing together the severed personal and cultural psyche.

I say many black people, even most black people, to acknowledge that there were some in the community who were uneasy with King's power and questioned his authority. He was not held uniformly in a positive light. Some saw him as a traitor to the race and called him an Uncle Tom, some argued that he was standing in the way of black empowerment rather than paving the way for it, and many took great issue with his advocacy of nonviolence, believing it further weakened the black psyche rather than strengthening it. Some were critical of the image he projected, and how he allowed himself to become a projection-carrier, and found this damaging to the goals of the Civil Rights Movement. We will explore these critiques in Chapter 8 when we look at the dangers of taking a man and making him into a myth.

Conclusion

It is very common for leaders to consciously seek out the projections of their constituencies by evoking powerful archetypes. Hitler was a master of this, consciously evoking the archetypal force of the Norse warrior-king Wotan. John F. Kennedy evoked and then benefited from the projection of Camelot onto his reign. A president who appears in military uniform standing in front of a group of soldiers, like George W. Bush did in the post-911 days, is evoking the archetype of the warrior, consciously seeking to benefit from the projections of his followers, especially those with a predilection for that particular archetype. In this case, leaders are taking possession of the archetypes, using them as a means to their own end; they may or may not personally be under their possession as a complex. It is very often difficult to distinguish the latter, to determine whether the person is consciously taking possession of an archetype for power or whether they are unconsciously under the control of a complex, and thus, possessed by the archetype. As mentioned before, archetypes are powerful currents, and many a person has been swept away when the current they stepped into became too powerful to control (again, Marilyn Monroe is a good example here).

There are three major archetypes that King evoked and embodied during his tenure as leader of the Civil Rights Movement: the deliverer, the prophet, and the martyr-savior. Whether he was possessed by these archetypes, and unconsciously under the control of a complex, or whether he simply identified with them and consciously evoked them for his own purposes, is something we'll try to determine in Chapter 8 after we've fully explored all three archetypes themselves.

What's undeniable is that King had a tremendous archetypal effect on both his foes and followers. Consider the words of Alice Walker when she recalled first seeing King.

At the moment I saw his resistance I knew I would never be able to live in this country without resisting everything that sought to disinherit me, and I would never be forced away from the land of my birth without a fight.

He was The One, The Hero, The One Fearless Person for whom we had waited. I hadn't even realized before that we *had* been waiting for Martin Luther King, Jr., but we had. And I knew it for sure when my mother added his name to the list of people she prayed for every night.

I sometimes think that it was literally the prayers of people like my mother and father, who had bowed down in the struggle for such a long time, that kept Dr. King alive until five years ago. For years we went to bed praying for his life, and awoke with the question "Is the 'Lord' still here?"

You can tell you're in the midst of archetypal and mythological projections when someone capitalizes titles such as The One, The Hero, and The Lord. So let's turn now to King's specific archetypal roles.

7 ARCHETYPES:

THE GOAL THAT OBSESSED HIM AND THE ROLES THAT POSSESSED HIM

Before we begin our exploration of the specific archetypes that King embodied, a few words about literal comparison. Remember that archetypes are universal patterns, and myths are the specific cultural carriers of those archetypes, carrying symbolic and psychological truths, not literal truths. Therefore, we are able to say that King was living out the archetype of the deliverer, and he carried that archetype to the people using the vehicle of Moses. While I will point out some of the literal direct parallels between Moses and King to help illustrate the connection, I will rarely point out aspects of the myth that do not fit. I do this, following the philosophy of Lionel Corbett:

> Mythic characters personify intrapsychic processes, but there are many characters and plots in any story on which attention can be focused, and only certain of them pertain to the individual self. . . . This helps to explain why different observers select different themes on which to focus; we are drawn to aspects of the story that resonate personally.

Therefore, we will focus on the aspects of the myths that resonated with King personally, those parts of the myths that King both carried *to* the people, and carried *for* the people.

The Archetypal Goal of the Beloved Community

All three of King's archetypal roles were in service to a single archetypal goal: the creation of utopia. In Christianity this archetype is found in the utopia of the past, the Garden of Eden, and the utopia of the future, Heaven. Plato made famous the myth of utopian Atlantis and several authors helped create Camelot as a perfect world. As we explored in Chapter 5, the Puritans came to this country to create a perfect world, guided by their utopian dreams. More examples abound in history, literature, mythology, and film, testifying to the archetypal nature and universal appeal of utopia. Many people are still captivated by these myths and have hope or faith that these once and future societies will rise again.

A typical feature of the utopian myth is that these places either existed in the past and/or will exist in the future—where utopia *is not* is in the present. This distinction is clear in the very definition of the word itself, which literally translates into "no place." When describing something as utopian now, we usually refer to projects that are considered impossible, or at least out of reach of humanity as we know it. While different cultures—or even different people within a culture—will have different definitions of what a utopian world would be like, the overarching goal of utopian societies is harmonious relationships: harmony in social relationships, in interpersonal relationships, in political relationships, in relationship with nature, and in relationship with God or the gods.

King's Vision of a Utopian Society

King called his vision and version of a utopian society "the beloved community."[16] Smith and Zepp, the authors of *Search for the Beloved Community,* stated that "the vision of the Beloved Community was the organizing principle of all of King's thought and activity." They defined King's vision of the beloved community as "a transformed and regenerated human society" where "unity would be an actuality in every aspect of social life" which "involves personal and social relationships that are created by love." King called the beloved community "a new nation where men will live together as brothers; a nation where all men will respect the dignity and worth of the human personality."

For King, the beloved community was an ideal he developed early in his life, and he spoke of it often throughout his life. In one of his first articles about the Montgomery Bus Boycott written in 1957, he declared the purpose of the boycott as "reconciliation; the end is redemption; the end is the creation of the beloved

---

[16] Some authors chose to capitalize Beloved Community, and capitalizing it does emphasize its archetypal nature. However, since King did not in his own publications, I will follow suit and not do it in mine.

community." In fact, he saw all social activism, not just the boycott, in this light. Explaining the purpose of the Southern Christian Leadership Conference, again in 1957, King said, "The ultimate aim of SCLC is to foster and create the 'beloved community' in America where brotherhood is a reality. . . . SCLC works for integration. Our ultimate goal is genuine intergroup and interpersonal living—*integration*."

He continued to keep this vision at the forefront of his thinking and teaching. At the start of the sit-in movement during the founding conference of the Student Nonviolent Coordinating Committee in 1960, he made this clear.

> It must be made palpably clear that resistance and nonviolence are not in themselves good. There is another element that must be present in our struggle that then makes our resistance and nonviolence truly meaningful. That element is reconciliation. Our ultimate end must be the creation of the beloved community.

Years later, when speaking during the Chicago movement in 1966, King returned to the same idea.

> There comes a time when we move from protest to reconciliation and we have been misinterpreted by the press and by the political leaders of this town as to our motives and our goals, but let me say once again that it is our purpose, our single purpose is to create the beloved community. We seek only to make possible a city where men can live together as brothers.

King found support for the ideal of the beloved community in the Bible, particularly in the concept of the kingdom of God. In fact, Smith and Zepp noted, "The kingdom of God and the Beloved Community were synonymous in King's thought." King said that

> the Kingdom of God will be a society in which men and women live as children of God should live. It will be a kingdom controlled by the law of love. . . . Many have attempted to say that the ideal of a better world will be worked out in the next world. But Jesus taught men to say, "Thy will be done in earth, as it is in heaven."

Following the teachings of Jesus, King believed that the kingdom was not simply a future utopia to be found in heaven, but something that we should strive to reach on earth.

Striving for the beloved community, then, was a profoundly moral and religious act. He believed that "although man's moral pilgrimage may never reach a destination point on earth, his never-ceasing strivings may bring him ever closer to the city of righteousness." He felt that the kingdom could come in the present or could be post-historical, but regardless of whether it comes "soon or late, by sudden crisis or through slow development," the beloved community

> will be a society in which all men and women will be controlled by the eternal love of God. When we see social relationships controlled everywhere by the principles which Jesus illustrated in his life—trust, love, mercy, and altruism—then we shall know that the kingdom of God is here. To say what this society will be like in exact detail is quite hard for us to picture, for it runs so counter to the practices of our present social life. But we can rest assured that it will be a society governed by the law of love.

King pointed out that "though the Kingdom of God may remain not yet as a universal reality in history, in the present it may exist in such isolated forms as in judgment, in personal devotion, and in some group life." It is clear that King saw the Civil Rights Movement itself as the "group life" in which the beloved community was manifesting itself. He had an early experience of this at the March on Washington in 1963; his wife Coretta captures the experience most clearly.

> As Martin ended [his "I Have a Dream" speech], there was the awed silence that is the greatest tribute an orator can be paid. And then a tremendous crash of sound as two hundred and fifty thousand people shouted in ecstatic accord with his words. The feeling that they had of oneness and unity was complete. They kept on shouting in one thunderous voice, and for that brief moment the Kingdom of God seemed to have come on earth.

She continued, "We all had felt that a great human milestone, a great spiritual communion, had taken place on August 28, 1963."

Another group experience of the beloved community was the march from Selma to Montgomery in 1965; King was very moved by it.

> When we marched from Selma to Montgomery, Alabama, I remember that we had one of the most magnificent expressions of the ecumenical movement I had ever seen. Protestants, Catholics, and Jews joined together in a beautiful way to articulate the injustices and the indignities that Negroes were facing.

After the march, there was a delay at the airport, and several thousand demonstrators waited for hours "crowding together on the seats, the floors, and the stairways of the terminal building." King was there with them, and he was struck by the obvious unity of the crowd.

> As I stood with them and saw white and Negro, nuns and priests, ministers and rabbis, labor organizers, lawyers, doctors, housemaids and shop workers brimming with vitality and enjoying a rare comradeship, I knew I was seeing a microcosm of the mankind of the future in this moment of luminous and genuine brotherhood.

It was precisely because the beloved community was predicated on harmonious social relationships that King always fought for inclusiveness in all aspects of the Civil Rights Movement, encouraging every type of person to participate.

> The people who attended the mass meetings and rallies, who participated in the demonstrations, and who worked in other innumerable ways were from every segment of American society. Professional leaders (teachers, lawyers, doctors, clergy, etc.) willingly walked and worked with domestics and day laborers. Every social class and every age group was represented. The educated and the illiterate, the affluent and the welfare recipient, white and black—people who had heretofore been separated by rigid social mores and laws—were brought together in a common cause.

Nothing could please King more than such a diverse gathering of people united peacefully around a common goal. Just as he knew that love could not be created from hate, and peace could not be created from violence, he knew that a unified community could not be created by a segregated movement. Therefore, when the Black Power Movement began to call for black-only marches, King refused to take part; we saw in Chapter 4 how King took issue with the whole idea of "Black Power" itself, saying that the Movement must "work for brotherhood, for true intergroup, interpersonal living, and black and white together": he reminded people that power itself was not the end they sought, but rather the "objective is a truly brotherly society, the creation of a beloved community."

King taught that the beloved community was intricately connected to the so-called "American dream" which itself was antithetical to racial segregation. "America is essentially a Dream," he said, "a dream of a land where men of all races, of all nationalities, and of all creeds can live together as brothers." In his "I Have a Dream" speech, he spoke most movingly of union and harmony as he evoked images of the beloved community. Just remember some of his powerful final lines of the speech.

- I have a dream that one day on the red hills of Georgia, sons of former slaves and sons of former slave-owners will be able to sit down together at the table of brotherhood.

- I have a dream that one day, down in Alabama . . . Little black boys and black girls will be able to join hands with little white boys and white girls as sister and brothers.

- With this faith we will be able to transform the jangling discords of our nation into a beautiful symphony of brotherhood.

- With this faith we will be able to work together, to pray together, to struggle together, to go to jail together, to stand up for freedom together, knowing that we will be free one day.

And of course, the final lines, the penultimate utopian vision of union:

And when we allow freedom to ring, when we let it ring from every village and hamlet, from every state and city, we will be able to speed up the day when all of God's children—black men and white men, Jews and Gentiles, Catholics and Protestants—will be able to join hands and to sing in the words of the old Negro spiritual, "Free at last, free at last; thank God Almighty, we are free at last."

The Beloved Community as the Archetype of Union

I mentioned the Latin word *coniunctio* in the last chapter. Jung used this word to represent the archetype of the union of opposites, and declared it one of the most powerful archetypes, writing that "the absorptive power of the archetype explains not only the widespread incidence of this motif but also the passionate intensity with which it seizes upon the individual, often in defiance of all reason and understanding." Precisely because of its power, "the image of the *coniunctio* has always occupied an important place in the history of the human mind."

Depth psychologist Erich Fromm also noted the power of the archetype of union.

> There is only one passion which satisfies man's need to unite himself with the world, and to acquire at the same time a sense of integrity and individuality, and this is love. Love is union with somebody or something, outside oneself, under the condition of retaining the separateness and integrity of one's own self. It is an experience of sharing, of communion, which permits the full unfolding of one's own inner activity.

Because of this universal human need, Jung wrote that "the free society needs a bond of an affective nature, a principle of a kind like *caritas*, the Christian love of your neighbor." Though Jung used the term "caritas" and Fromm used the word "love," both of them anticipate King's call for agape, which we discussed in Chapter 2. Jung said that in love resides a society's "real cohesion and consequently its strength. Where love stops, power begins, and violence, and terror."

Jung believed that integration, both within oneself and with one's neighbor, was incredibly difficult and ultimately achievable by very few, though a therapist still works with clients toward that goal.

Theologian Walter Rauschenbusch, in the book that was so influential to King, *Christianity and the Social Crisis,* taught the same thing.

> In asking for faith in the possibility of a new social order, we ask for no Utopian delusion. We know well that there is no perfection for man in this life: there is only growth toward perfection. . . . We make it a duty to seek what is unattainable. We have the same paradox in the perfectibility of society. We shall never have a perfect social life, yet we must seek it with faith. . . . At best there is always but an approximation to a perfect social order. The kingdom of God is always but coming. But every approximation to it is worthwhile. Every step toward personal purity and peace, though it only makes the consciousness of imperfection more poignant, carries its own exceeding great reward, and everlasting pilgrimage toward the kingdom of God is better than contented stability in the tents of wickedness.

King's short life was such a pilgrimage toward the beloved community, the promised land of freedom, the archetypal utopia, the *coniunctio* on the cultural level, the deepest expression of union and integration. As the deliverer, King wanted to take his people there; as the prophet, he wanted to announce its existence and decry all impediments to embodying it now; and as the martyr-savior, he was willing to die to save his people (and all were his people) from living anywhere else or living anything less.

The Therapeutic Parallels

Before we look at King's three archetypal roles, I want to draw some preliminary therapeutic parallels here; these will be discussed more in the final chapter of the book, but I believe evoking them here will help to contextualize the rest of this chapter inside of the main argument of this book, that King acted as a cultural therapist for America during one of her major times of crisis, the Civil Rights Movement.

What is the archetypal goal of therapy? Different schools of therapy, different theorists and practitioners, therapists from different times in history or in different cultural locations may all answer this question in different ways. Some may assert it is healing the psyche from its past childhood wounds; some may suggest it is helping people cope with present day problems; some may believe it is helping people adjust and adapt to their circumstances; some focus on helping people function in their lives; others on helping people live through existential despair; others on teaching people more healthy thought and behavior patterns; others on empowering people to work through addictive and/or destructive patterns in their lives; still others on helping people to improve the quality of their relationships.

Regardless of the specific focus, I want to suggest that the goals of therapy are very congruent with King's goal above, the creation of the beloved community, though obviously stated in very different language. The beloved community is marked by harmonious relationships—the relationship with self and others—a goal congruent with the goals of therapy. The beloved community is marked by integration—the integration of self, and the integration of that self with others—a goal congruent with the goals of therapy. The beloved community is marked by friendship and love and respect for the dignity of all people—all goals congruent with the goals of therapy. We could even imagine therapy as being the place where people go to work through all their issues, problems, thoughts, behaviors, everything and anything that keeps them from being a participant in and co-creator of the beloved community. Seen this way, King's main goal in working with the country was profoundly congruent with the goals of therapy, and in fact is a model (not *the* model, but *a* model) for what therapy done with a culture can look like.

Turning to look at the archetypal roles that therapists embody, these too can vary. Most therapists would recognize themselves as archetypal healers, as doctors of the psyche or soul. In the age of neuropsychology, some now may imagine themselves as the scientist or the brain technician. Others, both contemporary, historically, and cross-culturally, might imagine themselves as the witness, the shepherd, the minister, the midwife, the shaman, the counselor, the spiritual guide, etc. Each archetypal role carries a different nuance, and will sound different tones within the therapy. Each one will also come with a different set of expectations and projections in the dynamic field between therapist and client: for instance, what if the therapist sees herself in the role of the witness, and the client sees the therapist in the role of the shepherd? What conflicts will arise in therapy as a result?

As we explore the archetypal roles that King resonated with, those of the deliverer, the prophet, and the martyr-savior, we'll keep in mind how each one might play out in the therapeutic relationship, in this case, cultural therapy between a man and his country.

King as the Archetypal Deliverer

In the archetypal myth of delivery, a god or hero leads a group of people out of exile or bondage and into freedom. In Christianity, the myth of Moses leading the Israelites in their exodus from Egypt and into the Promised Land is considered by some "the greatest story of liberation from enslavement ever told." For obvious reasons, it's a myth that's been long at the heart of the black experience in America.

The belief that black people were called by God to redeem the United States was a part of their religious tradition: writer James Baldwin illustrated this when he wrote, "The more devout Negro considers that he is a Jew, in bondage to a hard taskmaster and waiting for a Moses to lead him out of Egypt." Before Emancipation, many black leaders wore that mantle, including Harriet Tubman and Frederick Douglass. Journalist and author Louis Lomax noted that the myth might have died out had Emancipation really meant freedom for black people, but because in so many ways they were still oppressed, "The myth not only continued but took on even greater significance." In the early 20th century, the mantle fell for a time on Marcus Garvey and his "Back to Africa" movement. By the middle of the century, the role of deliverer was both gifted to and received by Martin Luther King, Jr.

King saw the struggle of oppressed black people in America to gain their freedom as the archetypal embodiment of this biblical exodus myth.

> Oppressed people cannot remain oppressed forever. The yearning for freedom eventually manifests itself. The Bible tells the thrilling story of how Moses stood in Pharaoh's court centuries ago and cried, "Let my people go." This was an opening chapter in a continuing story. The present struggle in the United States is a later chapter in the same story.

This myth also runs through the chapters of King's life. Indeed, it acts as a set of bookends: it was the myth he referred to at his first major appearance on the public stage during the Montgomery Bus Boycott, and while he continued to use it throughout his life, he drew from it again most memorably in his last major public appearance, the night before his death in Memphis.

It was in Montgomery where he first drew the comparison of himself to Moses.

> And that is why down in Montgomery we could walk twelve months and never get weary, because we know there is a great camp meeting in the promised land of freedom and justice. . . . People today are standing in the wilderness. The masses of people [are] waiting to go over, go into the Promised Land. They've gained a vision of it, they've tasted freedom. Sometimes they can't speak for themselves, don't know the exact techniques, but they are ready to go. And any minister of the gospel who refuses at this point to lead his people is not worth having the name of "reverend" in the name of God.

Though he just hints at his affinity with Moses here, nearly four years later when he left Birmingham to return to Atlanta, he fully declares the connection. Reassuring his congregation that he was not leaving the Movement, he said, "I can't stop now. History has thrust something upon me which I cannot turn away. I should free you now."[17]

King created himself in the image of Moses, an image that was quickly embraced and propagated by the media. The popular black magazine *Jet* called him "a symbol of divinely inspired hope" and "a kind of modern Moses who has brought new self-respect to Southern Negroes." *Time* magazine, in naming King "Man of the Year" in 1964, wrote, "Another [King supporter] ecstatically calls

---

[17] Statements like these are the reason I titled this chapter in part, "the archetypal roles that possessed him." Archetypes can possess us, overwhelm us, cause us to lose our own identity and identify with something much larger than us. While some could interpret such a strong statement as "I should free you now" coming from such a young man as arrogant, preposterous, over-assuming and over-estimating of one's own power (imagine a therapist saying to a client, "I should heal you now"), I interpret it here as proof that King was possessed with the archetypal energy of the deliverer as it manifested in the myth of Moses.

him a 'Moses, sent to lead his people to the Promised Land of first-class citizenship.'" Countless individuals continued to promulgate the mythological connection. A black clergyman in Memphis prepared his congregation for the march to come, telling them "King is the man, O Lord, that has been sent to lead us out of the land of Egypt." T. J. Jimerson was a lifelong friend and associate of King's; he declared, "God only puts on the face of the earth a leader like that once in a number of years. He's never had more than one Moses at a time."

Learning From the Moses Myth

As we explored in the last chapter, myths often function as storehouses of wisdom for the culture and serve a teaching function. There are several lessons within the Moses myth that are particularly important to note here because they shaped the way King viewed the freedom struggle and his place within it. The first lesson was the soul's innate desire for freedom; King called it "a throbbing desire" that is "the essential basis" of personhood.

> There is something in the soul that cries out for freedom. There is something deep down within the very soul of man that reaches out for Canaan [the Promised Land]. Men cannot be satisfied with Egypt. They try to adjust to it for awhile. Many men have vested interests in Egypt, and they are slow to leave. Egypt makes it profitable to them; some people profit by Egypt. The vast majority, the masses of people, never profit by Egypt, and they are never content with it. And eventually they rise up and begin to cry out for Canaan's land.

King saw himself as answering the cry for freedom by leading his people toward the Promised Land; he would free their souls, an appropriate albeit lofty ambition for both a minister and a cultural therapist.

Secondly, the myth contains a lesson about the tactics one might have to use to gain freedom. Moses originally made an emotional appeal to Pharaoh to let his people go, but Pharaoh refused, instead hardening his heart against Moses and the Israelites. God sent nine different and devastating plagues to Egypt, and each time Moses told Pharaoh he could avoid the plagues if he would let the people go, but Pharaoh continually refused. Finally, the tenth plague was sent—the death of all the Egyptian first-born sons—and Pharaoh was finally forced to relent. King learned from this myth that while changing someone's heart is preferable and should be the first line of offense, much of the time freedom must be taken by force. He told his followers that there was something they must never forget as they found themselves "breaking aloose from an evil Egypt, trying to move through the wilderness toward the promised land of cultural integration"—that "the oppressor never voluntarily gives freedom to the oppressed. . . . Freedom only comes through persistent revolt, through persistent agitation, through persistently rising up against the system of evil." He would appeal to the hearts of the Pharaohs in the various cities where he fought for freedom, but ultimately he knew he would have to use (nonviolent) force, his plagues taking the form of persistent marches and boycotts and sit-ins and demonstrations.

Thirdly, there is a lesson about the power of suffering in the myth. Fromm stated that the story of Moses teaches us that "the beginning of liberation lies in man's capacity to suffer, and he suffers if he is oppressed, physically and spiritually. The suffering moves him to act against his oppressors, to seek the end of the oppression." Further, "the possibility of liberation exists only because people suffer and, in biblical language, because God 'understands' the suffering and hence tries to relieve it." King taught the value of what he variously called *redemptive suffering* or *unearned suffering* or *unmerited suffering*, suffering done by those who do not deserve it on behalf of the greater cause of liberation. He reassured his followers, consistent with the Moses myth, that God was on their side, that they had cosmic companionship in their struggles, that God struggled with them on behalf of the cessation of their suffering.

Even with God on their side, however, King knew that the struggle was never easy: "It comes through hard labor and it comes through toil. It comes through hours of despair and disappointment." He continued, "That's the long story of freedom, isn't it? Before you get to Canaan, you've got a Red Sea to confront. You have a hardened heart of a Pharaoh to confront. You have the prodigious hilltops of evil in the wilderness to confront."

The fourth lesson from this myth is closely related. Because there is so much struggle involved in freedom, King knew people would not always welcome their deliverers. Moses' followers often complained, doubted, disobeyed, and rebuked him. King summarized this part of the myth.

> About 2800 years ago Moses set out to lead the children of
> Israel from the slavery of Egypt to the freedom of the
> promised land. He soon discovered that slaves do not always
> welcome their deliverers. They become accustomed to being
> slaves. They would rather bear those ills they have, as
> Shakespeare pointed out, than flee to others that they know
> not of.

Understanding that people could easily come to resent the demands
put upon them by their deliverers, King was constantly aware of the
necessity of providing his followers enough victories to make the
demands of the suffering somehow worthwhile.

Finally, a fifth lesson from the myth that King certainly took to
heart is that the deliverer doesn't always make it into the land of
deliverance. Moses never made it to the Promised Land himself.
Instead, from a mountaintop God offered Moses a panoramic view
of the Promised Land, and then and there he took Moses' life. The
glory falls upon Joshua, the second in command, to lead the people
into that Promised Land.

On a literal level, while this may seem a cruel punishment to a
man who faithfully served his god, on the archetypal level, it does
make sense. Moses is the deliverer, the emancipator—not the
delivered, not the emancipated. And King knew this, knew very
early on that it was unlikely he would see the Promised Land. These
are words from a 1957 sermon.

> Moses might not get to see Canaan, but his children will see
> it. He even got to the mountaintop enough to see it and that
> assured him that it was coming. But the beauty of the thing
> is that there's always a Joshua to take up his work and take
> the children on in. And it's there waiting with its milk and
> honey, and with all of the bountiful beauty that God has in
> store for His children.

Eleven years later he returned to that idea in the speech given the
very night before his assassination. Caught up in the emotion of this
archetype, it was as if he sensed his imminent death and its
archetypal fatedness. He ended the last speech of his life by evoking
his role as Moses.

> Well, I don't know what will happen now. We've got some
> difficult days ahead. But it doesn't matter with me now.
> Because I've been to the mountaintop. And I don't mind.
> Like anybody, I would like to live a long life. Longevity has
> its place. But I'm not concerned about that now. I just want
> to do God's will. And He's allowed me to go up to the
> mountain. And I've looked over. And I've seen the promised
> land. I may not get there with you. But I want you to know
> tonight, that we, as a people, will get to the promised land.

As moving as those words are when juxtaposed to his own
death less than twenty-four hours later, it is important to note that
King actually used similar language eleven years earlier in
Montgomery. After his house was bombed, he spoke the same
words.

> So I'm not afraid of anybody this morning. Tell Montgomery
> they can keep shooting and I'm going to stand up to them.
> Tell Montgomery they can keep bombing and I'm going to
> stand up to them. If I had to die tomorrow morning I would
> die happy because I've been to the mountaintop and I've
> seen the promised land and it's going to be here in
> Montgomery.

He ended his speech the night before his real death much in the
same way he ended his speech the morning after the death attempt.
"And I'm happy tonight. I'm not worried about anything. I'm not
fearing any man. Mine eyes have seen the glory of the coming of the
Lord." The Moses myth not only helped to shape his thoughts and
imbue his life with the energy of the archetypal deliverer, but it also
gave him hope and courage throughout his abbreviated trek through
the American desert. It perhaps gave him comfort as he faced
continual assassination attempts and feared his own early death; his
death was archetypally prefigured, but so too was the fact that his
people would see the promised land.

King as the Archetypal Prophet

Though the archetype of the deliverer was one King frequently
hitched himself to in public, it was the archetype of the prophet that
seemed to propel him personally. Smith and Zepp asserted, "The

Hebrew prophets influenced King more than any other part of Scripture with the exception of the Sermon on the Mount. Sometimes by direct quotation, but mostly by tone and implication, the prophetic model is evident in most of King's speeches and writings." Before we compare King to the two specific prophets who were most important to him, Amos and Jeremiah, let's see how King conformed to the general archetypal pattern of the prophet.

Characteristics of the Prophet Archetype

In *How to Read the Prophets*, author Jean Pierre Prevost defined a prophet as someone who has been sent by God and who speaks to the community in God's name, delivering his message. King certainly resonated with this archetype: as his professor Harold DeWolf shared, "King believed that the Dream existed originally in the mind of God and that he saw himself as a medium for the communication of God's dream to God's people." King historian Stuart Burns stated that King "did not hesitate to inform meetings large or small that God was speaking through him. He would habitually interrupt staff meetings to divine God's answers to their strategic or tactical questions." Prevost noted that the prophets are not only men of God's Word, but they are "men of the word," both spoken and written, each expressive in his own style and distinctive genius. King, of course, was a gifted orator with a unique and charismatic style, and this ability and style allowed him to communicate God's message to the people eloquently and emotionally.

Prophets primarily speak about what needs to be done in the present to avoid a negative future or create a positive one, but they also take action, according to Prevost.

> To make the Word of God understandable to their contemporaries, the prophets did more than speak. They performed actions and translated the world by their lives. . . . So one is not a prophet at the level of lip service, but in one's flesh and one's tears.

King was undeniably a man of action, one who was concerned with walking his talk as much as he was concerned with the talk itself. In one of his characteristic coinages, he would say, "This is no day to pay lip service to integration, we must pay *life* service to it."

One place where the prophets commonly served was in the

political world, rarely as politicians themselves but more often as their consciences and guides. Fromm described this aspect of the prophet.

> His realm is never a purely spiritual one; it is always of this world. Or rather, his spirituality is always experienced in the political and social dimensions. Because God is revealed in history, the prophet cannot help being a political leader; as long as man takes the wrong way in his political action, the prophet cannot help being a dissenter and a revolutionary.

In this sense, King was a prophet as well. He served as an advisor to both Presidents Kennedy and Johnson, but when he was asked in 1967 to run for vice-president on a third party ticket with Dr. Benjamin Spock as the presidential candidate, King considered but ultimately refused, saying, "I have come to think of my role as one which operates outside the realm of partisan politics" because "I feel I should serve as a conscience of all the parties and all of the people, rather than a candidate myself." He was often criticized for serving as that conscience, particularly during the Vietnam War, when he was not afraid to speak out against President Johnson's policies, inviting and incurring Johnson's ire.

This is consistent with another of the characteristics of prophets: their emphasis on peace. Fromm defined what peace might mean to the prophet. "The idea of peace, in the prophetic view, cannot be separated from the idea of the realization of man's humanity. Peace is more than not-war; it is harmony and union between men, it is the overcoming of separateness and alienation." This echoes King's message about peace, that true peace "is not merely the absence of some negative force—war, tension, confusion, but it is the presence of some positive force—justice, goodwill, the power of the kingdom of God." Prophets are less concerned with preaching about the future realization of the peaceful kingdom of God in heaven; they are more concerned with preaching the possibility of realizing peace here and now on earth. King shared this emphasis, as we discussed earlier in this chapter and in Chapter 2.

King felt that the prophetic role was an important one for the minister, though not an easy one. He wrote, "Any discussion of the role of the Christian minister today must ultimately emphasize the need for prophecy. Not every minister can be a prophet, but some must be prepared for the ordeals of this high calling and be willing to suffer courageously for righteousness." King was clearly both prepared and willing. He explained, "I'm the pastor of a church and in that role I have a priestly function as well as a prophetic function, and in the prophetic role I must constantly speak to the moral issues of our day far beyond civil rights." He called his prophetic function a commission, and said, "Something said to me that the fire of truth is shut up in my bones, and when it burns me, I must tell it."

In general, King clearly falls into the archetype of the prophet. In specific, the two most important prophets to him were from the Christian tradition: Amos and Jeremiah. In his very first sermon as pastor at his very first church, the Dexter Avenue Baptist Church, he told his congregation, "I come with a feeling that I have been called to preach and to lead God's people. I have felt like Jeremiah, 'The word of God is in my heart like burning fire shut up in my bones.' I have felt with Amos that when God speaks who can but prophesy?" Looking a little closer at these two prophets reveals many reasons why King resonated with them so strongly.

Comparing King and Amos

The prophet King referred to most in his sermons and writings was Amos. While at Boston University, King took a class called "Religious Teachings of the Old Testament." He wrote hundreds of notecards for the class, and the two he wrote about Amos are particularly interesting because they serve as foundational themes for the opus of King's work. The first notecard is on Amos 5:21-24, which King thought "might be called the key passage of the entire book." The first two verses speak of God's criticism of religious rituals and sacrifices; that criticism, King noted, "reveals the deep ethical nature of God. God is a God that demands justice rather than sacrifice; righteousness rather than ritual. . . . Certainly this is one of the most noble ideas ever uttered by the human mind." King went on to note, "Unless a man's heart is right, Amos seems to be saying, the external forms of worship mean nothing."

Amos and the other prophets often critiqued the religious establishment of their time for being at best passive, ineffectual, and hypocritical, and at worst active in perpetuating social evils. King certainly proved himself worthy of the prophetic lineage in his attacks upon formal religion, which ranged from gentle nudging to scathing scolding. King criticized the black church in particular for its classism, for having "developed a class system [that] boasts of its dignity, its membership of professional people, and its exclusiveness." This classism freezes the church, where "the worship service is cold and meaningless, the music dull and uninspiring, and the sermon little more than a homily on current events."

He criticized the white church in particular for its racism and lack of concern with social justice.

> Millions of American Negroes, starving for the want of the bread of freedom, have knocked again and again on the door of so-called white churches, but they have usually been greeted by a cold indifference or a blatant hypocrisy. . . . One of the shameful tragedies of history is that the very institution that should remove man from the midnight of racial segregation participates in creating and perpetuating the midnight.

Finally, King criticized both the black church and the white church for not taking a stronger stand against militarism and materialism.

> What more pathetically reveals the irrelevancy of the church in present-day world affairs than its witness regarding war? In a world gone mad with arms buildups, chauvinistic passions, and imperialistic exploitation, the church has either endorsed these activities or remained appallingly silent.

Regarding materialism, he noted how often both the black and the white church had "aligned itself with the privileged classes and so defended that status quo," making itself the cause and not the cure of economic privation. King echoed Amos' style of prophecy—telling the truth, telling it blunting, and telling it as if God had revealed it directly to him—when he wrote, "The judgment of God is upon the church as never before."

The passage where Amos attacks the church ends with a sentence King used over and over again in his sermons, most famously in the "I Have a Dream" speech: "Let justice roll down like waters and righteousness like a mighty stream." In fact, King used these words so often that they were chosen for the Civil Rights Monument in Montgomery, Alabama, imprinted onto a wall of flowing water.

On his second note card about Amos titled "Social Ethics," he wrote, "Amos' emphasis throughout seems to be that justice between man and man is one of the divine foundations of society. Such an ethical ideal is at the root of all true religion. This high ethical notion conceived by Amos must always remain a challenge to the Christian church." Of course, this was King's challenge to the Christian church as well, as he called for it to "come to the aid of justice" and be willing to fight on behalf of righteousness.

After King became a minister, he referred to Amos in two contexts. First, he would term Amos as "an extremist for justice," categorizing him with other extremists such as Abraham Lincoln, Thomas Jefferson, the apostle Paul, and Jesus Christ. In "Letter from Birmingham City Jail," King revealed that he was initially disappointed to be dismissed as an extremist, but, "as I continued to think about the matter I gradually gained a bit of satisfaction from being considered an extremist" because of the good company he kept. "After all," he wrote, "maybe the South, the nation and the world are in dire need of creative extremists." Second, he often referred to Amos as "maladjusted," telling his followers, "I call upon you to be as maladjusted as Amos who in the midst of the injustices of his day cried out in words that echo across the generation, 'Let justice roll down like waters and righteousness like a mighty stream.'" Here again he linked Amos with other maladjusted individuals such as Lincoln, Jefferson, and Jesus, and asked for God to make more of us maladjusted so "we will be able to go out and change our world and our civilization."

Comparing King and Jeremiah

The other prophet King resonated with and referred to often in his sermons and speeches was Jeremiah. King's closest companion Ralph Abernathy drew the connection. King was a very funny man, according to Abernathy, but people outside of his inner circle rarely saw his humorous side. Abernathy attributed that to the circumstances of King's first call in Montgomery, where frivolity obviously would have struck the wrong tone. He said, "We were in serious trouble. So was the entire country. Martin felt that his public appearances had to reflect the grim realities of the situation. America needed a Jeremiah, not another black comedian. So he became Jeremiah, and continued in that role until the end."

King's interest in Jeremiah went back to his graduate school days at Crozer where he wrote a paper called "The Significant Contribution of Jeremiah to Religious Thought," calling Jeremiah "the greatest of them all." In the paper, King pointed out two significant interests of Jeremiah's that paralleled King's interests. First, Jeremiah was similar to Amos in that he saw and declared "that public religion is an organized hypocrisy. In it religion was divorced from morality." Jeremiah was not afraid to attack the religious establishment, and in particular the Jerusalem priests, whom he thought were more dedicated to the status quo than to God. Thus, King called Jeremiah "a shining example of the truth that religion should never sanction the status quo."

Secondly, King was interested in Jeremiah's idea of the establishment of a New Covenant, a concept analogous to the beloved community. When the New Covenant was established,

> the laws written in the heart will become an inseparable part of man's moral being. Principles would take the place of external ordinances. Such principles as truth, and justice, and purity, love to God and love to men, would be enshrined in the hearts of men. This, said Jeremiah, would lead to an ideal state.

King, like Jeremiah, believed that external laws were important, but he was also clear that legislation written in the heart was more important than legislation written on paper; indeed, it was only a change of heart that would lead to both Jeremiah and King's ideal state.

King found Jeremiah relevant to contemporary times, particularly in his striving for a more perfect world.

> He stepped on the religious stage sounding the trumpet for a new idea of God, and the signal for another forward march of the soul. He had seized on a great and revolutionary truth, and with that truth, like a pillar of cloud by day and of fire by night, went ahead of his times. In many instances the picture drawn by Jeremiah is an idealistic one, and an idea which has not yet been realized—the New Covenant for example. But the ideal is there; it at least serves as a standard by which we may measure ourselves, a goal which we may all strive to attain.

Substitute the term "Beloved Community" for "New Covenant" and those very same words could easily serve as a summary of King's life and mission.

At the end of his paper, King raised the question, "But what is society's reaction to such men?" His answer: "It has reacted, and always will re-act, in the only way open to it. It destroys such men. Jeremiah died a martyr." In the margins of the paper, Professor James Bennett Pritchard marked an "X" after "martyr" and wrote in the margins, "Not literally." Most scholars believe that Jeremiah did not die for the cause, but rather, fled to Egypt where he lived the rest of his life and died of natural causes. However, at least one scholar pointed out a different possibility. "Tradition says that he was stoned to death there [in Egypt] by exasperated and angry Judeans, whom he continued to rebuke for their cowardice and folly." Regardless of what happened to Jeremiah, it's psychologically interesting that King would choose the martyr's death, and in such unequivocal language, stating that killing the martyr was *the only way* open to society, that society would *always react* by destroying men such as Jeremiah.

Whether Jeremiah was destroyed literally by his call to prophecy, he certainly suffered. As scholar Mary Ellen Chase noted, "He endured more than did any other prophet; he was mocked, humiliated, rejected, heckled, scorned, persecuted, even tortured. He was surely one of the loneliest of men, sacrificing marriage, children, and friends for the sake of his calling." The same could be said of King: he was mocked, yelled at, spit on, threatened, stabbed, bombed, pelted with bricks and stones, verbally attacked and criticized left and right by black and white. He, too, was a lonely man, although this aspect of his biography is seldom highlighted. He traveled constantly, and was away from his family most days of the year. His marriage, though seemingly strong on the outside, was beset with difficulties, not the least of which were his multiple extramarital affairs. Biographer David Garrow quoted one of King's intimate friends, Dennie Drew, who called King "very, very lonely. . . despite the fact that he was surrounded by people all the time. He was still alone—he was apart." She attributed his growing girth and his struggles with his weight to "basic loneliness." Garrow described the changes in King towards the end of his life: "King had always been a formal, reserved man in public, but some friends now saw a more profound somberness in him, a melancholy that seemed to reflect a basic loneliness."

Writer Moshe Pearlman noted Jeremiah's struggles with darkness. "He suffered fits of depression. . . . but he could not repress his thoughts nor muzzle his lips. He had to speak out." King, too, struggled with depression, and though his struggles were hidden from the public, they were no secret to his inner circle of friends and colleagues. He was hospitalized several times with the diagnosis of "exhaustion"—but best friend and closest colleague Ralph Abernathy implied that depression might have been a more appropriate description. Garrow does a thorough job of chronicling King's bouts of depression throughout his life, but especially in his final days, when he was "dispirited," "despondent," and "melancholy." Garrow quoted civil rights leader Roger Wilkins, who met with King during that time and reported that King seemed "very tired and drained" and "very discouraged," that "a profound sadness" had descended over him. Abernathy also described King at that time as "sad and depressed." His wife Coretta said, "There were moments when he would feel depressed," sometimes to the point where he would contemplate taking a year off from the Movement, but he felt compelled to continue.

Though the public never knew how depressed King really was, he did speak publicly about his discouragement, like in this sermon.

> And I don't mind telling you this morning that sometimes I feel discouraged. I felt discouraged in Chicago. As I move through Mississippi and Georgia and Alabama, I feel discouraged. Living every day under the threat of death, I feel discouraged sometimes. Living every day under extensive criticisms, even from Negroes, I feel discouraged sometimes. Yes, sometimes I feel discouraged and feel my work's in vain.

But he never left his audience with his discouragement, always offering them a sense of the healing he felt with God: "But then the holy spirit revives my soul again. 'There is a balm in Gilead to make the wounded whole. There is a balm in Gilead to heal the sin-sick soul.'" What Mary Ellen Chase wrote of Jeremiah equally applies to King: "No other prophet experienced so often and so deeply dark nights of the soul; yet not one came out of those nights so triumphantly as did Jeremiah, or saw so clearly through the darkness the dawn of a new day for his country and for his people."

The archetype of the prophet is not an easy one. Though it was not part of the public persona that King presented, it is not surprising that privately and with his intimates he would experience loneliness, discouragement, and depression, and fear that he would be killed like other prophets before him. This is especially unsurprising given the third archetype he embodied: the martyr/savior.

King as the Archetypal Martyr-Savior

One of the most powerful and compelling archetypes is that of the savior, someone who gives of him or herself to save another. I have combined this archetype with that of the martyr, someone who endures great suffering, even death, to save souls, to further a cause, or to defend a principle. Of course not all saviors are martyrs, since it is possible to save someone without enduring any major suffering on your behalf, and not all martyrs are saviors, since it is possible to endure great personal suffering and not end up saving anyone or anything. However, it is common to see the two together—they were certainly linked in King's mind—and for these reasons, I use the term martyr-savior.

For any Christian, Jesus is the archetype *par excellence* of the martyr-savior, but even so, King seemed especially drawn to him, his life particularly informed by him. As explored in the last chapter, King didn't believe that Jesus was set apart from humanity, possessing any inherent metaphysical substance that would make him supernatural. Jesus embodied many qualities that King admired and aspired to emulate. Jesus provided King with all his main ethics: agape, nonviolence, preferential treatment for the poor, redemptive suffering, sacrifice, radical involvement, commitment to justice, compassion towards the dispossessed, and the belief that one should strive on earth to create heaven. In addition, King found in Jesus someone whose deeds matched his creeds, "a perfect alignment between words and action" that he sought to also embody.

What King revered and wanted to revive about Jesus was his revolutionary message, a message he thought modern Christianity had lost.

> We have the power to change America and give a kind of new vitality to the religion of Jesus Christ. . . . The great tragedy is that Christianity failed to see that it had the revolutionary edge. You don't have to go to Karl Marx to

learn how to be a revolutionary. I didn't get my inspiration from Karl Marx; I got it from a man named Jesus . . . And that is where we get our inspiration. And we go out in a day when we have a message for the world, and we can change this world and we can change this nation.

King saw in Jesus proof of the transformative power of a man and a message. Jesus modeled for him what King scholar Luther D. Ivory called, in his book by the same name, "a theology of radical involvement."

King saw Jesus as the radically involved personality, motivated by a strong God-consciousness, striving to live in harmony with divine will, exhibiting sacrificial love in personal conduct, and working to achieve redemption in interpersonal and committed relationships.

Perhaps "the radically involved personality" could be considered an archetype in and of itself, in which case it was this archetypal dimension of Jesus that magnetized King to him. However, though King referred to Jesus many times in his role as the radically involved personality, it was the martyr-savior dimension of Jesus that most people have come to associate with King, and King eventually came to associate most with himself.

How Others Compared King to Jesus

There are some interesting parallels between King's life and the life of Jesus. Some of those parallels were connections King drew himself, and others feel like synchronicities, sometimes eerie ones, and were drawn by others. Coretta and Ralph Abernathy wrote about one of the eerie ones, something that occurred a couple of days before King's assassination. He met with his staff to discuss the Poor People's Campaign, the plan to bring thousands of poor people of every color to occupy the National Mall in an anti-poverty protest. King was already depressed leading up to this meeting, and had made many "morbid comments about his death." There was much contention at that meeting; the staff was not supportive of King's campaign, thinking it ill-advised on many levels, and King felt betrayed by them, much in the same way Jesus was betrayed and denied by his disciples before his death.

Coretta described the meeting in detail.

It was a little like the Last Supper. Members of the staff still talk a lot about that meeting. They remember it so well and the emotional impact it had on them. Martin felt so much agony and experienced so much conflict because the staff was not cooperative and supportive of his going back to Memphis. There was no enthusiasm; they hoped he would give up on the project. He kept talking to them and trying to prevail upon them. He went around the room and told each person what they needed to do; he criticized them one by one. It was like the way the Last Supper is described, when Christ told Judas that he would betray Him and then spoke to Peter and the others. Martin said that he wanted anyone in the organization who turned to violence to be fired, and then pointed out who was getting out of line. The meeting got very emotional, and he got upset and left. He knew that if he did that they would probably come around.

Come around they did, under admonitions by Abernathy to support their leader. They called King back to the meeting to tell him they were ready to support him, but he took hours to return, and by then, Abernathy remembered, most of them were asleep, echoing the sleep of the disciples in the Garden of Gethsemane the night before Jesus was crucified.

Recall that the night before King was assassinated, he spoke as if he knew his own death was near, just as Jesus did. He talked in the speech about the time he was stabbed by the mentally ill woman, how the blade of the letter-opener she used had lodged so near his heart that the doctors said one sneeze would have killed him. He was glad he hadn't sneezed, he told the crowd, because he wouldn't have seen all the accomplishments that had come about in the last ten years. But after talking about how grateful he was to have lived, he did an abrupt reversal, and began to talk of his death. "Now it doesn't matter now. It really doesn't matter now," he repeated. He told of leaving Atlanta for the flight to Memphis, how the plane was delayed because there had been a bomb threat. When he arrived in Memphis there were more death threats. He repeated again, "But it doesn't matter with me now because I've been to the mountaintop. And I don't mind."

Why didn't he mind the idea of dying? Why didn't his own death matter to him anymore? Coretta offered an answer.

My husband had always talked of his own readiness to give his life for a cause he believed in. He felt that giving himself completely would serve as a redemptive force in its inspiration to other people. This would mean that he would be resurrected in the lives of other people who dedicated themselves to a great cause.

King was so possessed by the martyr-savior archetype that he had reconciled himself to his own crucifixion and seemed to welcome his subsequent resurrection.

In another eerie connection, Coretta drew a parallel between the timing of King's death and the timing of Jesus'. King's death happened during Lenten week, the week before the Passion. In Christianity, the Passion refers to the last days of Jesus' life and the events leading up to and including his crucifixion. According to Coretta,

Martin had felt a mystical identity with the spirit and meaning of Christ's Passion. And even in those first awful moments [when she heard of King's death], it went through my mind that it was somehow appropriate that Martin Luther King's supreme sacrifice should come at the Easter season.

Just days after his death at a Memphis rally, Coretta incorporated that symbolic language into a speech she delivered.

I would challenge you today to see that his spirit never dies and that we will go forward from this experience, which to me represents the Crucifixion, on toward the resurrection and the redemption of the spirit. How many times have I heard him say that with every Good Friday there comes Easter. When Good Friday comes, these are the moments in life when we feel that all is lost, and there is no hope. But then Easter comes as a time of resurrection, of rebirth.

This symbolic language was not missed by others. In fact, right after his death, a woman said, "I'm hoping Easter Sunday he'll rise again!"

King frequently drew connections between Good Friday as the

day of sorrows, and Easter as the morning of resurrection, the triumph of life over death. He would have hoped that his sacrificial death, his crucifixion, would awaken a passion for resurrection in his followers. It certainly did in his closest companion Ralph Abernathy. In a letter to King he read at a service three days after his death, Abernathy said "there were so many parallels" between King and Jesus.

> You were our leader and we were your disciples. Those who killed you did not know that you loved them and that you worked for them as well. . . . They thought that they could kill our movement by killing you, Martin. . . . There has been a crucifixion in our nation, but here in this spring season as we see the blossoms and smell the fresh air we know that the Resurrection will shortly appear.

Abernathy made a promise to King after he died, that his "disciples" would carry on his work in his name.

> When the masters left the disciples, they felt gloom at first. Then they gathered themselves together in a fellowship. . . . Many grew up overnight. They were covered with their ancient words and with despair. We promise you, Martin, just as the disciples tarried in that upper room, that we're going to. . . . wait until the Holy Ghost speaks. . . . [then] speak as Peter spoke. And others will be converted and added to the movement and God's kingdom will come.

The Poor People's Campaign was carried out by his disciples, and the name of the planned tent city, "City of Hope," was changed to "Resurrection City."[18]

---

[18] I have written about this campaign and compared it to the Occupy Wall Street movement which began, synchronistically enough, at the same time the Martin Luther King, Jr. National Memorial was dedicated on that same National Mall in Washington D.C. where the Poor People's Campaign convened. The essay, "'Out of a Mountain of Despair, A Stone of Hope': Reflections on our Next (?) Civil Rights Movement" can be found in the book *Occupy Psyche: Jungian and Archetypal Perspectives on a Movement*, edited by Jordan Shapiro and Roxanne Partridge.

How King Compared Himself to Jesus

King resonated with both facets that hyphenate the martyr-savior archetype: the crucifixion facet, which conferred upon a person the status of a martyr, and the resurrection facet, which conferred upon a person the status of a savior. First, he spoke often of the honor given to a martyr. One of his personal heroes was Gandhi, another martyr-savior. He wrote, "Gandhi's death at the hand of an assassin added to the number of distinguished martyrs for a noble cause." King believed that "if physical death is the price that some must pay to free their children from a permanent life of psychological death, then nothing could be more honorable." He stated, "You may even give your body to be burned, and die the death of a martyr. Your spilt blood may be a symbol of honor for generations yet unborn, and thousands may praise you as history's supreme hero." If King were to die for the cause, "Once more it might well turn out that the blood of the martyr will be the seed of the tabernacle of freedom."

It was important to King that the suffering and death of the martyr was not for naught, but rather that it coupled with the resurrection facet of the myth, the martyr reborn as a savior. He hoped that if he died a martyr's death, his death would have redemptive power. In an interview with *Playboy* magazine, he said, "I feel, though, that my cause is so right, so moral, that if I should lose my life, in some way it would aid the cause." He noted that "I may be crucified for my beliefs, and if I am, you can say, "He died to make men free."" He stated unequivocally that "if physical death is the price I must pay to free my white brothers and all of my brothers and sisters from a permanent death of the spirit, then nothing can be more redemptive. And I'm determined."

Given King's fascination with crucifixion and resurrection, with martyrdom and saviorhood, it makes sense that the cross was an important symbol to him. Very early in the Civil Rights Movement, right after his house was bombed in Montgomery, King began to use the cross as a symbol of redemptive suffering. He wrote, "We must not return violence under any condition. I know this is difficult advice to follow, especially since we have been the victims of no less than ten bombings. But this is the way of Christ; it is the way of the cross. We must somehow believe that unearned suffering is redemptive." Just contemplating the image of Christ on the cross could be redemptive, he believed. "What is the cross but God's way of saying to a wayward child, 'I still love you [and] if you will see within the suffering Christ on the cross my power, you will be able to be transformed, you will be redeemed.'"

What makes the suffering of Christ so powerful is that he did not deserve to suffer, that his suffering was sacrificial. King was drawn to this sacrificial nature of the cross, and saw in it a symbol of the love of God for man.

> The divine love, in short, is sacrificial in its nature. This truth was symbolized, as stated above, by the death of Christ, who, because of his unique relation to God and his moral perfection, made this truth more efficacious than any other martyr. . . . Some of life is an earned reward, a commercial transaction, *quid pro quo*, so much for so much, but that is not the major element. The major element arrives when we feel some beauty, goodness, love, truth poured out on us by the sacrifices of others beyond our merit and deserving. It is at this point that we find the unique meaning of the cross. It is a symbol of one of the most towering facts in life, the realm of grace, the sacrificial gifts bought and paid for by one who did what we had no right to ask.

This was true love, he thought, and true grace—to sacrifice yourself for someone who has no right to ask for or expect this from you.

King often connected the cross of the martyr with the crown of the savior.

> Christianity has always insisted that the cross we bear precedes the crown we wear. To be a Christian one must take up his cross, with all its difficulties and agonizing and tension-packed content, and carry it until that very cross leaves its mark upon us and redeems us to that more excellent way which only comes through suffering.

Though it might be the more excellent way, King knew it was not an easier way. He often talked of "taking up" the cross, or "bearing" the cross, aware of its weight and burden.

> When I took up the cross, I recognized its meaning. . . . The cross is something that you bear and ultimately that you die on. The cross may mean the death of your popularity. It may mean the death of a foundation grant. It may cut down your

budget a little, but take up your cross, and just bear it. And that's the way I have decided to go.

He wrote to Coretta during his confinement in a Georgia prison that it was "the cross we must bear for the freedom of our people." And in an interesting anecdote, Coretta revealed how King literally bore a cross as well. During King's surgery to repair his stab wound, the doctor "made the incision over Martin's heart in the form of a cross. 'Since the scar will be there permanently and he is a minister, it seemed somehow appropriate,'" the doctor told her.

What's so fascinating about King's Christ-connection and the symbolism connected to it is just how early it appeared in King's life. After more than a decade of marching, of laying his life on the line for the cause, of suffering daily from death threats and constant verbal abuse and yet continuing on with sacrificial self-determination, deserved comparisons could be made between King and Jesus. However, those comparisons were there from the beginning, as early as March of 1956, when King was merely 27 years old and only in the very early days of the Montgomery Bus Boycott. Historian Stewart Burns tells the story of King's arrest under a 1921 conspiracy law that prohibited boycotting local businesses. He was released on bond after he was found guilty and his sentence stayed. King walked into a church, and the minister who was at the podium hushed the singing crowd, declaring, "He who was nailed to the cross for us this afternoon approaches." One woman muttered upon seeing him come down the aisle, "He's next to Jesus himself." Another said, "He's right there by God." The audience sang heartily "I Want to Be Near the Cross Where They Crucified My Lord." He was introduced to the audience by Dr. Moses Jones, who said, "He is part of us. Whatever happens to him, happens to us. Today he was crucified in the courts." Then King himself spoke of Easter and the cross and suffering—all themes he would continue to work for the next twelve years of his life.

I call attention to the fact that this archetype of martyr-savior appeared so early and so powerfully in King's career because it hints at the presence of a martyr-savior complex. How else can we explain how being arrested on a conspiracy charge got elevated to the martyrdom of being nailed to a cross? That black people carried such a complex, historian Lewis V. Baldwin finds inarguable.

The identification of King as a kind of savior was only

natural for a people who had had a "messiah complex" for so long. The idea that God raises up individual messiahs to challenge the Pharaohs of this world was deeply rooted in the religious traditions of the folk.

Examples abound where people projected onto King the martyr-savior archetype. One of the members of King's Dexter Avenue Baptist Church congregation said of King, "I can't see what's the difference between him and the Messiah. That's just the truth about it, and I am not a real religious man." Another member talked about how "the old folks saw in him a black Jesus"—some women in the congregation called him "Little Lord Jesus." A man who knew King back in his Montgomery days talked of King's impact on the black community: "He lifted them so high, and they just can't help but think he is a messiah. They can't help it, no matter how smart they are." Coretta stated that people saw her husband as "almost like a Messiah to them." One time she heard someone shout, "There he goes, just like Jesus."

Conclusion

King denied having a martyr-savior complex, but I believe he did protest this point too much. He certainly courted and capitalized on the projections, both at the church that fateful day in 1956, and throughout the rest of his life until the very night before his death in 1968. Added to the archetypal role of the martyr-savior was that of the deliverer and the prophet, and all were intimately intertwined in King's mythology and connected to his archetypal goal of achieving the beloved community: the prophet in King spoke the word of God, announcing the presence of the beloved community and denouncing obstacles in the way; the deliverer spent over a decade marching through the desert of discrimination with his people in order to lead them to the promised land; and the martyr-savior sacrificed his life to expedite the delivery of the people to the beloved community, thus fulfilling the prophet's pronouncements.

However, the last forty-plus years of history have shown us that the prophet's pronouncements have indeed not been fulfilled. We know the Civil Rights Movement disintegrated after King's crucifixion, and his dream of the psychological integration of all God's children has never been fully realized. We'll turn in the next chapter to examine some psychological reasons why, exploring the dangers of myth-making to a man, to a movement, to a message, and to history itself.

8 ANALYSIS:

THE DANGERS OF MAKING A MAN INTO A MYTH

Now that we have examined the three major archetypal roles that King embodied, we can return to the question of whether King was consciously or unconsciously controlled by psychological complexes, or whether he wisely chose to control and exploit the myths he knew would be most effective to his leadership and goals. Exploring this question will lead us into a discussion of the fourfold dangers of making a man into a myth—dangers to the man, to the Movement, to history, and to the message—and suggest ways America might remember King in order to continue the therapeutic process of her own integration.

King and the Complexes

In consciously and constantly evoking the archetypes of the deliverer, the prophet, and the martyr-savior, and in courting comparisons between himself and those archetypes, King both drew upon the power, and drew to himself the projections of those archetypes. Jung was very clear that in order for someone to carry a projection, they must have a "hook" themselves. That hook comes in the form of a complementary complex, since the archetypes, when activated, can manifest themselves inside our psyches as complexes. As we discussed in Chapter 6, because the archetypes are so powerful and magical, they often take on a kind of numinous spirituality. Thus, it is not surprising that King as a Christian minister would carry a deliverer complex, a prophet complex, and/or a martyr-savior complex, since these are imbued with numinous power and deeply embedded within the spiritual and cultural tradition to which he was drawn.

It may be helpful here to distinguish between being affiliated with an archetype versus being controlled by a complex. There are four major distinctions: irrationality, intensity, identification, and compulsion. Let's take the example we used earlier of the coach pumping up his football team with the archetypal energy of the warrior. The team members accepts the role and while on the field, they are fierce, competitive warriors doing battle with the enemy or rival. But after the game is over, they can take off the role, shake hands with the other team, and return to being sons, lovers, brothers, students, etc. They can draw on the power of that identity when that identity is called for, but they don't over-identify with it. For those with a *warrior complex,* they *are* the warrior. Being a warrior is their go-to position. Even when the situation doesn't call for a warrior, even when to fight or go to battle is an irrational response, they will do it anyway because they are compelled to do so.

Hair-triggered, knee-jerk, and overly intense responses are often indicative of a complex. In the last chapter, I shared my suspicion that King in fact did have a martyr-savior complex that was most evident in the early days of the bus boycott when he hadn't done enough yet to deserve such an identification with the crucified Christ. "He who was nailed to the cross for us this afternoon approaches"—that response to a man being falsely accused of conspiracy, briefly jailed and then released—the intensity, the identification, and the irrationality of this response all suggest that a complex was constellated.

Jung was careful when elucidating his theory on the complexes to explain that complexes are normal and in fact ubiquitous; there is not a person without them. The question is not "Do I have any complexes?" but instead is "Am I aware of the complexes I have?" If a complex is unconscious, we are out of control and possessed by it; if it is conscious, we have some control and possession of it, and can respond to situations that trigger our complexes rather than blindly reacting to them. This knowledge doesn't stop us from irrational feelings, but at least we know they are irrational, and we can strive for enough psychological vigilance to avoid projecting them onto others, or accepting others' projections onto us.

King was familiar with the language of complexes, and he publicly denied that he had them. As Garrow notes, King "felt compelled to rebut one particular rumor: 'I have no Messiah complex.'" King once said, "A person who constantly calls attention to his trials and sufferings is in danger of developing a martyr complex" and for that reason, he shared his reluctance to refer to his own sacrifices. [19] But King *did* refer to his own sufferings and sacrifices, not constantly but consistently, and he *did* elevate suffering to the level of spirituality, and he *did* expect to die a martyr's death, and he *did* identify with the savior in his mission to save the soul of America. As we saw in Chapter 6, he not only accepted the projections of others onto him but he actively courted those projections by comparing himself frequently to the deliverer, the prophet, and the martyr-savior.

King's denial that he had the complexes can be interpreted psychologically in two ways. The first interpretation is simple: King was unconscious about his own complexes, and in denial about their existence. The second interpretation is more complex because it moves us into the realm of fate. Perhaps King denied having a complex because he didn't *want* to have the complexes that were projected onto him. At times he quite naturally must have resented the sacrifices and suffering that came with the roles he embodied, and didn't relish the idea of dying a prophet's death, murdered as a martyr in order to become a savior who in his death could deliver souls to the promised land that he would never reach. In this case, we could imagine him as an actor who is conscious of playing a very difficult role day and night on the public stage, compelled to do so because he knows it is good for the audience.

Stated another way, King didn't select his complexes, but the complexes selected *him*. Jung noted that "archetypes are complexes of experience that come upon us like fate," and when they do, he added, "We know the gods have claimed another victim." This is especially true of the great personality. Jung didn't think that the projection of the archetypes could be avoided by the person under the grip of "the eternal laws" of the psyche. He wrote, "Actually, I do not believe it can be escaped. One can only alter one's attitude and thus save oneself from naively falling into an archetype." In certain periods of history, Jung noted that "collective contents, such as religious, philosophical, political and social conflicts, select projection-carriers of a corresponding kind." Perhaps King's denial that he had the complexes was his way of saying that he had not

---

[19] Feeling compelled to explain and defend yourself is often a sign of a complex; the compulsive need to rationalize what others find irrational often indicates an unconscious complex.

naively fallen into them, but had instead accepted the call to be a projection-carrier, and had "chosen to be chosen," as we explored in the first chapter.

In this statement, we can see how fully he surrendered to the archetypes that claimed him:

> At times I think I'm a pretty unprepared symbol. But people cannot devote themselves to a great cause without finding someone who becomes the personification of the cause. People cannot become devoted to Christianity until they find Christ, to democracy until they find Lincoln and Jefferson and Roosevelt, to Communism until they find Marx and Lenin. . . . I know that this is a righteous cause and that by being connected to it I am connected with a transcendent value of right.

However, this connection did not come without a great cost to the man behind the myth.

The Dangers to the Man Behind the Myth

It is very common in the therapeutic process for clients to project their own mythology and complexes onto the therapist. For example, a woman with a Cinderella complex might project the role of Prince Charming onto the therapist, thinking he is her true love come to sweep her away from her ordinary household life. Therapists are trained to spot such projections, and to make the distinction between "is" and "as if." For the client, the therapist *is* a prince, but the therapist knows it's *as if* he is a prince. This is the distinction between literal thinking, which people under the control of a complex are wont to do, and symbolic thinking. In that case, the work of the therapist is to bring to light the symbolic role the client is projecting, to help the client see the difference between the symbol and what is symbolized.

It is not particularly dangerous to the therapist in this example to be literally seen by his client as Prince Charming, as long as he remains clear he is a symbol. However, if he had a hook, a unconscious complex of his own that complements hers—for instance a "Don Juan" complex—he might be wont to literalize the myth and allow himself to fall into a dangerous and unethical relationship with the client. If you are a cultural therapist like Martin Luther King, Jr. and have accepted the role of projection-carrier for your client/country of the martyr-savior complex, you face a particularly grave danger, because the inevitable outcome of the myth is literally your own death.

This raises some interesting psychological questions. By accepting and allowing these three mythological roles of men who died martyrs' deaths, did King consciously court his own death, making it inevitable? Could King have benefited from making his client/country conscious of the myths he carried for them? Instead of saying, "I am Moses and I should free you now," what if he said "I am a symbol of Moses for you, and you want me to free you now"? Taking his therapeutic role one step further, he might have helped his client/country become conscious of their role in projecting the myth of Moses onto him and expecting him to free them, when in fact they should withdraw the projection and hightail it to the Promised Land themselves. What if he refused to accept the inevitability of his death, and had in his speeches and sermons set the stage for his long life, for his own entrance into the Promised Land with the people? Psychological wisdom suggests a symbolic interpretation of the myth might have saved him from the danger of drawing to himself the literalization of the myth through dying a martyr's death.

Of course as we've explored above, King already had that wisdom; he knew the difference between symbolizing and literalizing an archetype. He was highly aware that he served as a symbol for the people, that he served an archetypal function. At one point he was exhausted, on the edge of breaking down, and felt like he needed a sabbatical, but he said, "If I have to go through this to give the people a symbol, I am resigned to it." But what he was also resigned to was his martyrdom, was his death, and that was not symbolic but was all too literal.[20]

If his death was effected, even fated, by the archetypes he carried, so too was his life. Carrying an archetype exacts a heavy burden on a person, particularly if that person is carrying it for as many people as King did. Jung wrote that being a projection-carrier for the masses forces someone "to act a part at the expense of one's humanity. Possession by an archetype turns a man into a flat

---

[20] I am not suggesting he caused his own death, or his death was the effect of his own complexes—that kind of cause-effect thinking is too simplistic—but it is one psychological perspective on the tragedy.

collective figure, a mask behind which he can no longer develop as a human being, but becomes increasingly stunted."

King chose to mask many of his personal qualities that weren't congruent or appropriate for the archetypes he was embodying. Humor was one of them. I quoted his friend Ralph Abernathy in Chapter 7 who said King knew the Movement needed a serious man like the prophet Jeremiah, not another black comedian. Both Abernathy and King's wife stress how funny King was, and how warm, two sides of him that most of the world never saw. Others have also mentioned King's lighter side, as well as his less-than-perfectly virtuous side: he drank whiskey, he smoked, he overate, he plagiarized many of his papers and sermons, he had extramarital affairs, his feelings about women in general were often sexist, and he loved dirty jokes and stories. Certainly carrying these mythological roles came at the expense of his humanity, as he chose to mask his more human side in order to appear more divine.

Masking aspects of his humanity was just one of many personal sacrifices King would make on behalf of the projections he carried. He lost time to reflect and relax, he lost much of his good health to stress and self-medicating through overeating, he lost hope and struggled with serious depression. He lost his basic trust and privacy as he was hounded by J. Edgar Hoover's FBI, constantly under surveillance and betrayed by insider informants. He took on enormous amounts of responsibility in his roles, and he flagellated himself for every failure, small and large. He never fulfilled his dream of becoming a college professor; there was simply no time, nor did it fit with the archetypal roles that hooked him.

Then, there is the unimaginable toll it took on his roles of husband, then father. Yolanda, the first of his four children, was an infant when King accepted the mantle of the Movement, and was twelve when he died. King was rarely home during those twelve years, and missed births and birthdays and everything in between. As his son Dexter Scott King wrote in his memoir *Growing Up King*, "the Cause had taken over his life." Dexter recalled his father's burgundy-colored robe that he wore to breakfast. "Whenever he wore his robe, I was happy, because it meant he wasn't going anywhere for a while." King lost the creature comforts of home, living most of those twelve years in hotels and motels. His extensive travels away from home and exhaustive demands upon him when he was home caused an estrangement from his family, and ultimately, he became estranged from part of himself: as he once told an old college mentor, "Martin Luther King the famous man [is] a kind of stranger to me."

The losses were of course accompanied by gains, and the sacrifices came with rewards—we could place them on the scale and debate which way it tilts—but what is not debatable is the personal danger to King, the man, of allowing himself to become a myth.

The Dangers of Myth-Making to a Movement

The costs to King are clear, but couldn't we argue that King's loss was the Cause's gain, that King as the great personality catalyzed the Civil Rights Movement? Certainly this is the popular position, one that is perpetuated in every public school history book, but it is too simplistic. So let's take the opposite position and look at where the mythic status of King was detrimental to the Movement. Turning again to the Moses myth for a moment will provide a good example.

Erich Fromm discussed the time in the myth when Moses was gone for forty days and forty nights receiving the Ten Commandments. During this time, the people faltered and asked Aaron, Moses' older brother, to create a god for them. "The people felt relatively secure as long as he, the powerful leader, the miracle worker, the feared authority, was present. Once he is absent, even for only a few days, they are gripped again with the fear of freedom" and they wanted another symbol. Aaron fashioned a symbol that gave them unity, melting all their jewelry down and creating the golden calf, which the people worshipped as a new god. Fromm writes, "If a relatively short absence of the leader results in making the people regress fully to idol worship then, indeed, how can one expect that they will ever become free?"

This myth points to the dangerous dependency people have upon their leaders, illustrating both how they depend upon them while they are there, and how they can fall apart when they are gone. Both aspects can apply to King: the dependency fostered during his life, and the falling apart after he was gone.

There was a concern from within various factions of the Civil Rights Movement about the people's dependency on King's leadership. The problem with putting all your leadership eggs in one basket, with projecting all the power onto one man and elevating him to mythological status, was pointed out by historian Paula Giddings. The Student Nonviolent Coordinating Committee (SNCC) was a grass-roots activism group active in the Civil Rights

Movement. In the mid 1960's, they were already working in Albany when some people wanted to invite King into the movement there. Many of the students in SNCC were against it. According to Giddings, "They felt King's presence would elicit a 'Messiah Complex': make the unusually high number of local and grass-roots people who were participating in the demonstrations feel 'that only a particular individual could save them [so they] would not move on their own.'" They knew the mythological truth at the core of a messiah complex: if someone bears the cross for you, it becomes unnecessary for you to bear it yourself, for the sacrifice has already been made for you in a form of vicarious atonement.

Civil rights activist Ella Baker echoed this truth when she said, "People have to be made to understand that they cannot look for salvation anywhere but to themselves." Baker once worked for King for two years in SCLC, but she became disenchanted with the idol worship that surrounded King and went to work instead for SNCC. Baker believed in group-centered leadership, rather than a leader-centered group. In a 1968 interview, she explained her belief: "The thrust is to try and develop leadership out of the group. . . you're organizing people to be self-sufficient rather than to be dependent upon the charismatic leader." She pointed to some interesting dangers of mythologizing a leader.

> I have always felt it was a handicap for oppressed peoples to depend so largely upon a leader, because unfortunately in our culture, the charismatic leader usually becomes a leader because he has found a spot in the public limelight. It usually means he has been touted through the public media, which means that the media made him, and the media may undo him. There is also the danger in our culture that, because a person is called upon to give public statements and is acclaimed by the establishment, such a person gets to the point of believing that he *is* the movement. Such people get so involved with playing the game of being important that they exhaust themselves and their time, and they don't do the work of actually organizing people.

Ironically, as much as King courted his role as the archetypal Messiah bringing salvation to the people, remember that he also believed that we are all Jesuses, called upon to live our lives fully in accordance with divine principles and in relationship with divine power. Theoretically, he would have wanted to go into Albany or any town and spawn more Moses and Amoses and Jeremiahs and Jesuses, knowing that if he did, the Movement would carry on without him just fine, and would in fact spread even faster. Of course there were people who took King's message to heart and became empowered themselves, who didn't rely upon King to carry their own personal power for them. Would there have been more, significantly more, if King had taken a grassroots, SNCC-approach to leadership and downplayed his own role? Would the world have rallied behind a movement with a thousand anonymous faces rather than a movement with one recognizable face in front of the thousands? These questions, while important to ask, can only be answered by armchair speculation; what's important here is that some people in the Civil Rights Movement then and still today believe that King the myth did the Movement more harm than good.

In understanding such an assertion, we might look what happened after King's death. If you ask the average American when the Civil Rights Movement ended, many would mark King's assassination as that moment in time. Of course historians debate this point, some saying it died earlier, and others that it died later. Reality is less important than perception here, and perception says that the Movement died with the man. We can look at three examples that may prove illustrative: the violence that broke out after King's death, the complete failure of the Poor People's Campaign, and the inability of any one person to pick up King's mantle of leadership and carry the Movement forward.

First, let's look at the violence that broke out after King's death. Though Coretta Scott King noted the "tremendous outpouring of concern" from all over the world immediately following her husband's death, calling it a period of "genuine love and brotherhood throughout the world," there were also some very dark days and nights of violence that followed as well. There were riots in sixty-three cities across the country; the worst one lasted for three days in Washington, D.C. and caused President Johnson to order several thousand army paratroopers to defend the city. Several blocks of the capital were destroyed. To the west, fires gutted thirty blocks of downtown Chicago. Around the nation, twenty thousand soldiers and eighty thousand national guardsmen attempted to assist local police in keeping the peace and battling looters, snipers, and arsonists. In total, at least forty people were killed, and thousands were arrested. A Paris newspaper watched the devastation in the United States and called it "the disintegration of everything that makes up the life of a civilized collectivity." It was certainly the disintegration of many of the things King stood for, fought for, and died for.

James Lawson was typical of the many close friends and followers of King "who spoke over and over again. . . beseeching people to stay faithful to their slain hero's nonviolent creed" and reminding the people that King "died on behalf of us all." Even Coretta noted that the riots were "an ironic tribute to the apostle of nonviolence." Many of those rioters reasoned that if King was dead, a victim of violence, so too were the Movement's principles of nonviolence and passive resistance dead. Though it is important to note that the vast number of Americans did stay nonviolent, the riots and the violence eerily echoes Fromm's question from above: "If a relatively short absence of the leader results in making the people regress fully to idol worship then, indeed, how can one expect that they will ever become free?" In the history of the United States since King's death, nonviolence has never been taken as seriously and used as effectively as it was during the Civil Rights Movement. Without King to carry it, that aspect of the Movement, if not the entire Movement itself, ground to a halt.

The second incident-turned-argument that the Movement died with King is the failure of the Poor People's Campaign. The SCLC began planning this campaign in November of 1967 under King's visionary leadership. As stated in the last chapter, the intention was to bring as many poor people of every different race across the country and into the Mall at the Capital where they would live in "tent cities" to illustrate the plight of the poor in a way that couldn't be ignored. This would be the first major campaign to address the struggles of a cross-section of American minorities; it would also be the first to use King's more radical vision of massive civil disobedience meant to disrupt or even shut down Washington until the goals were met.

The slogan for the campaign was "Jobs or Income." King wanted a simple rallying cry, something that every American could not help but support. His goal was an "economic bill of rights": specifically, the campaign requested a thirty-billion-dollar anti-poverty package that would include a commitment to full employment or a guaranteed annual income, and increased construction of low-income housing. There was much contention in the ranks of SCLC over this campaign. Many of King's staff thought it too broad in scope, too ill-planned and unorganized, with a goal that was unreachable. Many wanted to stick to "the black cause" where the Movement had its greatest successes and the most authority. Some supported King in theory but simply did not believe there was enough time to build the necessary momentum to ensure the campaign's success. However, King marched ahead, resolute. The campaign would be launched in May of 1968, and King would spend the intervening months traveling the country, speaking about poverty and recruiting participants.

King's full-time attention was pulled away from the campaign in March, when he decided to give his support to striking garbage workers in Memphis. He was assassinated there on April 4, 1968, just one month before the Poor People's Campaign was slated to begin. The SCLC leadership decided to honor King by moving forward with the campaign. On May 12, the first wave of demonstrators arrived in Washington, and one week later, "Resurrection City" was built on the Mall, a settlement to house the protestors. Demonstrators attempted to lobby Congress and various federal agencies, to no avail. Eliciting no response from legislators, SCLC cut its losses and closed Resurrection City on June 19. In his book *The Last Crusade: Martin Luther King, Jr., the FBI, and the Poor People's Campaign*, Gerald D. McKnight calls the campaign an "almost perfect failure: It was poorly timed, poorly organized, and poorly led."

History will point to many reasons why the campaign failed, including bad press, FBI infiltration and manipulation, Robert Kennedy's assassination, and an underwhelming number of protestors. Some members of SCLC would see it as proof that it was ill-conceived from the start. However, the lack of King's presence and leadership surely played a part in its failure. Although Ralph Abernathy had taken over as SCLC president following King's death, he was unable to provide the charismatic leadership, vision, and inspiration that King would have provided. No one will ever be sure how the campaign might have had different results had King been alive; however, we can be sure that it was deeply unfortunate, as well as symbolic, that the first campaign in the Movement after King's death was such a failure.

Though Abernathy was a capable leader, he was unable to garner the followers, nor the media spotlight, that King could. After King's death, there has been no single leader of his stature leading the Movement since, though many have tried, most notably

Abernathy, Reverend Jesse Jackson, and Reverend Al Sharpton. Certainly there has been no one, including those three, who has carried the archetypes of deliverer, prophet, and martyr-savior with anywhere near the same effective and affective intensity.[21] In fact, the case of Ralph Abernathy, King's best friend and right-hand man, is quite instructive.

After King died, his staff members in Memphis left the hospital and returned to the motel where King had been assassinated. James Bevel stood up and said, "Our leader is dead. In many respects I loved Dr. King more than Jesus." But King was gone, and they needed to elect a new leader. Abernathy "inherited the throne," taking over as president of SCLC. He led the march in Memphis that King had intended to lead, and when he addressed the crowd, he told them, "I have been to the top of the mountain. I have talked with God about it, and God told me that Martin did not get there but you have been so close to Martin I am going to help you get there. If God will lead me I am going to lead my people to the promised land." Here we see Abernathy attempting to take on the archetype of prophet, claiming he has spoken directly with God and has a message to deliver to the people, and that of the deliverer, invoking the Moses myth.

Sixteen months later, Abernathy continued to invoke that Moses myth. He announced to the delegates of the annual meeting of SCLC that "our 'sixteen months of wandering in the wilderness of mourning for Martin' were over. We were now leaving the desert . . . through to the Promised Land.'" Then Wyatt Tee Walker changed the allusion, comparing Abernathy's role to Joshua. "Joshua was entirely different from Moses. He didn't try to do Moses' job; he just did Joshua's job." In the myth, Joshua was the one who led the Israelites into the Promised Land after Moses, and helped them conquer their enemies at Jericho. Abernathy picked up on the allusion, stating his intention "to press on until the walls [of Jericho] came tumbling down." Abernathy came to enjoy the comparison to Joshua and capitalized on it often, even naming his autobiography *And The Walls Came Tumbling Down*.

---

[21] Barack Obama is certainly a black leader of tremendous charisma and archetypal power, but I am writing here about the dangers to the Civil Rights Movement, and he was far too young at the time of King's assassination—six years old—to further that leg of the Movement.

Wyatt Tee Walker was right in his intuition that Abernathy could not successfully take on the same archetypal roles as King. Abernathy was never able to inspire people the way King did, or to work the themes with the same resonance and authority, though he was King's best friend and closest to him during every one of the twelve years of the Movement. He tried to draw the projections of the people to himself in the way King did, but his personality was not magnetic enough, not "great" enough in the sense of Jung's great personality, to make them stick. While there may have been many small movements afterwards, and many people that stepped forward to lead them, the Movement at large, bereft of its King, became history.

The Dangers of Myth-Making to History

This brings us to the third level where we can see the dangers of making a man into a myth, and that is the level of history itself. Clayborne Carson, Stanford historian and editor of *The Martin Luther King, Jr. Papers Project*, has clearly articulated these dangers, offering at least three arguments for why it is dangerous to mythologize King, and by extension, other "Great Men" or "Great Women" in history.

First, he argued that we must be careful about attributing King's unique role in the black struggle to his charismatic leadership and his archetypal affect. King *was* a charismatic leader,

> but emphasis on his charisma obscures other important aspects of his role in the black movement. . . . Emphasis on his charisma conveys the misleading notion of a movement held together by spellbinding speeches and blind faith rather than by a combination of rational and emotional bonds.

King was also a good tactician, an effective community mobilizer, and an excellent fund-raiser, among other qualities, but these, Carson argued, get lost when one focuses solely on his charismatic appeal and his numinous qualities. Since we tend to view charisma as a magical quality that few people naturally possess, focusing on it as a catalyst for transformation disempowers people from studying other important leadership qualities with an eye toward developing these themselves to change the course of history.

Secondly, focusing exclusively on the mesmerizing power of King and allowing him to carry the success of the entire Civil Rights

Movement burden fails to recognize the thousands of other leaders who emerged during that time on the local and national level. Yet, as Carson noted, "Directing attention to the other leaders who initiated and emerged from those struggles should not detract from our appreciation of King's historical significance; such movement-oriented research reveals him to be a leader who stood out in a forest of tall trees." While very few of us can aspire to the stature of a King, all of us can be part of the forest, and many of us can be tall trees; relativizing any great leader's role in history using this analogy allows us to stand up and take our rightful place in our own future historical movements.

Carson contrasted the "great man perspective" with a "movement-centered perspective" such as the Student Nonviolent Coordinating Committee (SNCC) fostered. SNCC became "increasingly critical of [King's] leadership style, seeing it as the cause of feelings of dependency that often characterize the followers of charismatic leaders." SNCC had a different approach: "To instill in members of local communities the confidence that they could lead their own struggles." They felt they had failed if the community became dependent upon their presence. "As the organizers put it, their job was to work themselves out of a job."

This concept has its parallels to something depth psychologist Edward Edinger put forward in *The Christian Archetype*: "Christ, as a particular concrete manifestation of the Holy Spirit, must die in order for the disciples to develop an individual relation to the Holy Spirit, that is, the projection must be withdrawn." But this didn't happen historically, he continued. "The individual did not become the vessel for the Holy Spirit. Instead, a collective container, the Church, emerged as vessel of the Holy Ghost." That was precisely the worry of SNCC, that people would project leadership onto King rather than developing their own leadership potential, and that he would be the carrier of the collective container called "The Civil Rights Movement." If King fell, the container would fall as well, and the Movement could shatter.

This is still Carson's worry about the ongoing way we mythologize the man: if King is seen as the archetypal carrier of the Civil Rights Movement and if people buy into the theory that history only changes significantly when Great Men or Women step onto the stage, we will disempower ourselves right out of the ongoing work of creating the very beloved community for which King gave his life.

The notion that appearances by Great Men (or Great Women) are necessary preconditions for the emergence of major movements for social change reflects a poor understanding of history and contributes to a pessimistic view of the possibilities for future social change. Waiting for the Messiah is a human weakness that is unlikely to be rewarded more than once in a millennium.

When Barack Obama was running for president in 2008, he articulated this same cautionary message about waiting for a Great Man or Woman to save the country. He said, "The challenges we face will not be solved with one meeting in one night. Change will not come if we wait for some other person or some other time. We are the ones we've been waiting for. We are the change that we seek." Moving from "I will free you now" to "We will free ourselves" takes the onus for cultural transformation off the great personality and places it in the hands of the people, who then become great themselves by striving. In a therapeutic analogy, the goal of therapists is never to have their clients become dependent on them, but rather, to help midwife a more whole, or functional, or healthy, or authentic human being, thus working themselves out of a job.

The third danger of mythologizing King, according to Carson, is the reverse side of idolizing a man—the tendency of some people to tear down the idol. He argued, "Idolizing King lessens one's ability to exhibit some of his best attributes, or, worse, encourages one to become a debunker, emphasizing his flaws in order to avoid embracing his virtues." Thus, there are people who relish in exposing all of King's flaws, people who will immediately discount the message by attacking the messenger. While someone will say that King was one of the greatest men of the 20th century, others will counter that he was a plagiarist, a philanderer, a man who did not practice all that he preached. One extreme position calls out the other. King himself would have recognized this tendency, as it is simple Hegelian thesis and antithesis. What Carson calls for is a synthesis: King is not a god nor a devil, but rather, he is a third thing, something that King himself might be comfortable calling simply human. It is important to history that we recognize the humanity of even our most revered leaders so that their greatest contributions do not get thrown out that like proverbial baby in the bathwater. It is also important in this day and age of intense media scrutiny because if we wait for leaders whom we can idolize for their perfection, we will have no more leaders.

The Dangers of Myth-Making to the Message

The fourth and final danger is arguably the one most important one for America to pay attention to now if she wants to continue King's integration process: the danger of losing the message while mythologizing the man. Ironically, while much of the private side of King has now been exposed, the more public side of his message has undergone quite a repression. In many ways, it was to be expected. As scholar C. Eric Lincoln wrote in the introduction to his book *Martin Luther King, Jr.: A Profile*, "America was on trial—self-consciously on trial, and America developed a defensive psychosis which inevitably led to the removal of Dr. King. He was the symbol—the unbearable symbol—of what is wrong with ourselves and our culture."

Extending the analogy, it can be argued that when the prosecutor died, America stepped down from the witness stand and ended the trial. The revolution in values that King called for never took place; the wheel turned, but only a degree. The defensive psychosis that called for King's death is the same one that still calls for the repression of his truly revolutionary message.

It is bitterly ironic that a country embodying only a fraction of what King called for is the same country that's enshrined him in the myth of a national hero. For people who don't know better, they might imagine that if King were still alive, he would celebrate the national holiday that his birthday has become by draping the American flag around his shoulder and congratulating the country on fulfilling his dream. "I had a dream," they might hear King saying, "And we did it! Now, let's all take the day off and celebrate!" In order to perpetuate this myth of the successful hero, King's message had to be sanitized, purged of much of its powerful indictment on the country, making him an "antiseptic hero," according to civil rights leader Julian Bond. In order to make the country comfortable, King must be remembered as the gentle dreamer from the 1963 March on Washington, rather than the fiery prophet who was killed just a few days before planning to give a sermon called "Why American May Go to Hell."

This is one of the dangers of myth-making. Let me quote again the words of Lionel Corbett from Chapter 6 about our tendency to be selective when we work in the realm of myth.

> Mythic characters personify intrapsychic processes, but there are many characters and plots in any story on which attention can be focused, and only certain of them pertain to the individual self. . . . This helps to explain why different observers select different themes on which to focus; we are drawn to aspects of the story that resonate personally.

We might also add that psychologically we are drawn to aspects of the story that resonate *safely*, that provide us with just the right amount of challenge our psyches can hold. In the case of the still-neurotic American psyche, it is obvious that she can hold very little of the challenge that King the man provided, so she selected certain aspects and themes of his story to mythologize, certain places where she can safely worship the King.

A brief list of the revolutionary reforms that King called for but have been ignored or forgotten include:

- A end to all war
- An end to international poverty
- Reparations for slavery in the form of affirmative action, including quotas, and other massive government compensatory measures
- The demise of capitalism and the rise of democratic socialism
- Closure of the income gap
- Closure of the educational gap
- Guaranteed income or full employment for all citizens

King scholars and historians and former Civil Rights Movement survivors and those well-versed in King's life may be the only ones reminding us every year on King's birthday that none of the above, *none of the above*, have been achieved, and in some cases, like the income gap, things have gotten worse, not better. Yet it seems the country may have bitten off all it can chew at the banquet table where King laid out his dream. Shhhh. . . . go back to sleep. It's best to forget the rest of the dream.

America has utilized the defense mechanisms of denial, repression, and suppression of these aspects of King's message that failed to thrive in the country while upholding him as a victorious hero for where he succeeded. And where exactly is that? In the realm of racism.

I have written about this before, in an essay titled "America's Selective Remembering and Collective Forgetting of Martin Luther King, Jr." In that essay, I recount the story of asking my then nine-year-old niece Hayley around the time of the King holiday what she was learning about him in school. This is her unedited response.

> He wanted to have the right to have freedom from the white people, because the white people have always bossed the black people around, and he felt that that was wrong. And so he told the other black people that they are strong. They need to have the right to become free. And, it worked! And so that made them all happy, and so that made life easier. And that's how it is now.

Her response shows us the myth of King that is perpetuated in the country, the self-congratulatory story we tell ourselves, the victory we celebrate, the part of King's message that we embrace. It makes us feel good to think of King this way, as a man who helped us come to our senses about the most overt forms of racism and discrimination. It is our defensive story, allowing us to keep our neurosis in place by patting our ideal selves on the collective back. We remember just the part of King's message that we can bear to remember. And no more.

But even that story is problematic. First, though tremendous strides were made against institutional racism in the 60's, arguably little has been done since then: racism still exists as a national presence and problem. Life may be easier for black people now, but white privilege is still an insidious problem. Second, while white people may not "boss black people around" like they used to, there are still racist Americans, and no, not all black people are happy now in their relationship with white America. Third, while the majority of Americans will agree that we *should* end discrimination and close any gaps that exist purely because of race, there is dissent about *how* we should do it, with both the right and the left wings using King as a poster-boy for their racial policies. On the right, King has been used to refute affirmative action, since he called for us to be judged "not by the color of our skin, but by the content of our character." The right wing makes this argument while ignoring the fact that King not only called for affirmative action, but also for reparations for slavery and other compensatory measures for her black citizens. And fourth, while the fight against racism was King's early focus, he later came to see that the three "triplets of evil," as he called them—racism, materialism, and militarism—were not equal, that both racism and militarism were subsumed under the greatest evil—materialism.

This part of King's message is the most silenced. That King was nonviolent, every school child will learn. That King was anti-materialistic, the majority will not. They won't hear the part of King's message where he came to believe that both racism and militarism were ultimately driven by greed, that even slavery itself was driven more by materialism than racism and that this held true for current manifestations of racism as well. This is why King came to believe that restructuring the entire American economic system was the only solution systemic enough to weed out the triple evils and bring about true and full psychological and social integration. Perhaps King died before he was able to fully convey this message to the American people, since he came to this realization later in his short life, or perhaps the American psyche applied selective hearing to the message so she could hold onto her neurotic pride.

That America would choose to coronate and celebrate as one of its heroes a man with such a radical message as King, then choose to ignore the vast majority of his message, can only be seen as evidence that she is still just as neurotic, if not more so, than she was during King's day, with the gap between her ideal self and her real self as large, if not larger, than it was then. For though King certainly helped close the gap in American racism during his lifetime, since his death, the gap has become even more widespread in the other of his two evil triplets of materialism and militarism. King called for nothing less than a "radical restructuring of the architecture of American society." He believed that "for the evils of racism, poverty and militarism to die, a new set of values must be born." This became his rallying cry, his most important message, yet it's not what we hear in the mythological narrative.

In one of the most bizarre moments in our country's history, it was one of our most conservative presidents, Ronald Reagan, who gave one of our most radical revolutionaries his own national holiday. Slightly before the King Holiday was signed into law, Governor Meldrim Thompson of New Hampshire wrote a letter to Reagan expressing concerns about King's morality and Communist connections. Reagan responded, "I have the reservations you have, but here the perception of too many people is based on an image, not reality. Indeed, to them the perception *is* reality." U. S.

Representative Charles Rangel raised a provocative question.

> Could it be that Mr. Reagan understood that the ease-ee-est way to get rid of Martin Luther King, Jr. is to worship him? To honor him with a holiday that he never would have wanted. To celebrate his birth and his death, without committing ourselves to his vision and his love. It is easier to praise a dead hero than to recognize and follow a loving prophet. The best way to dismiss any challenge is to exalt and adore the empirical source through which the challenge has come.

To *exalt* and *adore* the source, I would add the words to *fix* and *freeze* the source. From the start of the Montgomery Bus Boycott in 1955, King was seen as an archetypal warrior, fighting the dynamic and dramatic battle against racism through the weapon of nonviolent resistance. I would argue that King became fixed and adored in 1963 during the March on Washington in the archetype of the dreamer, and became frozen and exalted in 1968 through his assassination in the archetype of the martyr. What he did between 1963 and 1968 is mostly forgotten. Certainly his radical prophetic message about militarism and materialism has been repressed and forgotten, a form of cultural collective amnesia.

If there is a solution to this obvious repression, denial, and dishonoring of King's message, it may be to change the focus of Kingian mythology, selecting a different archetypal aspect of the man to uphold, study, and draw inspiration from. For example, we discussed earlier how King was drawn to Jesus as an archetype of the radically involved personality before he chose to focus on his martyr-savior aspect. This aspect of King's life is honored by the King Holiday and Service Act, passed in 1994 by Congress, designating the King Holiday as a national day of volunteer service. The motto is "Make It A Day On, Not A Day Off," a motto which would please King, though he would argue that one day on is not enough. This is one example of how shifting the mythological emphasis would remind us of another aspect of King's life and message. However, while the talk is good, it means nothing without the walk. The majority of Americans who are given the day off stay off, not on.

Another way we could honor King's message by changing the

mythological focus follows the lead of Lewis who called King a great American gadfly. The gadfly is a social critic, similar to the prophet but without the necessity for religious belief in God. The task of the gadfly is to open up dialogue; the intention of that dialogue is to stimulate awareness followed by action on behalf of improving societal conditions. Instead of seeing King as Moses, Amos, Jeremiah, or Jesus, we could compare King to Socrates, the 5th century Greek teacher and philosopher who said of himself, "I am that gadfly which God has attached to the State, and all day long and in all places am always fastening upon you, arousing and persuading and reproaching you."

Here we are not creating a mythological role where none exists, for it's clear that King saw himself as this sort of gadfly. He wrote, "If something doesn't happen soon, I'm convinced that the curtain of doom is coming down on the U.S." And he wouldn't allow that to happen.

> America, I don't plan to let you rest until that day comes into being when all God's children will be respected, and every man will respect the dignity and worth of human personality. America, I don't plan to allow you to rest until from every city hall in this country, justice will roll down like waters and righteousness like a mighty stream. America, I don't plan to let you rest until from every state house . . . Men will sit humbly before their God. America, I don't plan to let you rest until you live it out that "all. . . . are created equal and endowed by their creator with certain unalienable rights." America, I don't plan to let you rest until you believe what you have read in your Bible that out of one blood God made all [people] to dwell upon the face of the earth.

These words illustrate King at his gadfly-finest.

Whether we honor King by *agreeing* with or *accepting* all aspects of his message is less important than our agreement to *examining* all aspects of his message; otherwise, we freeze him in a myth. In doing so, we freeze our own opportunity for psychological and social growth, healing, transformation, and integration. If we came to focus on King in his role as gadfly, it would radically shift the way we approach his message. For example, every year when the King holiday came around, we could honor King by spending the day in rigorous self-reflection. Each year we could take a different speech of his or a different aspect of his message to study and debate. The country would be well-served by putting a moratorium on listening to King's "I Have a Dream" speech and instead focusing its attention on other speeches or sermons, particularly his later ones. For example, what would happen if we focused instead on one of King's last documents, written in March of 1968, during his final month on earth? Imagine the whole country reading and meditating on these words.

> Millions of Americans are coming to see that we are fighting an immoral war that costs 30 billion dollars a year, that we are perpetuating racism, that we are tolerating almost 40 million poor during an overflowing of material abundance. Yet they remain helpless to end the war, to feed the hungry, to make brotherhood a reality. This has to shake our faith in ourselves. . . . If we look honestly at the realities of our national life it is clear that we are not marching forward, we are groping and stumbling. We are divided and confused. Our moral values and our spiritual confidence sink even as our material wealth ascends. In these trying circumstances the black revolution is much more than a struggle for the rights of Negroes. It is, rather, forcing America to face all its interrelated flaws: racism, poverty, militarism, and materialism. It is exposing evils that are rooted deeply in the whole structure of our society. It reveals systemic rather than superficial flaws, and it suggests that radical reconstruction of society itself is the real issue to be faced.

In this excerpt, King speaks of the real work of integration, the work that the United States of America has never done and may never do until it remembers *all* of King's message, until it stops denying two of the evil triplets and perpetuating the myth that it has successfully disciplined and transformed one of them.

Conclusion

We might say that America got it right in honoring King as one of its most important heroes, but she got it right for the wrong reasons. Rabbi Abraham Heschel, introducing King in Memphis right before his death, said "The whole future of America will depend upon the impact and influence of Dr. King." Some may pass this off as hyperbole, but if it is true, the future of America will depend not on King the man, not on King the myth, and not on King the leader of the Movement, but on King's message, a message which did not originate with King and thus cannot die with King, a message that perhaps needs a forest of committed messengers and a few tall trees. For that to occur, we must not make of King a temple and worship there, but instead see his work as a template, and continue to define and refine that template and apply it to psychological and cultural transformation and integration. It is the only way we can begin to live out King's dream—the creation of the beloved community.

9 INTEGRATION:

THE THREE DIMENSIONS OF A COMPLETE LIFE

In 1954, Dexter Avenue Baptist Church in Montgomery was searching for a new pastor, and they invited the 25-year-old Martin Luther King, Jr. to give a "trial" sermon before the congregation. The sermon he chose to deliver was called "The Three Dimensions of a Complete Life"; it was by all accounts a success, and King was unanimously called to the ministry of the church, a fateful vocational move that would in a year thrust him into the heart of the action of the Montgomery Bus Boycott. It was a sermon he repeated often, including thirteen years later—one year before his death—in front of a Chicago congregation. The sermon serves as a good conclusion for this book, for it speaks most directly to our theme of integration, the theme that bookended King's all-too-short life.

In psychology, one parallel term for integration comes from C. G. Jung, who called it *individuation*. To individuate is to become our own self in our incomparable uniqueness. It is a process of a lifetime, and to the extent to which we achieve it, we become a united personality—we become integrated, we become our real selves. Jung described this process using alchemy, an ancient practice of transforming base metals to gold in which he saw a symbol for psychological transformation. Jung took his three dimensions of an individuated life, which he called *unions*, from the three stages of alchemy. As we examine King's three dimensions of a complete or integrated life, we will find parallels with the three unions of the individuated life. We'll look at how these dimensions apply to the integration of an individual, and then, in keeping with the conceit of this book, we'll look at how they can apply to the integration of a nation as well.

The Three Dimensions of Individual Individuation and Integration

Though King is primarily remembered for his social activism, he was fond of reminding people that first and foremost, he was a preacher. As a preacher, his concern was also with the individual souls of his parishioners, and thus his emphasis on the three dimensions of a complete life. In his 1954 original sermon, he explained the dimensions using the imagery of a triangle.

> The Length of Life, as we shall use it, is not its duration, not its longevity. It is rather the push of a life forward to its personal ends and ambitions. It is the inward concern for one's personal welfare. The Breadth of Life is the outward concern for the welfare of others. The Height of Life is the upward reach toward God. These are the three dimensions of life, and, without the due development of all, no life becomes complete. Life at its best is a great triangle. At one angle stands the individual person, at the other angle stands other persons, and at the tip top stands God. Unless these three are concatenated, working harmoniously together in a single life, that life is incomplete.

King defined the first dimension as the concern with our personal well-being. In this dimension, "We are concerned with developing our inner powers." He called it the "selfish dimension of life," though I think he is using the word "selfish" in the same way a depth psychologist might use "Self-centered": in other words, focused on the discovery of the Self's center. In this stage, King preached, the goal is to learn to love yourself. People who don't love themselves "go through life with deep and haunting emotional conflicts." In order to love yourself, he told his congregation, you must accept yourself, accept everything about yourself.

Accepting everything about yourself means knowing yourself, for how can you accept what you do not know? He suggested, "And we must pray, 'Lord, Help me to accept myself every day; help me to accept my tools.'" He shared the story of a time he had to accept his own tools, or rather, his *lack* of tools. He had a college classmate who was better than him in statistics. Every night he could do his homework in about an hour, while King would take two or three hours. King kept trying to do his work in one hour like his peer, but he reported, "The more I tried to do it in an hour, the more I was flunking out in the course. And I had to come to a very hard conclusion. I had to sit down and say, 'Now, Martin Luther King, Leif Cane has a better mind than you.' Sometimes you have to acknowledge that." King's identified his problem: "I was not willing to accept myself. I was not willing to accept my tools and limitations." He explained that some people are Cadillacs, and some are Fords, and the point is to know yourself and to accept the kind of vehicle you are, for "the principle of self-acceptance is a basic principle in life."

This stage corresponds with Jung's first stage of individuation in which one achieves a state of interior oneness, a state of being united with oneself. This stage includes the confrontation with one's personal shadow.

> Since the soul "stands between good and evil," [an individual] will have every opportunity to discover the dark side of his personality, his inferior wishes and motives, childish fantasies and resentments. . . . he will be confronted with his shadow.

The goal of this stage is "the attainment of full knowledge of the heights and depths of one's own character."

Though King does not discuss good and evil directly in this sermon, he did so in many other places, particularly in his sermon "Unfulfilled Dreams," which we discussed in detail in Chapter 4. There, he talked about what happens when you set out to build a great temple, another symbol for the individuation process or a complete life. He said, "Whenever you set out to build a creative temple, whatever it may be, you must face the fact that there is a tension at the heart of the universe between good and evil." It's not only in the external universe, but it is in our internal lives, and he likened the struggle with good versus evil to a civil war. It's important that we remain conscious of the tension in our souls: "Whenever we set out to dream our dreams and to build our temples, we must be honest enough to recognize it." King was realistic enough to know that we'd never overcome this tension, and he eased the minds of his parishioners when he reassured them, "In the final analysis, what God requires is that your heart is right. Salvation isn't reaching the destination of absolute morality, but it's being in the process and on the right road."

Jung wrote that this first union, where one becomes united

with oneself, "was not the culminating point but merely the first stage of the procedure." For Jung, the second stage occurs when the insights made in the first union become fully realized and embodied. In this union we take our integrated self into the world and we embody it authentically, living our ethics, our morals, our values, and "walking our talk" in our relationships with others. The same was true for King; he was concerned that people do not stop at the first "self-centered" stage of individuation. He cautioned, "You know, a lot of people get no further in life than the length. They develop their inner powers; they do their jobs well. But do you know, they try to live as if nobody else lives in the world but themselves?" These people use other people like objects; they are attached to themselves, but detached from others. If we could categorize Jung and King's first union or dimension as primarily *psychological* in nature, both of them saw the second union or dimension as primarily *sociological* in nature: it was the integration of the individual through relationships with others.

King called this dimension of a complete life its breadth, which he defined as concern for one's fellow men and women. He said, "A man has not begun to live until he can rise above the narrow confines of his own individual concerns to the broader concerns of all humanity." This second state was embodied for King as well as for Jung: "The preacher must be concerned about the whole man. Not merely his soul but his body. It's all right to talk about heaven. I talk about it because I believe firmly in immortality. But you've got to talk about the earth."

King's language when describing this second dimension is full of examples of literally taking care of the bodies of others. He started with the story of the Good Samaritan who stopped to help a man who had been attacked by thieves. On Judgment Day, he said, God will not care if the world honored you for doing your job, or making a lot of money, or achieving academic accolades. Instead,

> it seems as if I can hear the Lord of Life saying, "But I was hungry, and ye fed me not. I was sick, and ye visited me not. I was naked, and ye clothed me not. I was in prison, and you weren't concerned about me. So get out of my face. What did you do for others?" This is the breadth of life.

In this famous passage from the Bible, it is clear that whatever you do for other people, you do for Christ. When you care for another's body, you care for the body of Christ. This passage takes on even deeper meaning when we remember that Christ himself was used by both King and Jung as a symbol of the integrated life. Thus, we can imagine the second stage of an integrated life as the union of an individual with the body of Christ as it manifests on earth in the bodies of our fellow humans.

But neither Jung nor King stopped there. There is one more stage of a complete life, one more union to be complete. Jung called it "the union of the whole man with the *unus mundus*," a term he used to mean the spiritual world, however it may manifest to an individual. It could be the Tao, the Atman, our Buddha-nature, our relationship with Gaia, or Mother Earth, or, in Christian symbolism, the union with God, whom Jung called a symbol of "unity *par excellence*." If the first union is *psychological* and the second *sociological*, the third union is *spiritual*.

And so for King, the third stage was the height of life, where we "move beyond humanity and reach up, way up for the God of the universe, whose purpose changeth not." We neglect God, he said, when we do not turn our attention upwards, and he gave several examples of how some people stay earth-bound that I'd like to quote here in length because they demonstrate King at his poetic finest.

> They deny the existence of God with their lives and they just become so involved in other things. They become so involved in getting a big bank account. They become so involved in getting a beautiful house, which we all should have. They become so involved in getting a beautiful car that they unconsciously just forget about God. There are those who become so involved in looking at the man-made lights of the city that they unconsciously forget to rise up and look at that great cosmic light and think about it—that gets up in the eastern horizon every morning and moves across the sky with a kind of symphony of motion and paints its technicolor across the blue—a light that man can never make. They become so involved in looking at the skyscraping buildings of the Loop of Chicago or Empire State Building of New York that they unconsciously forget to think about the gigantic mountains that kiss the skies as if to bathe their peaks in the lofty blue—something that man could never make. They become so busy thinking about radar and their television that they unconsciously forget to think about the stars that

bedeck the heavens like swinging lanterns of eternity, those stars that appear to be shiny, silvery pins sticking in the magnificent blue pincushion.

The third dimension of a complete life, the looking upwards and experiencing union with God, cannot be escaped, for as he said, "We were made for God, and we will be restless until we find rest in him."

Thus, we see that both Jung and King defined the individuated/integrated life as one in which we are united in our relationships with ourselves, with others, and with our spiritual source. The terms shift when we move from looking at an individual to a culture, but only slightly.

The Three Dimensions of Cultural Individuation and Integration

In the 1967 version of "The Three Dimensions of a Complete Life," King added a new twist. He discussed the chapter in the Bible when John was in prison on the island of Patmos and had a vision where "descending out of heaven, [came] a new heaven and a new earth. . . . the holy city, the new Jerusalem." King quoted John as saying that the holy city was complete: "The length and the breadth and the height of it are equal." King interpreted this description by saying, "This new city of God, this new city of ideal humanity, is not an unbalanced entity but is complete on all sides." This holy city, this new Jerusalem, the city of ideal humanity, is the Biblical symbol of King's beloved community. With this connection, we can see how his three dimensions of a complete life apply to cultural integration as well as individual integration. As much as King was a preacher concerned with the individual souls of his parishioners, he was also a leader and a visionary concerned with the soul of a nation—and larger, the world—and in the transformation of that world, the same basic processes of integration apply. Using America again as our case study, let's see how.

The first dimension of an integrated life, again, was the honest recognition of one's character, a confrontation with the shadow sides of one's personality and the potential for good and evil, and the synthesis of the opposites within the personality. The synthesis of opposites in America's case can be seen as the uniting of black people and white people, indeed of *all* people in the country into a harmonious relationship based on equality. We discussed in depth this whole process in Chapter 5, so just a brief summary here.

King awakened the country to an honest recognition of its character by pointing out the gap between its ideal self and its real self. He and the Movement used marches and other forms of nonviolent resistance and civil disobedience to awaken America to its shadow side and force it to confront the evil and injustice within. Once she saw her shadow, King hoped that a sense of shame and guilt would develop which would bring about "transformation and change of heart." This change of heart would lead to a more harmonious relationship between black and white people based on love and justice.

The Movement became the vessel that held the potential for this transformation—in particular, the March on Washington took on gargantuan proportions in the cultural psyche, and King's "I Have a Dream" speech most especially. Recall from Chapter 7 Coretta's description of the numinosity of that speech, how when it was complete, there was an outburst of applause as

> two hundred and fifty thousand people shouted in ecstatic accord with his words. The feeling that they had of oneness and unity was compete. They kept on shouting in one thunderous voice, and for that brief moment the Kingdom of God seemed to have come on earth.

Recall that a great number of participants at the March were white. Recall other times mentioned in that same chapter where King marveled at the unity of white and black people during the Movement. The Civil Rights Movement at its finest was an integrated movement, bringing together black and white and all shades in between, and can be see as the first dimension, or the first union, in the process of integrating the cultural psyche.

The second dimension or union would happen when the insights of the first union were made real or embodied in our relationships with others—Jung called it "the reunion of the spirit with the body." If the spirit achieved in the first dimension of the Civil Rights Movement was the spirit of brotherhood, then that spirit needed to be united with the body of laws of the nation, the body politic; in other words, brotherhood needed to be *embodied*, and that would be done through the justice system, through the transformation of sociological institutions.

King wanted full citizenship rights for black Americans, which included complete desegregation, equal opportunity for employment and housing, and equal and fair ballot access. He was realistic enough to know that a change of heart was not enough, but must be embodied by a change in laws, that in fact the natural reflection of a changed heart *would be* changed laws. He called for nothing less than a revolution in America, and that would require more than just good feelings. He stated this clearly: "A social movement that only moves people is merely a revolt. A movement that changes both people and institutions is a revolution." Some second dimension successes were such obvious victories as the Civil Rights Acts of 1957, 1960, 1964, and 1968, each with their own ever-widening scope of legislation protecting equality and justice; the Voting Rights Act of 1965; uncountable individual city, state, and federal commission rulings; and the thousands of court victories and dozens of Supreme Court rulings.

After the first union of black and white in the spirit of brotherhood, and the second union of the spirit of brotherhood with the body politic, the third union became possible: the union with the *unus mundus*, or what Jung called "the potential world." King languaged this potential world, this third dimension, in several ways. Sometimes he would refer to the final product of cultural integration as the creation of the beloved community. He also referred to it as the fulfillment of the American dream. Sometimes he would refer to the *imago dei*, "the idea that all men have something within them that God injected"—a country living its promise would recognize the *imago dei* in every person. He was fond of Martin Buber's idea of the "I-Thou" relationship as the fulfillment of the potential world. Often he described it in biblical language, calling it the New Jerusalem, the Promised Land, or God's Kingdom on Earth. He sometimes quoted the words of an old spiritual: "In Christ there is no East or West/In Him no North or South/But one great Fellowship of Love/Throughout the whole wide world." No matter how he languaged it, the final stage of this cultural integration would occur when we know our essential unity, when "one day all men everywhere will recognize that out of one blood God made all men to dwell upon the face of the earth." In its simplest sense, this would be the birth of a world soul.

In this third stage, not only would God and humans experience and rejoice in unity, but the very soul of the world would recognize, rejoice, and reflect our collective integration as well. When that day came, King said, "the morning stars will sing together," and in the animal world, "the lamb will lie down with the lion." Nature would reflect our consciousness, as "every valley will be exalted, and every hill and mountain will be made low; the rough places will be made plain, and the crooked places straight." This would be the true union of all aspects of the *unus mundus*: the personal, the interpersonal, and the transpersonal linking together humanity, nature, and spirit. It would happen when people become psychologically, sociologically, and spiritually united to themselves, their neighbors, and God. And it would bring about the mythological heaven on earth, the beloved kingdom.

King's sermons and speeches bring us glimpses of that third and final union. Perhaps the most touching example is his "farewell speech" to the country on the night before his assassination, these final words.

> Well, I don't know what will happen now. We've got some difficult days ahead. But it really doesn't matter with me now. Because I've been to the mountaintop. And I don't mind. Like anybody, I would like to live a long life. Longevity has its place. But I'm not concerned about that now. I just want to do God's will. And He's allowed me to go up to the mountain. And I've looked over. And I've seen the promised land. I may not get there with you. But I want you to know tonight, that we, as a people will get to the promised land. And I'm happy, tonight. I'm not worried about anything. I'm not fearing any man. Mine eyes have seen the glory of the coming of the Lord.

His final public words echo the words of Jungian analyst and author Jeffrey Raff, who wrote of the third and final union of the integrated life, "There is simply nothing the individual lacks, and no joy that is denied him. Whatever life may bring such an individual, he or she rests secure in the bonds of sacred marriage." In King's language that night, his life was complete.

Conclusion

Though King's life was complete, his life's work was not—he did not set foot in the Promised Land; he did not live to see the beloved community thrive. He had a dream, and when the assassin's bullet shattered his life, it was mostly unfulfilled.

In his sermon "Unfulfilled Dreams," given just a month before his assassination, he discussed another great King, the Bible's King David, who set out to build a great temple but was not able to complete it. King called this "one of the great agonies of life . . . that we are constantly trying to finish that which is unfinishable." And yet, King preached, God offered David reassurance.

> Your dream will not be fulfilled. The majestic hopes that guided your days will not be carried out in terms of an actual temple coming into being that you were able to build. But I bless you . . . because it was within thine heart. You had the desire to do it; you had the intention to do it; you tried to do it; you started to do it. And I bless you for having the desire and the intention in your heart.

King clearly needed that reassurance himself. It made him happy, he said, to hear "a voice crying through the vista of time" telling him it was well that it was within his heart.

King is a man in a long history of men and women who have struggled as cultural therapists and alchemists to bring about their culture or their country's or their world's transformation, to build the great and golden temple of heaven on earth where we are whole, where we are integrated. Jung said that the "alchemists were consciously performing an *opus divinum* [divine work] when they sought to free the 'soul in chains'. . . and restore him to his original condition of unity." We can see King in this way, as an alchemist and therapist attempting to free and unite the individual souls of his fellow citizens, to free and unite the soul of America, and eventually to free and unite the soul of the world. This was his *opus divinum*; this was what was within his heart.

And what a heart he had. Though King is remembered more for his focus on concepts like justice, freedom, equality, and the achievement of the American Dream, he spoke just as often and as eloquently of love. As we discussed in Chapter 2, King thought love was the value that would save us all—love for ourselves, love for others, love for God all brought together in *cosmic love*, for he believed it was "only love that can generate a peace that will 'transform our imminent cosmic elegy into a psalm of creative fulfillment.'" Jung expressed something very similar when he wrote, "For we are in the deepest sense the victims and the instruments of cosmogonic 'love.'" I like to imagine King in this way, as a willing victim and instrument on which the cosmos played its love song.

For King, the final stage of individual and cultural integration he preached for and reached for was love, love as a cosmic psalm, an experience of the divine song on earth as it is sung in heaven, "a beautiful symphony of brotherhood" and "the *summum bonum* of life."

It was, and remains, a beautiful dream and the song of songs.

ACKNOWLEDGEMENTS

This book project was born during my years as a student at Pacifica Graduate Institute along the central coast of California, where I earned my doctorate in depth psychology, and I owe a debt of gratitude to my professors and classmates there who educated, inspired, and encouraged me. Thank you in particular to Stephen Aizenstat, founding president of the Institute, for his vision in creating a graduate school with the motto *animae mundi colendae gratia*, "for the sake of tending the soul in and of the world." Special thanks to Mary Watkins and Veronica Goodchild from Pacifica Graduate Institute, and to Clayborne Carson from Stanford University, the esteemed historian and director of the Martin Luther King, Jr., Research and Education Institute, and senior editor of the Martin Luther King Papers Project, for helping to shape this work and sealing it with your approval when it was in doctoral dissertation form. It's come a long way since then, but the imprint of your individual touches is still there.

I regret missing the Civil Rights Movement, and I owe a huge debt of gratitude to two groups of people: those who participated in it, for putting your hearts and your lives on the line, and those who have written about it, for sharing your keen minds which created such invaluable scholarship. I live with your books as close companions; this book would not be possible without yours.

Finally, I want to thank my mother, Peggy Meyers Selig, for two of the usual reasons—her unconditional love and support—and for one unusual reason. Thank you for conceiving me on the west coast around the time of the March on Washington on the east coast, thus imbuing me with a dream. You are my Queen to his King.

NOTES

INTRODUCTION NOTES

"taps into our engaged practical understanding of an entity": Packer, *Tracing the Hermeneutic Circle*, p. 106.

"No single account can include all the different forms": Ibid. p. 113.

"To give an interpretive account covering all of them": Ibid.

"Thinking about him is like thinking about the prism": Jackson, cited in Schulke & McPhee, *King Remembered*, p. 274.

BIOGRAPHY: CHAPTER 1 NOTES

"A political, social, philosophical, and religious": Jung, *Flying Saucers* (1978), pp. 108-109.

"it is not for nothing that our age cries": Jung, "Epilogue" (1989), pp. 82-83.

Jung's Great Personality

Jung wrote in some detail about what he called "the great personality": Jung, "The Development of the Personality" in *The Essential Jung* (1983), pp. 192-210.

"Martin Luther King Jr. ranks as one of the most important": Ivory, *Toward a Theology of Radical Involvement*, p. 13.

"acts upon society to liberate, to redeem, to transform, and to heal": Jung, *The Essential Jung* (1983), p. 208.

"To Redeem the Soul of America": Fairclough, *To Redeem the Soul of America*.

"God's instrument to save the soul of America": King, cited in Cone, *Martin & Malcolm & America*, p. 71.

"We can help America save her soul": King, cited in Dyson, *I May Not Get There With You*, p. 39.

"I can't stop now. History has thrust something": King, cited in R. H. King, "Martin Luther King, Jr. and the Meaning of Freedom," p. 133.

"But what has the individual personality to do with": Jung, *The Essential Jung*, (1983), p. 202.

"All the usual explanations and nostrums of psychology": Ibid., p. 205.

"In 1957 when a group of us formed the Southern Christian": King, "A Time to Break Silence," (1986), p. 233.

The Making of a Great Personality: Rational Explanations

"To understand the history that Martin": Cone, *Martin & Malcolm & America*, p. 20.

"It is quite easy for me to think of a God": King, "Autobiography of Religious Development," (1992), p. 360.

"It is impossible to get at the roots of one's religious attitudes": Ibid, pp. 360-

361.

"The church was the dominant institution": Cone, *Martin & Malcolm & America*, p. 20.

"the economic, educational, and moral development": Ibid., p. 21.

He grew up in a "wholesome community": King, *The Autobiography*, (1998), p. 2.

"I was much too young to remember the": King, "Autobiography of Religious Development," (1992), p. 359.

"determined to hate every white person": Ibid., p. 362.

"his father had demanded that he would play with me no more": Ibid.

"We'll either buy shoes sitting here": M. L. King, Sr., cited in King, *The Autobiography*, (1998), p. 8.

"My father had not adjusted to the system": Ibid.

"Let me make it clear to you that you aren't talking to a boy": M. L. King, Sr., cited in King, *The Autobiography*, (1998), p. 8.

He described his mother as "very devout": King, *The Autobiography*, (1998), p. 3.

"in general, protected from the worst blights of discrimination": Ibid.

"My mother never complacently adjusted herself": Ibid.

"I have always been somewhat precocious": King, "Autobiography of Religious Development," (1992), p. 359.

"At an early age, he became fascinated by language": Cone, *Martin & Malcolm & America*, pp. 25-26.

his speech was called "The Negro and the Constitution": King, *The Autobiography*, (1998), p. 9.

"a little above the average in scholarship": Tobin, "Lucius M. Tobin to Charles E. Batten," p. 151.

"stemmed from the interaction of large social and historical": Morris, "A Man Prepared for the Times," p. 36.

The Making of a Great Personality: Irrational Explanations

"There is always something irrational": Jung, *The Essential Jung*, (1983), pp. 205-206.

"I can't really understand it": Smiley, cited in Schulke & McPhee, *King Remembered*, p. 69.

"I will always believe that the Lord": Henderson, cited in Schulke & McPhee, *King Remembered*, p. 70.

"represents something quite special to us": Huggins, "Commentary," p. 88.

"We do not honor nonrational behavior": Ibid., p. 89.

"sophisticated means of analyzing and understanding the religious": Ibid.

"but psychology is poor for this sort of thing because psychologists": Ibid.

The fact is that the approach to the numinous": Jung, cited in Corbett, *The Religious Function of the Psyche*, p. 13.

"What is it, in the end": Jung, *The Essential Jung*, (1983), p. 199.

The Vocational Response of the Great Personality

"it is quite clear that I joined": King, "Autobiography of Religious Development," (1992), p. 361.

"But this uncritical attitude could not last long": Ibid.

he planned to be a lawyer or a doctor instead: King, *The Autobiography*, (1998), p. 14.

However, at liberal Morehouse, "the shackles of fundamentalism": Ibid., p. 15.

"My call to the ministry was quite different": King, "Application for Admission to Crozer," (1992), p. 144.

"Conversion for me was never an abrupt something": King, "Autobiography of Religious Development," (1992), p. 361.

"It was in my senior year of college": Ibid., p. 363.

"concern about experiences which are regarded as of supreme": Brightman, cited in King, "A Conception and Impression of Religion," (1992), p. 408.

"How I long now for that religious experience": King, "A Conception and Impression of Religion," (1992), pp. 415-416.

"I do remember moments that I have been awe awakened": Ibid., p. 416.

"Maybe after all I have been religious for a number of years": Ibid.

First, he was critical of the fundamentalism: King, *The Autobiography*, (1998), p. 15.

"revolted against the emotionalism": Ibid.

"unlettered, not trained in seminaries": Ibid.

"Both were ministers, both deeply religious": Ibid., p. 16.

"I had had a great deal of satisfaction in the pastorate": Ibid, p. 41.

"nothing so special to offer": Ibid., pp. 45-46.

"I come to you with only the claim of being a servant of Christ": Ibid., p. 46.

For a year, King was an active pastor in his church: King, *The Autobiography* (1998).

According to Abernathy: Abernathy, *And the Walls Came Tumbling Down*.

"Well, if you think I can render some service, I will": Ibid, p. 148.

"The action had caught me unawares. It had happened": King, *The Autobiography*, (1998), p. 56.

Within a month and a half: King, *Stride Toward Freedom*, (1958), p. 112.

"as the weeks passed, I began to see that many of the threats": Ibid., p. 113.

"They can be taken away from me at any moment": Ibid., p. 114.

"Listen, nigger, we've taken all we want from you": Ibid.

"It seemed that all of my fears": Ibid.

"I am here taking a stand for what I believe is right": Ibid.

"experienced the presence of the Divine": Ibid.

"Almost at once my fears began to go": Ibid., p. 115.

"Since that morning I can stand up without fear": King, cited in Garrow, "Martin Luther King, Jr., and the Spirit," p. 22.

"It is a very different thing when the psyche": Jung, *The Essential Jung*, (1983), p. 201.

"And it seemed at that moment that I could here: King, "Why Jesus Called a Man a Fool," (1998), p. 162.

a "profoundly spiritual transformation" and "the most central and formative event in his life": Garrow, "Martin Luther King, Jr., and the Spirit," p. 19.

"the most important thing to grasp and appreciate": Ibid., p. 34.

"go forward with feelings of companionship, self-assurance": Ibid, p. 21.

"He never really says what it is; he describes it": Huggins, "Commentary," p. 88.

"the original meaning of 'to have a vocation'": Jung, *The Essential Jung*, (1983), p. 200.

"The archetypes come to independent": Jung, "Psychotherapists or the Clergy," (1933), p. 242.

"To the patient it is nothing less than a revelation": Ibid.

"If there is any one fear I have conquered, it is the fear of death": King, in C. S.

King, *My Life With Martin*, p. 280.

Another noteworthy incident when he "saw the light": King, *The Autobiography* (1998).

"so distressing that it threatened to ruin the movement": Ibid., p. 181.

I thought I was standing at the center of all that my life": Ibid., pp. 182-183.

"said a few words that lifted a thousand pounds from my heart": Ibid., p. 185.

"I was aware of a feeling that had been present": Ibid., pp. 185-186.

"like a law of God from which there": Jung, *The Essential Jung*, (1983), p. 199.

Choosing to be Chosen

"history has thrust something upon me": King, cited in Garrow, "Martin Luther King, Jr., and the Spirit," p. 21.

"Unknowingly and unexpectedly, I was catapulted": King, *The Autobiography*, (1998), p. 136.

"History has thrust me into this position": King, cited in Garrow, "Martin Luther King, Jr., and the Spirit," p. 25.

"If anybody had asked me a year ago to head this movement": King, cited in Garrow, *Bearing the Cross*, pp. 84-85.

"personality can never develop unless the individual": Jung, *The Essential Jung*, 1983, p. 198.

"the chosen fulfillment of our destined nature": King, "The Ethical Demands for Integration," (1986), p. 121.

"That is the great and liberating thing": Jung, *The Essential Jung*, (1983), p. 203.

"greatest possible freedom for self-determination": Ibid., p. 195.

"This is not the life I expected to lead": King, in C. S. King, *My Life With Martin*, p. 151.

Remaining Faithful to the Call

"a sacred symbol because it is the psychological": Jung, *The Essential Jung*, (1983), pp. 204-205.

"fidelity to the law of one's own being": Ibid., p. 197.

Nonviolence was a doctrine King studied during college: King, *The Autobiography*, (1998).

"I've decided that I'm going to do battle": King, cited in Schulke & McPhee, *King Remembered*, p. 218.

"then and there he lost me. Dr. King": Jordan, *Moving Towards Home*, p. 195.

"Nevertheless, and five years later, when I heard": Ibid.

"a man can make a moral decision to": Jung, *The Essential Jung*, (1983), p. 198.

However, when King initially began to speak out against Vietnam: Garrow, *Bearing the Cross*; Garrow, "Martin Luther King, Jr., and the Spirit."

"King knew full well that his new, aggressive stance": Garrow, "Martin Luther King, Jr., and the Spirit," p. 26.

"At times you do things to satisfy your conscience": King, cited in Garrow, "Martin Luther King, Jr., and the Spirit," p. 27.

"I can no longer be cautious": Ibid.

"More than anything else, the Vietnam War": Garrow, "Martin Luther King, Jr., and the Spirit," p. 26.

"I was politically unwise but morally": King, cited in Garrow, "Martin Luther King, Jr., and the Spirit," p. 27.

"To develop one's own personality is indeed an unpopular undertaking": Jung,

The Essential Jung, (1983), p. 198.

"When I took up the cross, I recognized its meaning": King, cited in Garrow, "Martin Luther King, Jr., and the Spirit," p. 28.

"growing inclination to sacrifice himself to his larger mission": Levison, cited in Garrow, "Martin Luther King, Jr., and the Spirit," p. 29.

"an actor in history at a particular moment that called": Ibid.

The Mythological Power of the Great Personality

"the legendary heroes of mankind, the very ones": Jung, *The Essential Jung*, (1983), pp. 198-199.

"Martin Luther King, Jr. was not a god": Jordan, *Moving Towards Home*, p. 193.

"the ideal of personality is one of the ineradicable needs of the human soul": Jung, *The Essential Jung*, (1983), p. 205.

"for the miracle of a man being able": Ibid, p. 199.

"Keep Martin Luther King in the background": King, cited in Schulke & McPhee, *King Remembered*, p. 24.

"The listeners didn't move. There was": Angelou, *The Heart of a Woman*, p. 55.

"Strangers embraced tightly; some men": Ibid., pp. 56-57.

"Martin Luther King was sacred": Ibid., p. 97.

"The young people just envisioned a new hope": Nesbitt, cited in Schulke & McPhee, *King Remembered*, p. 69.

The Great Personality's Relationship With Death

"We have the strange feeling down in Montgomery": King, "Non-Aggression Procedures to Interracial Harmony," (1997), p. 327.

"the universe is under the control": King, "Pilgrimage to Nonviolence," (1963), p. 153.

"I don't think anyone in a situation": King, cited in Garrow, *Bearing the Cross*, p. 171.

"But he who cannot lose his life, neither shall": Jung, *The Essential Jung*, (1983), pp. 209-210.

"The truer you are to your daimon, the closer": Hillman, *The Soul's Code*, p. 212.

"If one day you find me sprawled out dead": King, *Toward Freedom,* (1958), p. 113.

"Remember, if I am stopped, this movement": Ibid., p. 118.

"It may be that some of us have to die": King, cited in Garrow, *Bearing the Cross*, p. 83.

"Once you become dedicated to a cause": Ibid., p. 84.

"stand up for what I think is right": Ibid., p. 108.

"It may get me crucified": King, cited in Ansbro, *Martin Luther King, Jr.*, p. 97.

"I was urged to cancel the trip, but I": King, *The Autobiography*, (1998), p. 250.

"I'm tired of marching for something": King, cited in Garrow, *Bearing the Cross*, p. 515.

"Well, I don't know what will happen": King, "I See the Promised Land," (1986), p. 286.

"a recurring fear that her husband": Garrow, *Bearing the Cross*, p. 84.

"talked about it [death] in his ": C. S. King, *My Life With Martin*, p. 301.

"My husband often told the children that if a man": Ibid.

"If he hearkens to the voice": Jung, *The Essential Jung*, (1983), p. 202.

"I think that Martin always felt": Young, cited in Garrow, "Martin Luther King, Jr., and the Spirit," p. 24.

"Martin was driven by a sense of": C. S. Scott, *My Life With Martin*, p. 139.

"This is what is going to happen to me also. I keep telling you": Ibid., p. 227.

"that as the leader of the Movement he would be killed": Young, cited in Ansbro, *Martin Luther King, Jr.*, p. 97.

SPIRITUALITY: CHAPTER 2 NOTES

"deals with both earth and heaven, both time": King, *Toward Freedom,* (1958), p. 21.

The Therapist as Minister: The Minister as Therapist

"rightly seeing in the cure of souls the real purpose": Jung, "Psychoanalysis and the Cure of Souls," (1975), p. 220.

"as the suffering of a soul which has not discovered": Ibid., pp. 198-199.

For Jung, the rediscovery of meaning was the cure: Ibid., p. 198.

"psychology without the psyche": Ibid.

"It is safe to say that every one of them fell ill": Ibid., p. 202.

"healing may be called a religious problem": Jung, "Psychotherapists or the Clergy," (1933), p. 237.

"Man is never helped in his suffering": Ibid, pp. 240-241.

"dogmatic and traditional biases": Ibid., p. 203.

"Many of our abnormal fears can be dealt with": King, *Strength to Love*, (1963), p. 122.

"man has never yet been able single-handedly": Jung, "Psychotherapists or the Clergy," (1993), p. 240.

In fact, Jung's father was a minister: Jung, *Memories, Dreams, Reflections*, (1989), Chapter 3.

"No one has the ears of as many people": King, cited in L. V. Baldwin, *There Is A Balm in Gilead*, p. 336.

"an important single force in shaping public": Ibid., p. 289.

The Four Spiritual Graces

Jung believed that religion's greatest gift was giving people: Jung, "The Modern Spiritual Problem," (1933).

"these four highest achievements of human endeavor are so many gifts": Ibid., p. 199.

"help the sufferer to attain the liberating": Ibid., p. 200.

"And where are the great and wise men": Ibid.

"The way to experience, moreover, is anything": Ibid.

Faith

"Which of you who has a friend will go to him at": King, "A Knock at Midnight," (1998), p. 65.

"It is midnight in the parable": Ibid.

"The traveler asks for three loaves of bread": Ibid., pp. 69-70.

"Midnight is a confusing hour": Ibid., p. 76.

"We have moved all of these months in the daring faith": Ibid., p. 77.

"we [keep] going with the faith that as we struggle": King, *The Autobiography*, (1998), p. 96.

"a creative force in the universe": King, "Where Do We Go From Here?," in *A Testament of Hope*, (1986), p. 252.

"When our days become dreary with low-hovering clouds": Ibid.

"for making people believe that they had a moral gift": Dyson, *I May Not Get There*, p. 35.

"at the root of King's civil rights": Schulke & McPhee, *King Remembered*, p. 270.

"The Negro himself no longer believes": Baldwin, *The Fire Next Time*, p. 115.

"I had been ready to resent the whole white race": King, *The Autobiography*, (1998), p. 14.

"to awaken the dozing conscience of many": Ibid., p. 140.

"distrust of all white people": King, "I Have a Dream," (1986), p. 218.

"the dedicated whites who had suffered, bled": King, *The Autobiography*, (1998), pp. 318-319.

"We must not lose faith in our white brothers": King, "Eulogy for the Martyred Children," (1986), p. 222.

"we must never forget that there are some": King, cited in Garrow, *Bearing the Cross*, p. 488.

"that some of the most implacable and vehement": King, *The Autobiography*, (1998), p. 48.

"I accept this award today with an abiding": King, "Nobel Prize Acceptance Speech," (1986), p. 225.

"If any new principle is to gain power": Rauschenbusch, *Christianity and the Social Crisis*, pp. 351-352.

"I confess that I do not believe this day": King, *"Playboy* Interview," (1986), p. 375.

"walk on in the days ahead with an audacious faith": King, "Where Do We Go From Here?," in *A Testament of Hope*, (1986), p. 252.

"The therapist embodies for the patient": Friedman, *The Healing Dialogue*, p. 34.

"He challenged us to be better people": Jackson, "Afterward," p. 150.

Hope

"a movement based on hope": King, "Love, Law, and Civil Disobedience," (1986), p. 52.

"an exciting age filled with hope": Ibid.

"We have difficult days ahead": King, "The American Dream," (1998), p. 224.

"hew out of the mountain of despair": Ibid.

"he became a symbol, and disenfranchised people": Smiley, cited in Schulke & McPhee, *King Remembered*, p. 67.

"a symbol of divinely inspired hope": *Jet* magazine, cited in C. E. Lincoln, "Martin Luther King, Jr.: A Profile," p. 43.

"Genuine hope," in his definition": King, cited in Franklin, "An Ethic of Hope," p. 49.

"Realistic hope," in another of his definitions: Ibid.

"Hope," as he further defined it: Ibid., p. 50.

"the analyst must realize and explicitly": Horney, *Our Inner Conflicts*, p. 186.

"always has a 'we' quality": King, cited in Franklin, "An Ethic of Hope," p. 50.

"We, the black people, the most displaced": Angelou, *The Heart of a Woman*, p. 56.

"Martin King had been a hero": Ibid., p. 94.

"The period was absolutely intoxicating": Ibid., p. 196.

"We raised the hopes tremendously but": King, cited in Garrow, *Bearing the Cross*, p. 537.

"deep despair and deep frustration": Ibid.

"I think that it was a hope that died aborning": Angelou, *The Heart of a Woman,* p. 72.

"Hope is the final refusal to give up": Ibid., p. 594.

"I can't lose hope. I can't lose": Ibid., p. 596.

"The only healthy answer lies in one's honest": King, *Do We Go From Here,* (1967), p. 53.

"Martin King's greatest contribution was his ability": Cone, "Martin Luther King, Jr. and the Third World," p. 221.

Love

"and now these three remain [faith, hope and love]": 1 Corinthians, 13:13.

agreeing with the apostle Paul that it is "the greatest of all": King, "Paul's Letter," (1998), p. 36.

"the most durable power in the world": Ibid, p. 34.

"the highest good": Ibid.

"the *summon bonum* of life": Ibid.

"the only absolute": King, "The American Dream," (1998),p. 97.

"the key that unlocks the door which leads to ultimate reality": King, "A Time to Break Silence," (1986), p. 242.

"the ethics of love to the center of our lives": King, "Nonviolence and Racial Justice," (1986), p. 8.

"Love *must* be at the forefront of our movement": King, "Walk for Freedom," (1986), p. 82.

"As I look into your eyes, and into the eyes of all of my brothers": King, "Loving Your Enemies," (1998), p. 59.

hooks would come to call King "a prophet of love": hooks, *Salvation*, p. 6.

"A coward is incapable of exhibiting love": Gandhi, cited in Hollis, *The Eden Project*, p. 57.

"You hear it said some of us are agitators": King, cited in Wexler, *An Eyewitness History*, p. 151.

"But even more, Americans, you may give your": King, "Paul's Letter to American Christians," (1998), p. 35.

"not in love with money, but in love": King, cited in Cone, *Martin & Malcolm & America,* p. 74.

"this call for a world-wide fellowship that lifts": King, "A Time to Break Silence," (1986), p. 242.

"As a society we are embarrassed by love": Ackerman, cited in hooks, *All About Love*, introduction.

"creative, redemptive sort of love": King, "Walk for Freedom," (1986), p. 82.

"The Greek language, as I've said so often": King, "Loving Your Enemies," (1998), pp. 47-49.

"The divine love, in short, is sacrificial in its nature": King, "A View of the Cross," (1992), p. 267.

"you love every man because God loves him": King, cited in Cone, *Martin &*

Malcolm & America, p. 130.

"And when you come to the point": King, "Loving Your Enemies," (1998), p. 46.

"an absolute necessity for the survival of our civilization": Ibid., p. 42.

"Jesus was very serious when he gave this command": Ibid.

"Hate for hate only intensifies": Ibid., pp. 49-50.

"hate distorts the personality of the hater": Ibid., p. 51.

"We usually think of what hate does for the individual hated": Ibid.

"becomes a pathological case": Ibid., pp. 52-53.

"the very structure of the personality of the hater": Ibid.

"Never hate, because it ends up in tragic, neurotic responses": Ibid., p. 52.

"the world's greatest psychologist"—Jesus: King, "'Loving Your Enemies'": Sermon Delivered at Dexter Avenue Baptist Church, " (2000), p. 321.

"many would go so far as to say": Ibid, p. 41.

"And it's significant that he does not say": Ibid., p. 49.

"You come to the point that you love the individual": Ibid.

"there is a power there that eventually transforms": Ibid., p. 53.

"And I'm foolish enough to believe that through": Ibid., p. 59.

"I believe firmly that love is a transforming power": King, "Walk for Freedom," (1986), p. 83.

"the only way to ultimately change humanity": King, "The Power of Nonviolence," (1986), p. 13.

Meaning

"The soul longs to discover its meaning" Jung, "Psychotherapists or the Clergy, CW 11, ¶497).

"In the same way the body needs food": Jung, "The Philosophical Tree," (Jung, "The Philosophical Tree," CW 13, ¶476).

"it is love that will save our world and our civilization, love even for enemies": King, "Loving Your Enemies," (1998), p. 42.

"We must discover the power of love, the power, the redemptive": Ibid., p. 57.

"to suffer in a righteous cause is to grow to our humanity's full stature": King, "A Creative Protest," (2005), p. 369.

"the opportunity to transfigure himself": King, *Stride Toward Freedom,* (1958), p. 197.

"the choice is no longer between violence and nonviolence": King, "The American Dream," (1998), p. 215.

"by following this method, we may also be able": Ibid.

"a special American phenomenon which must be understood": King, *Where Do We Go From Here,* (1967), p. 197.

"on another and more important level, what is happening": Ibid.

"a major turning point in history": Ibid., p. 198.

"of offensive on the part of oppressed people": Ibid.

"been caught up by the spirit of the times, and with his black brothers of Africa": Ibid., p. 199.

"not to be detached spectators, but involved participants": King, "The American Dream," (1998), p. 215.

"the widest liberation movement in history": King, *Where Do We Go From Here,* (1967), p. 198,

"a great *hour* for the Negro. The challenge is here": King, *Stride Toward Freedom,* (1958), p. 200.

"Arnold Toynbee says in *A Study of History*": Ibid., p. 200-201.

"the Negro may be God's appeal to this age": Ibid., p. 201.

"a higher and more noble order": King, *Strength to Love*, (1963), p. 22.

"History has thrust upon our generation an indescribably": King, *Stride Toward Freedom*, (1958), p. 173.

"We are here in the general sense because first": King, *The Autobiography*, (1998), p. 60.

"We will win our freedom because the sacred heritage of our nation": King, "Letter From Birmingham City Jail," (1986), p. 301.

"our most powerful weapon for world respect and emulation": King, *Stride Toward Freedom*, (1958), pp. 173-174.

"How we deal with this crucial situation will determine our moral": Ibid.

"There comes a time when we move": King, cited in Garrow, *Bearing the Cross*, p. 523.

TEACHINGS: CHAPTER 3 NOTES

King's Psychological Credentials

He took his first college psychology course: Carson, *The Papers, Vol. 1*, p. 39.

The following semester, he took "Educational Psychology": Ibid.

In 1946-1947, he took "Social Psychology": Ibid.

"the deeper insight it gave me into the psychological": King, "Book Review of *Personality*," (1992), p. 357.

"This was the first time that I was able to read the psychologies": Ibid., pp. 357-358.

"Jung and Adler were given quite a bit": Ibid., p. 358.

"For instance, Adler, Jung and Freud": Ibid.

King was not comfortable with a fundamentalist approach: Carson, *The Papers, Vol. 1*.

"merely mythological" and called the stories therein "one of": King, "Light on the Old Testament," (1992), p. 180.

"It seems more reasonable to hold that the fall": King, "The Place of Reason and Experience," (1992), p. 232.

While at BU, King fully embraced the philosophy of Personalism: King, *The Autobiography*, (1998), Chapter 4.

"Personalism affirms that human nature": Ansbro, *Martin Luther King, Jr.,* p. 121.

Brightman taught, "Human nature is no definite substantial entity": Ibid.

Finally, Personalism teaches that the personal: Smith & Zepp, *Search for the Beloved Community*, pp. 121-122.

"Many of our abnormal fears can be dealt with by": King, "Antidotes for Fear," (1963), p. 122.

In a classic example, he would refer to the tension: King, "Unfulfilled Dreams," (1998), p. 195.

"a desire to be out front": King, "The Drum Major Instinct," (1998), pp. 170-171.

"We all want to be important, to surpass others": Ibid., p. 171.

"Hate is injurious to the hater": King, "Kenneth B. Clark Interview," (1986), p. 334.

Fromm was also well known for his work: Fromm, *The Sane Society, On Being*

Human.

"Especially common in our highly competitive society": King, "Antidotes for Fear," (1963), p. 116.

"There are certain technical words in the vocabulary": King, "The New Negro of the South," (1997), p. 286.

"Well, there are some things in our social": Ibid.

"If I am right that a major task of therapy": Hillman, in Hillman & Ventura, *We've Had a Hundred Years*, p. 156.

"If his repressed emotions are not released": King, "Letter From Birmingham City Jail," (1986), p. 298.

"Everyone underestimated the amount of violence": King, *The Trumpet of Conscience*, (1967), p. 7.

"With the growth of slavery it became necessary": King, "Non-Aggression Procedures," (1997), p. 323.

"they rationalized—insisting that the unfortunate": King, "Our Struggle," (1986), p. 75.

"His depth was the thing that was beyond": Vivian, cited in Schulke & McPhee, *King Remembered*, p. 67.

"Dear Reverend": King's Brief Stint as Advice Columnist

the editors note that while it is unclear how the arrangements: Carson, *The Papers of Martin Luther King, Jr.: Vol. 4* , footnote, p. 267.

"Let the man that led the Montgomery boycott": Ibid.

His December advice column, completed shortly after: Ibid., p. 540

Race

"Why did God make Jesus white?": Ibid., p. 279-280.

Religion

"Is there a one and only way to God?": Ibid., p. 375.

"Christianity," he wrote, "is an expression": Ibid., p. 471-472.

Social Inquiries

When the deacon of a church asked a question: Ibid., p. 268.

One woman wrote in complaining about the shallowness: Ibid., p. 306.

Philosophical Inquiries

it was "Why do people suffer?": Ibid., p. 280.

Political Inquiries

One was written by a GI in an army camp in Alabama: Ibid., p. 268.

Another reader wrote in wondering why even: Ibid., pp. 459-460.

Alcoholism

A woman wrote in who had an alcoholic husband: Ibid., p. 444.

In the second letter dealing with alcoholism: Ibid., p. 503.

Homosexuality

When a boy wrote that he had feelings for other boys: Ibid., pp. 348-349.

Birth Control
King received a letter from a woman in Harlem: Ibid., p. 326.

Interracial Marriage
a reader wrote in and asked King where such passages: Ibid., p. 357.
A black woman in love with a white man wrote: Ibid., p. 269.

The Death Penalty
when King was asked if he thought God approved of death: Ibid., p. 305.

Gambling
A woman wrote in concerned about her husband: Ibid., p. 280.

Nuclear Weapons
Of course, as an unrelenting pacifist: Ibid., p. 327, 471.

Rock and Roll Music
A 17-year-old musician who belonged to: Ibid., pp. 392-393.

Premarital Sex
To one he wrote that the problems created: Ibid., p. 306.
In an interesting twist on his answer: Ibid., p. 504.

Extramarital Sex
In the first, a woman who was married to a handsome: Ibid., p. 268.
A second question came from a woman whose husband: Ibid., p. 417
Finally, a woman whose husband wouldn't give up: Ibid., p. 459.

Divorce
King again took a more liberal position: Ibid., p. 349.

The Importance of a Rational Approach to Problem-Solving
In the most startling example, a 28-year-old: Ibid., p. 504.
A widow in her mid-fifties wanted to know: Ibid., pp. 327-328.
A man described how he was in love: Ibid., p. 305.

The Primacy of Self-Analysis
For example, a woman said her husband was a great pillar of the church: Ibid.,
    p.305.
Another time a man shared, "I have been married": Ibid., p. 348.
When a woman wrote in saying her husband mocked: Ibid., p. 541.
The woman mentioned in a section above whose husband: Ibid., 459.
In another letter, a child shared that she was in pain: Ibid., pp. 401-402.

The Importance of Dialogue
For instance, with the woman above whose husband: Ibid., p. 305.
To the 18-year-old boy with the alcoholic father: Ibid., p. 503.
In the letter from the woman whose husband mocked her and her family: Ibid.,
    p. 541.
For the woman who had an alcoholic husband, King suggested: Ibid., p. 444.

Combining Secular and Religious Therapies

For instance, a woman who had a child out of wedlock: Ibid., pp. 374-375.
One reader wanted to know how to stop worrying so much: Ibid., p. 445.

Always Seek the Root of the Problem

A man wrote in saying that the harder he worked, the further: Ibid., p. 349.
When a man who was separated from his wife for nine years complained: Ibid., p. 418.
In another letter, a black person confessed that he disliked all Jews: Ibid., p. 460.

The Importance of Knowing the Other

One woman wrote in that her new husband and her daughter did not: Ibid., p. 401.
To the man who disliked Jews: Ibid., p. 460.
When a 17-year-old girl expressed that she didn't like: Ibid;, p. 521.
He gave similar advice to a couple wondering: Ibid., p. 520.

Never Run Away From Problems

He stated this clearly to the 18-year-old boy: Ibid., p. 503.
He gave similar advice to a 15-year-old boy: Ibid., pp. 443-444.
A woman who had conflict with her pastor: Ibid., p. 521.
For instance, a preacher in a small town in Mississippi: Ibid., p. 326.

Concentrating on Higher Virtues

When a person asked how to overcome a bad temper: Ibid., p. 268-269.
To the woman who had a child out of wedlock: Ibid., p. 374-375.
To the woman who had lost her 5-year-old son in the horrible: Ibid., p. 504.
In an uncharacteristically poetic response: Ibid., p. 306.

Conclusion

"notion of sermonizing involved": L. V. Baldwin, *There is a Balm*, p. 288.

PREACHING: CHAPTER 4 NOTES

"A Tough Mind and a Tender Heart"
The Sermon

"The strong man holds in a living blend strongly marked opposites": King, "A Tough Mind," 1963, p. 13.
"the idealists are not usually realistic, and the realists": Ibid.
"Life at its best is a creative synthesis": Ibid.
He quotes one of his favorite philosophers, Georg Hegel: Ibid.
He quotes Matthew 10:16. "Be": Ibid.
"We must combine the toughness of the serpent": Ibid., pp. 13-14.
"characterized by incisive thinking, realistic appraisal": Ibid., p. 14.
"has a strong, austere quality that makes for firmness": Ibid.
and those religious people who reject science "with a dogmatic passion": Ibid., p. 15.
"The shape of the world today does not permit us the luxury": Ibid., p. 17.

detached from "the mainland of humanity": Ibid.

"To have serpent-like qualities devoid of dovelike qualities": Ibid., p. 18.

"acquiesce and resign themselves to segregation," but if they are too hardhearted, they will "combat": Ibid.

"When days grow dark and nights grow dreary, we": Ibid., p. 20.

Psychological Theory

For example, King did not believe in white power or black power: King, *The Autobiography*, (1998), "Black Power."

he did not believe that the truth could be found in communism: King, *The Autobiography*, (1998), pp. 19-22.

Harmony does not necessarily come through compromise: Jung, "The Transcendent Function," (1969).

Nonviolent resistance is also offered as a third: King, "A Tough Mind," (1963), p. 19.

Jung believed opposition was inherent: Sharp, *Psychological Types*.

Applying the Sermon and the Psychology to King

"My studies had made me skeptical, and I could": King, *The Autobiography*, (1998), p. 15.

"the shouting and stamping. I didn't understand it": Ibid.

"wondered whether it [religion] could serve as a vehicle": Ibid.

Though he always had a deep urge to serve humanity, he began: Ibid, p. 14.

"I came to see that behind the legends and myths": Ibid, p 16.

He was always intellectually against the war: Garrow, *Bearing the Cross*, p. 543.

"Unfulfilled Dreams"
The Sermon

"In the preface to that volume, King writes: King, *Strength to Love*, 1963, p. 11.

Yet God said to David, "'Whereas it was in thine": King, "Unfulfilled Dreams," (1998), pp. 191-192.

"temples of character, temples of justice, temples of peace": Ibid., p. 192.

"one of the great agonies of life": Ibid.

"a continual story of shattered dreams": Ibid.

he provides several examples: Ibid., pp. 192-193.

"must face the fact that there is a tension at the heart": Ibid., p. 194.

In his typical intellectual style, he gives several examples: Ibid., pp. 194-195.

King terms this struggle "a civil war": Ibid., p. 195.

"I don't care who you are, I don't care where you live": Ibid., p. 195.

"And whenever we set out to dream our dreams": Ibid., p. 196.

"In the final analysis, God does not judge us": Ibid.

"Salvation isn't reaching the destination of absolute morality": Ibid.

"Is your heart right?": Ibid., p. 198.

"He may not have reached the highest": Ibid.

"I'm a sinner like all of God's children. But": Ibid., p. 199.

"a strong boat of faith": Ibid.

Psychological Theory

"Man *is* neither good nor evil. If one": Fromm, *The Heart of Man*, p. 123.

"One can no longer avoid the realization that evil": Jung, *The Essential Jung*, (1983), p. 396.

"the unfathomable union of good and evil": Ibid., p. 271.

"Within the best of us, there is some evil": King, "Loving Your Enemies," (1998), p. 46.

Applying the Sermon and the Psychology to King

King shared in his sermon that he was no saint himself: King, "Unfulfilled Dreams," (1998), p. 198.

"His conscience was a formidable thing that kept him": C. S. King, *My Life With Martin*, p. 58.

"My husband was what psychologists might call": Ibid., p. 158.

"He criticized himself more severely than anyone": C. S. King, cited in Garrow, *Bearing the Cross*, p. 587.

"I subject myself to self-purification and to endless self-analysis": King, cited in Ansbro, *Martin Luther King, Jr.*, p. 146.

He felt that having been born into what was a middle-class: C. S. King, *My Life With Martin*, p. 59.

"Martin could be described as an intensely guilt-ridden": Levison, cited in Garrow, *Bearing the Cross*, p. 588.

"I am *conscious of two Martin Luther Kings*": Barbour, cited in Garrow, *Bearing* the Cross, p. 289.

"a kind of dualism in my life" and that "Martin Luther King": Ibid.

"a great liability for all us Negroes" and said "Satan could not do more": Garrow, *Bearing the Cross*, p. 373.

Garrow reports that King's initial response: Garrow, *The FBI and Martin Luther King, Jr.*, p. 134.

"Sex is sacred. It's beautiful, it's holy": King, cited in Burns, *To the Mountaintop*, p. 408.

"Each of us is two selves. And the great burden of life": King, cited in Garrow, *The FBI and Martin Luther King, Jr.*, p. 219.

"guilt will accompany us when we sin": Ibid.

"What I do is only between me and my God": Ibid., p. 134.

"I want to hear a voice saying to me": King, "Unfulfilled Dreams," (1998), p. 198-199.

"During our whole marriage we never had one single serious discussion": C. S. King, cited in Garrow, *Bearing the Cross*, p. 374.

"Others have speculated about Dr. King's relationships with women": Powers, *I Shared the Dream*, p. 235.

"Overcoming an Inferiority Complex"
The Sermon

Here, King relates the Biblical story of Zacchaeus: King, "Overcoming an Inferiority Complex," (2004), p. 304.

"love failures and because of moral failures": Ibid., p. 305

King notes that some ways of overcoming the feeling of inferiority are not constructive: Ibid., pp. 305-306

"Individuals become so accustomed and absorbed in running": Ibid., p. 305.

Some act like the fox in Aesop's fable: Ibid., pp. 305-306.

Others use what King called the "smoke-screen" method: Ibid., p. 306.

The first way is through "the principle of self-acceptance": Ibid., p. 307.

"individuals find a sort of impassable gulf": Ibid.

"with all limitations and with all of the endowments": Ibid.

"I had to just come to the point of accepting myself": Ibid.

"anything that you do for the upbuilding of humanity": Ibid., p. 308

"No matter how small you consider it, you can dignify anything": Ibid.

"can do more with just shining shoes than most people can do": Ibid.

substitutionary compensation," whereby you take your inadequate points and transform them into something adequate: Ibid., p. 309.

"into the channel of great scientific research": Ibid.

by absorbing yourself in some cause, in some principle, in some ideal": Ibid.

"And because of his being embedded in this cause": Ibid., p. 314.

"develop an abiding religious faith because there is": Ibid., p. 315

"Of all of the hundreds and thousands of patients": Ibid.

"it's so easy to feel that we are sort of": Ibid.

"for the race problem and for every Negro who stands in America": Ibid.

"the assurance that you belong and that you count": Ibid.

"go out of this church with a new faith in yourself": Ibid., p. 316.

Psychological Theory

King called the feeling of inferiority "one of the first and basic conditions of life": King, "Overcoming an Inferiority Complex," (2004), p. 304.

"one of the most stagnating and strangulating and crushing conditions of the human" : Ibid.

"Individuals can use safeguarding devices": Stein & Edwards, "Classical Adlerian Theory and Practice," ¶32.

"You can sublimate and take these inadequacies": King, "Overcoming an Inferiority Complex," (2004), p. 309.

for example, when King's shy young man directs his shyness: Ibid.

"substitutionary compensation"; for example, when King's homely girl: Ibid.

In the healthy forms of defenses, what Adler called a "minus situation": Stein & Edwards, "Classical Adlerian Theory and Practice," ¶16.

King offered other ways to turn the minus into a plus: King, "Overcoming an Inferiority Complex," (2004), p. 308-314.

The other pathway Adler suggested to curing the complex is through positive social interaction: Stein & Edwards, "Classical Adlerian Theory and Practice," ¶54.

King offered this cure as well, telling his parishioners: King, "Overcoming an Inferiority Complex," (2004), p. 308-315.

For Adler, any kind of social discrimination such as classism, racism, or sexism can exacerbate inferiority feelings. Stein & Edwards, "Classical Adlerian Theory and Practice," ¶42, 43.

"And so being a Negro in America is not a comfortable existence": King, *Where Do We Go From Here*, (1967), p. 141.

"It is impossible for white Americans to grasp the depths": Ibid., pp. 121-122.

the Negro's most potent weapon in achieving self-respect," and he encouraged them to develop "this spirit": Ibid., pp. 145-146.

"to unite around powerful action programs to eradicate the last vestiges of racial injustice": Ibid., p. 151.

"structures of evil do not crumble by passive waiting": Ibid.

"work passionately for group identity:" Ibid, p. 146.

Applying the Sermon and the Psychology to King

"very congenial home situation," where he uses the word "intimate": King, "An Autobiography of Religious Development," (1992), p. 359.

Physically, he was "an extraordinary healthy child" and mentally: Ibid.

"behind the scene setting forth those motherly cares, the lack of": Ibid., p. 360.

In front of the scenes was his father, whom King called "a real father": Ibid.

"exposed to the best educational conditions in my childhood": Ibid.

Adler wrote that if parents could help instill in children a satisfactory Stein & Edwards, "Classical Adlerian Theory and Practice," ¶20, 24.

"I grew up in a family where love was central": King, "An Autobiography of Religious Development," (1992), p. 360.

She explained the facts of slavery, discrimination and segregation, and then she assured King, "You are as good as anyone." King, *Stride Toward Freedom*, (1958), p. 5.

King learned from him that rugged sense of somebodiness: Ibid, pp. 5-6

"The most highly gifted black student": Dyson, *I May Not Get There*, p. 148.

Dyson discusses the concept of "stereotype threat": Ibid., pp. 151-152.

"terribly tense, unable to escape the fact that he was a Negro": Oates, *Let the Trumpet Sound*, p. 24.

"If I were a minute late to class, I was almost morbidly": King, cited in Oates, *Let the Trumpet Sound*, p. 24.

"Conquering Self-Centeredness"
The Sermon

"to suggest certain ways to conquer self-centeredness": King, "Conquering Self-Centeredness," (2000), p. 250.

"He who finds his life shall lose it": Ibid.

"An individual has not begun to live until he can rise above": Ibid.

Showing his understanding of child psychology, he makes reference to psychologist: Ibid..

After stating the problem, King then points out the effects, which he termed "tragic": Ibid., p. 251.

"to ominous proportions [leading] to a tragic sense of persecution": Ibid., p. 252.

First, he points to the importance of discovering "some cause": Ibid., p. 253.

"all human beings have a desire to belong": Ibid.

He quotes Ralph Waldo Emerson, "O, see how the masses of men": Ibid., p. 254.

"by having the proper inner attitude toward your position": Ibid.

"gives man a sense of belonging and on the other": Ibid., p. 256.

God could say "I am that I am": Ibid., pp. 256-257.

He quotes from the song "Amazing Grace": Ibid., p. 258.

"He who seeks to find his ego will lose it. But he who loses his ego": Ibid.

Psychological Theory

"Jung believed that the development of the ego": Hopcke, *A Guided Tour*, p. 79.

Jung termed this the process of individuation: Ibid., pp. 63-65.

For King, this meant "to extend the ego into objectively meaningful channels": King, "Conquering Self-Centeredness," (2000), p. 253.

"just move around in their little circles": Ibid.

"bounded all around by themselves": Ibid., p. 251.

"an indispensable condition, for without the conscious acknowledgment": Jung, "The Psychology of the Transference," (1963), p. 71.

King believed that "the proper religious faith": King, "Conquering Self-Centeredness," (2000), p. 256.

Applying the Sermon and the Psychology to King

"one of the problems that I have to face and even fight every day": King, "Conquering Self-Centeredness," (2000), pp. 254-255.

"Living over the past year, I can hardly go into any city": Ibid., p. 256.

"inescapable urge to serve society": King, "Application for Admission to Crozer Theological Seminary," p. 144.

"You have to give yourself entirely": C. S. King, *My Life With Martin,* p. 163.

"If every Negro in the United States turns to violence": King, cited in Albert & Hoffman, *We Shall Overcome,* p. 100

"that where I stand today, I stand": King, "Conquering Self-Centeredness," (2000), pp. 254-255.

"to see myself in my true perspective. Help me, O God": Ibid., p. 255.

"I couldn't walk out with arrogance": Ibid, p. 257.

"ringing in my heart saying, 'But for'": Ibid.

THERAPY: CHAPTER 5 NOTES

Diagnosing America

"Increasingly, the vocabulary King used": King, R. H., "Martin Luther King, Jr., and the Meaning of Freedom," p. 140.

"America has been something of a schizophrenic": King, "The American Dream," (1998), p. 87.

"We live in a sick, neurotic": King, cited in Garrow, *Bearing the Cross,* p. 584.

"If America would come to herself": King, *Where Do We Go From Here,* (1967), p. 99.

King referred to this book in a sermon: King, "A Knock at Midnight," (1998), p. 67.

The task of the therapist is to help: Horney, *Our Inner Conflicts,* p. 114.

Horney argues that neuroses come: Ibid., p. 187.

Defining Neurosis

"a disturbance in one's relation to self and to others": Horney, *Neurosis and Human Growth,* p. 368.

Because of their disruptive potential: Horney, *Our Inner Conflicts,* p. 34.

Horney states you can spot a neurotic: Ibid.

The Genesis of a Neurosis

If a child grows up and doesn't feel: Horney, *Neurosis and Human Growth,* p. 18.

"Harassed by these disturbing conditions": Horney, *Our Inner Conflicts,* p. 43.

She delineates three trends in the neurotic personality: Ibid., p. 42-46.

The Idealized Self

For neurotics, when safety is: Horney, *Neurosis and Human Growth,* p. 21).

Needing a new sense of identity: Ibid., pp. 21-22.

"Conscious or unconscious, the [idealized]": Horney, *Our Inner Conflicts*, p. 96.

"to bridge the gap and whip himself into perfection": Ibid., p. 98.

The idealized image the neurotic: Horney, *Neurosis and Human Growth*, p. 23.

This happens when the actual self is too painful: Ibid., p. 24.

To maintain the ideal, the neurotic turns: Ibid., pp. 24-28.

All these drives are compulsive: Ibid., pp. 28-33.

"The development of pride is the logical outcome": Ibid., p. 109.

"As soon as we go off on the search": Ibid., p. 94.

"into the fantastic, into the realm of unlimited": Ibid., p. 34.

"It [America] had a future that was destined by God": Lubbrage, "The Components of Manifest Destiny," ¶2.

"had a reputation that they were": Johanssen, "A Go-Ahead Nation," ¶4.

"In many ways, this was also an age of paradox": Ibid..,¶9.

"an imaginative creation interwoven with and determined": Horney, *Our Inner Conflicts*, p. 108.

The Civil War

He knew the country conceived eighty-seven years: A. Lincoln, "House Divided Speech," ¶1.

"that these dead shall not have died": A. Lincoln, "The Gettysburg Address," ¶1.

The Birth of the Civil Rights Movement

"The distinction of race has always been used in American life": S. Steele, *The Content of Our Character*, p. 5.

Horney argues that we cannot underestimate the power: Horney, *Neurosis and Human Growth*, pp. 188-189.

"Racial segregation is buttressed by": King, *The Autobiography,* (1998), p. 330.

"bring to an end a painful disparity": Washington Post, cited in Wexler, *An Eyewitness History*, p. 50.

"The Supreme Court has finally reconciled": Schlesinger, Ibid., p. 48).

"a strange paradox in a nation founded": King, "The Negro and the Constitution," (1992), p. 109-110.

"the nation in 1865 took a new stand": Ibid, p. 110.

"Black America still wears chains": Ibid.

we cannot have "an enlightened democracy": Ibid.

"cast down the last barrier to perfect freedom": Ibid.

"deep-seated belief that democracy": King, *The Autobiography,* (1998), p. 60.

"had achieved the ideals of our democracy": Ibid., p. 139.

"the greatest American patriot of the twentieth": Jackson, "Afterward," p. 150.

Smith and Zepp assert that King: Smith & Zepp, *Search for the Beloved*, p. 91.

"There is never a time in our American": King, *The Autobiography,* (1998), p. 60.

"has been torn between selves—a self": King, *Where Do We Go From Here*, (1967), p. 80.

Buber wrote that when you meet someone: Buber, *The Knowledge of Man*, p. 170.

"I must take the other person in his dynamic existence": Ibid, pp. 170-171.

"We will reach the goal of freedom in Birmingham": King, "Letter From Birmingham City Jail," (1986), p. 301.

"may have to wrestle with the patient": Friedman, *The Healing Dialogue*, p.

137.
let's remember Horney's admonition: Horney, *Neurosis and Human Growth*, p. 334.
"I'm still convinced that there is nothing": King, "Meet the Press," (1986), p. 388.

The Entrenchment of the White Ego
Horney lists several common fears that plague neurotics: Horney, *Our Inner Conflicts*, pp. 144-151.
"terror of the unknown": Ibid., p. 153.
"All experience hath shewn, that": "Declaration of Independence," ¶2.
"Clearly, no one develops his personality": Jung, *The Essential Jung*, (1983), p. 197.
"I soon saw that I was the victim of ": King, *The Autobiography*, (1998), pp. 69-70.
"Now it might be true that old man segregation": Ibid., p. 89.
"America will not admit the Negro to equal rights": Niebuhr, cited in Smith & Zepp, *Search for the Beloved Community*, p. 99.
"King had been greatly influenced by Gunnar": Early, "Martin Luther King and the Middle Way," p. 816.

The New Civil War
"Neurosis is an inner cleavage": Jung, "Psychotherapists or the Clergy," (1993), pp. 236-237.
"since no war was ever won on the defensive": Jung, "The Psychology of the Transference," (1963), p. 17.
"We did not hesitate to call our movement": King, *The Autobiography*, (1998), p. 179.
"an army without guns, but not": Ibid., p. 222.
"violence only serves to harden the resistance": Ibid., p. 294.
"Please don't be too soft.": King, cited in Garrow, *Bearing the Cross*, p. 386.

Bringing the Tension to the Surface
Socrates taught that it was necessary to create tension to stimulate growth: King, "Letter From Birmingham City Jail," (1986), p. 291.
"The injustice was there under the surface": Ibid., p. 264.
"We who engage in nonviolent direct action are not": Ibid., pp. 246-247.
He often defended himself by returning: King, "Meet the Press," (1986), p. 383.
"You have had a sort of negative peace": King, *Stride Toward Freedom*, (1958), pp. 24-25.
"Consciousness is really nothing more than maintaining conversation": Hillman, in Hillman & Ventura, *We've Had a Hundred Years*, p. 99.

The Importance of Seeing
"concerned with the act of seeing": Jung, *The Essential Jung*, (1983), pp. 262-263.
"only the tiniest fraction of the population learns anything from reflection": Jung, *Flying Saucers*, (1978), p. 39.
"conveniently sink into the sea of": Jung, *The Essential Jung*, (1983), p. 395.
"an eye for an eye but one that summoned": King, *Stride Toward Freedom*, (1958), p. 21.

"I can see the effects of this early childhood experience": King, The Autobiography, (1998), p. 2.

"I remember seeing the Klan actually beat a Negro": Ibid., p. 10.

"Here I saw economic injustice firsthand": Ibid., p. 11.

"How can one avoid being depressed when he sees": Ibid., p. 124.

"the ritual arena for the drama of race": Gates, "Prime Time," p. 160.

"The tactic of mass nonviolent direct action that disrupted": Morris, "A Man Prepared for the Times," pp. 53-54.

"carried pictures of prostrate women, and policemen": King, The Autobiography, (1998), pp. 208-209.

Often, it was the national and international media: Garrow, Bearing the Cross.

"Millions of white Americans, for the": King, The Autobiography, (1998), pp. 227-228.

"Like a good omen for the future, the face": Walker, The Way Forward, p. 124.

Awakening the Conscience, Stirring the Soul

"You just have to uncover the unrecognized sympathy": cited in Warren, "Segregation: The Inner Conflict," p. 198.

"This courageous willingness to go to jail may": King, The Autobiography, (1998), p. 140.

"Maybe it will take this type of self-suffering": Ibid., p. 145.

Here they saw blacks doing nothing but marching nonviolently across a bridge: Garrow, Bearing the Cross, pp. 397-399.

As King said simply, if white Americans have any conscience: King, "Playboy Interview," (1998), p. 348.

The irony of the situation is that ABC: Garrow, Bearing the Cross, p. 399.

"More white people learned more about the shame of America": King, "Black Power Defined," (1986), p. 304.

"This amazing unity, this profound self-respect": King, "Facing the Challenge of a New Age," (2000), p. 87.

"less ashamed of their prejudices toward Negroes": King, Where Do We Go From Here, (1967), p. 70.

In his book Violence: Reflections on a National Epidemic, James Gilligan argues: Gilligan, Violence: Reflections, p. 47.

In the classic 1979 study The Nature: Allport, The Nature of Prejudice, pp. 150-152.

"We must appreciate our great heritage": King, cited in Garrow, Bearing the Cross, p. 492.

"One must not overlook the positive value": King, Where Do We Go From Here, (1967), p. 47.

"the possibilities of life" and to their own possibilities: Walker, In Search of Our Mother's Gardens, p. 121.

"Through his dramatic efforts to contrast": Dyson, I May Not Get There, p. 34.

"Therapeutic work cannot avoid meeting the": Hillman, Loose Ends, p. 185.

"The white soul slumped to repressed guilt": Dyson, I May Not Get There, p. 34.

The Power of Guilt

"by a deep sense of guilt for what it has done to the Negro": King, "Playboy Interview," (1986), p. 358.

"The psychological use of the word 'guilt' should": Jung, "After the Catastrophe," (1989), p. 51.

"Psychological collective guilt is a tragic fate": Ibid., p. 53.

Jung thought it important to publicly acknowledge the: Ibid.

But he also cautions against the victims then rubbing: Ibid., p. 58.

"stagnant passivity and deadening": King, *The Autobiography*, (1998), p. 99.

"When we are conscious of our guilt we are": Jung, *The Essential Jung*, (1983), pp. 72-73.

Reconstructing the Real Self

"consciences must be enlisted in our movement": King, *Where Do We Go From Here*, (1967), p. 33.

For example, when the Civil Rights Act passed: King, *The Autobiography*, (1998), p. 245.

"the racial struggle in America has always been primarily": S. Steele, *The Content of Our Character*, p. 5.

"blacks used the innocence that grew out of their long subjugation": Ibid., p. 6.

Steele argues that historically, blacks have handled racism: Ibid., p. 11.

"A bargainer says, I already believe you are innocent": Ibid., pp. 10-11.

"must be earned through sacrifice while the latter": Ibid., p. 18.

"because of its belief in the capacity of whites to be moral": Ibid.

"Now suddenly the movement itself was using race": Ibid., p. 19.

King understood that racial power subverts moral power: Ibid.

"The sacrifices that moral power demands are difficult to sustain": Ibid.

"But even though I can understand it psychologically": King, cited in Cone, "Martin Luther King, Jr., and the Third World," p. 76.

"white guilt became so palpable you could see it on people": S. Steele, *The Content of Our Character*, p. 78.

"road back to innocence—through actions and policies": Ibid., p. 79.

"the redemption of innocence, [and] the reestablishment": Ibid., p. 84.

"In the final analysis the weakness of Black Power": King, *Where Do We Go From Here*, (1967), p. 61.

"In short, we, the black and the white": J. Baldwin, *The Fire Next Time*, p. 131.

Conclusion

"between his pride system and his real self, between his drive": Horney, *Neurosis and Human Growth*, p. 356.

Horney calls the "most turbulent period of analysis": Ibid., p. 356.

MYTHOLOGY: CHAPTER 6 NOTES

Martin Luther King, Jr.'s Understanding of Myths and Archetypes

In one paper he wrote that many things in the Bible must be seen as "merely mythological," calling the Bible an "allegory": King, "Light on the Old Testament," (1992), p. 180.

He made a distinction between finding it "true," which would make it "full of errors": Ibid.

"it seems more reasonable to hold that the fall of man is psychological": King, "The Place of Reason and Experience in Finding God," (1992), p. 232.

he wrote that it is important not to see Jesus as possessing some metaphysical substance: King, "The Christian Pertinence of Eschatological Hope,"

(1992), p. 262.
"true significance of the divinity of Christ lies in the fact": Ibid.
did not see his "substantial unity with God": Ibid., p. 261.
"his filial consciousness and in his unique dependence upon God": Ibid.
"at last realized his true divine calling: That": Ibid.
"inherent metaphysical substance within him" that made him one with God, but it was "actually harmful": Ibid., p. 262.
this divine quality or this unity with God was not something thrust": Ibid.

The Power of Archetypes

"form the structures of our consciousness with such force": Hillman, *Re-Visioning Psychology*, p. 129.
"But one thing is absolutely essential to the notion of archetypes": Ibid., p. xix.

King as a Projection-Carrier

"The adulation which King received in 1957 [during the Montgomery": Bennett, "When the Man and the Hour are Met," p. 38.
"those for affirmation and confirmation of our value, for emotional": Corbett, *The Religious Function of the Psyche*, p. 26.
"We must appreciate our great heritage": King, cited in Garrow, *Bearing the Cross*, p. 492.
"the need for alliance with, or to be psychologically": Corbett, *The Religious Function of the Psyche*, p. 26.
As an extreme example, one black man: cited in Schulke & McPhee, *King Remembered*, p. 258.
"These involve the need for sameness with others": Corbett, *The Religious Function of the Psyche*, p. 27.
"They used to love to call him 'My boy'": cited in Schulke & McPhee, *King Remembered*, p. 69.
"To be in a community of people of shared beliefs": Corbett, *The Religious Function of the Psyche*, p. 27.
"to feel that we can have an effect on the other person": Ibid.
"to the extent that the Self cannot embody": Ibid., p. 28.
"because they are aspects of the Self which are intended": Ibid., p. 26.

Conclusion

"At the moment I saw his resistance I knew I would": Walker, *In Search of Our Mother's Gardens*, p. 144.

ARCHETYPES: CHAPTER 7 NOTES

"Mythic characters personify intrapsychic processes, but there": Corbett, *The Religious Function of the Psyche*, p. 79.

King's Vision of a Utopian Society

"the vision of the Beloved Community was the organizing principle": Smith & Zepp, *Search for the Beloved Community*, p. 129.
"a transformed and regenerated human society" where "unity would be an actuality in every aspect of social life" which "involves: Ibid., pp. 130-131.

"a new nation where men will live together as brothers": King, cited in Smith & Zepp, *Search for the Beloved Community*, p. 155.

"reconciliation; the end is redemption; the end": King, cited in Smith & Zepp, *Search for the Beloved Community*, p. 130.

"The ultimate aim of SCLC is to foster and create": Ibid.

"It must be made palpably clear that resistance and nonviolence": King, *The Autobiography*, (1998), p. 140.

"There comes a time when we move from protest to reconciliation": King, cited in Garrow, *Bearing the Cross*, p. 523.

"The kingdom of God and the Beloved Community were synonymous in King's thought": Smith & Zepp, *Search for the Beloved Community*, p. 141.

"The Kingdom of God will be a society in which men and women": King, cited in Smith & Zepp, *Search for the Beloved Community*, p. 142.

"although man's moral pilgrimage may never reach": King, cited in Ansbro, *Martin Luther King, Jr.*, p. 191.

"soon or late, by sudden crisis or through slow Development," the beloved community "will be a society": King, "The Christian Pertinence of Eschatological Hope," (1992), pp. 272-273.

"though the Kingdom of God may remain not yet as a universal": King, cited in Ansbro, *Martin Luther King, Jr.*, pp. 191-192.

As Martin ended [his "I Have a Dream" speech]: C. S. King, *My Life With Martin*, p. 223.

"We all had felt that a great human milestone": Ibid., p. 225.

"When we marched from Selma to Montgomery, Alabama": King, *The Autobiography*, (1998), p. 287.

"crowding together on the seats, the floors": Ibid.

"As I stood with them and saw white and Negro": King, *Where Do We Go From Here*, (1967), p. 132.

"The people who attended the mass meetings and rallies": Smith & Zepp, *Search for the Beloved Community*, p. 132.

"work for brotherhood, for true intergroup, interpersonal": King, cited in Garrow, *Bearing the Cross*, p. 488.

America is essentially a Dream," he said, "a dream": King, cited Smith & Zepp, *Search for the Beloved Community*, pp. 138-139.

Just remember some of his powerful final lines of the speech: King, "I Have a Dream," (1986), pp. 219-220.

The Beloved Community as the Archetype of Union

"the absorptive power of the archetype explains not only the widespread": Jung, "The Psychology of the Transference," (1963), p. 130.

"the image of the *coniunctio* has always occupied": Ibid., p. 6.

"There is only one passion which satisfies": Fromm, *The Sane Society*, p. 31.

"the free society needs a bond of an affective nature": Jung, *The Essential Jung*, (1983), p. 400.

"real cohesion and consequently its strength": Ibid.

"In asking for faith in the possibility of a new social order": Rauschenbusch, *Christianity and the Social Crisis*, pp. 420-421.

King as the Archetypal Deliverer

"the greatest story of liberation from enslavement ever told": Meier, *Moses— The Prince*, p. 1.

"The more devout Negro considers that he is a Jew": J. Baldwin, *Notes of a Native Son*, p. 67.

"The myth not only continued but took on even greater significance": Lomax, "When 'Nonviolence' Meets 'Black Power,'" p. 272.

"Oppressed people cannot remain oppressed forever. The yearning": King, *Where Do We Go From Here*, (1967), pp. 198-199.

"And that is why down in Montgomery we could walk twelve months and never get": King, "Facing the Challenge of a New Age," (2000), p. 83.

"I can't stop now. History has thrust something upon me": King, cited in R. H. King, "Martin Luther King, Jr. and the Meaning of Freedom," p. 133.

"a symbol of divinely inspired hope" and "a kind of modern Moses": *Jet*, cited in Miller, "The Broadening Horizons," p. 43.

"Another [King supporter] ecstatically calls him a 'Moses, sent to lead his people to the Promised Land of first-class citizenship'": "Martin Luther King, Jr.: Never Again Where He Was," n. p..

"King is the man, O Lord,": cited in Lomax, "When 'Nonviolence' Meets 'Black Power,'" p. 178.

"God only puts on the face of the earth a leader like that once": cited in Schulke & McPhee, *King Remembered*, p. 274.

Learning From the Moses Myth

King called it "a throbbing desire" that is "the essential basis" of personhood: King, "Birth of a New Nation," (2000), p. 156.

"There is something in the soul that cries out for freedom": Ibid.

"as we ourselves find ourselves breaking aloose from an evil": Ibid., p. 161.

"the beginning of liberation lies in man's capacity to suffer": Fromm, *You Shall Be As Gods*, p. 92.

"the possibility of liberation exists only because people suffer": Ibid, p. 106.

"It comes through hard labor and it comes through toil": King, "Birth of a New Nation," (2000), p. 163.

"That's the long story of freedom, isn't it?": Ibid.

"About 2800 years ago Moses set out to lead the children of Israel": King, *Stride Toward Freedom*, (1958), p. 188.

"Moses might not get to see Canaan, but his children will see it": King, "Birth of a New Nation," (2000), p. 163.

"Well, I don't know what will happen now. We've got some difficult": King, "I See the Promised Land," (1986), p. 286.

"So I'm not afraid of anybody this morning. Tell Montgomery": King, cited in Burns, *To the Mountaintop*, p. 151.

"And I'm happy tonight. I'm not worried about anything": King, "I See the Promised Land," (1986), p. 286.

King as the Archetypal Prophet

"The Hebrew prophets influenced King more than": Smith & Zepp, *Search for the Beloved Community*, p. 34.

Characteristics of the Prophet Archetype

Jean Pierre Prevost defines a prophet as someone who has been sent by God: Prevost, *How to Read the Prophets*, pp. 7-8.

"King believed that the Dream existed originally": Smith & Zepp, *Search for the Beloved Community*, p. 138.

"did not hesitate to inform meetings large or small that God": Burns, *To the Mountaintop*, p. 308.

Prevost adds that the prophets are not only men of God's Word: Prevost, *How to Read the Prophets*, p. 8.

"To make the Word of God understandable": Ibid., pp. 14-15.

"This is no day to pay lip service to integration": King, *Stride Toward Freedom*, (1958), p. 177.

"His realm is never a purely spiritual one": Fromm, *You Shall Be As Gods*, p. 118.

"I have come to think of my role as one which operates": King, cited in Garrow, *Bearing the Cross*, p. 559.

"The idea of peace, in the prophetic view": Fromm, *You Shall Be As Gods*, pp. 125-126.

"is not merely the absence of some negative": King, "When Peace Becomes Obnoxious," (1997), p. 208.

"Any discussion of the role of the Christian minister": King, *Stride Toward Freedom*, (1958), pp. 186-187.

"I'm the pastor of a church and in that role": King, cited in L. V. Baldwin, *There is a Balm in Gilead*, p. 322.

"Something said to me that the fire of truth": Ibid., 324.

"I come with a feeling that I have been called": King, *The Autobiography*, (1998), p. 46.

Comparing King and Amos

"might be called the key passage of the entire book": King, "Notecards on Books of the Old Testament," (1994), p. 165.

"reveals the deep ethical nature of God": Ibid.

"Unless a man's heart is right, Amos": Ibid.

"developed a class system [that] boasts": King, "A Knock at Midnight," (1998), p. 64.

"the worship service is cold and meaningless": Ibid., pp. 64-65.

"Millions of American Negroes, starving for the want: Ibid., p. 63.

"What more pathetically reveals the irrelevancy": Ibid.

"aligned itself with the privileged classes and so": Ibid.

"The judgment of God is upon the church as never before": King, "Letter From Birmingham City Jail," (1986), p. 300.

"Let justice roll down like waters and righteousness like a mighty stream": King, "I Have a Dream," (1986), p. 219.

"Amos' emphasis throughout seems to be that justice between": King, "Notecards on Books of the Old Testament," (1994), p. 165.

"come to the aid of justice": King, "Letter from Birmingham City Jail," (1986), p. 300.

"an extremist for justice": Ibid, p. 297.

"as I continued to think about the matter": Ibid., p. 298.

"After all," he wrote, "maybe the South": Ibid.

"I call upon you to be as maladjusted as Amos": King, "The Power of Nonviolence," (1986), p. 14.

"we will be able to go out and change": Ibid., p. 15.

Comparing King and Jeremiah

"We were in serious trouble. So was the entire country": Abernathy, *And the*

Walls Came Tumbling Down, p. 468.

"the greatest of them all": King, "The Significant Contributions of Jeremiah," (1992), p. 195.

"that public religion is an organized hypocrisy. In it religion": Ibid., p. 186.

"a shining example of the truth that religion": Ibid., p. 194.

"the laws written in the heart will become an inseparable": Ibid., p. 185.

"He stepped on the religious stage sounding the trumpet": Ibid., p. 194

"But what is society's reaction to such men?" His answer: "It": Ibid., p. 195.

"Not literally": Pritchard, cited in King, "The Significant Contributions of Jeremiah," (1992), footnote on p. 195.

"Tradition says that he was stoned to death there": Chase, *The Prophets for the Common Reader*, p. 109.

"He endured more than did any other prophet": Ibid., p. 104.

"very, very lonely. . . . despite the fact": Drew, cited in Garrow, *Bearing the Cross*, p. 603.

"She attributed his growing girth and his struggles": Ibid.

"King had always been a formal, reserved man in public": Ibid.

"He suffered fits of depression": Pearlman, *In the Footsteps of the Prophets*, pp. 178-179.

"exhaustion"—but best friend and closest colleague Ralph Abernathy: Abernathy, *And the Walls Came Tumbling Down*.

"dispirited," "despondent," and "melancholy": Garrow, *Bearing the Cross*, pp. 577-578.

"very tired and drained" and "very discouraged," that "a profound sadness": Wilkins, in Garrow, *Bearing the Cross*, p. 599.

"sad and depressed": Abernathy, cited in Garrow, *Bearing the Cross*, p. 599.

"There were moments when he would feel depressed": C. S. King, cited in Garrow, *Bearing the Cross*, p. 602.

"And I don't mind telling you this morning": King, "Why Jesus Called a Man a Fool," (1998), p. 164.

"But then the holy spirit revives my soul again": Ibid.

"No other prophet experienced so often": Chase, *The Prophets for the Common Reader*, pp. 104-105.

King as the Archetypal Martyr-Savior

"a perfect alignment between words and action": Ivory, *Toward a Theology of Radical Involvement*, p. 82.

"a theology of radical involvement": Ivory, *Toward a Theology of Radical Involvement*.

"We have the power to change America": King, *The Autobiography*, (1998), p. 351.

"King saw Jesus as the radically involved personality": Ivory, *Toward a Theology of Radical Involvement*, p. 54.

How Others Compared King to Jesus

"morbid comments about his death": Garrow, *Bearing the Cross*, p. 602.

"It was a little like the Last Supper. Members of the staff": C. S. King, *My Life With Martin*, p. 289.

"Now it doesn't matter now. It really doesn't matter now": King, "I See the Promised Land," (1986), p. 286.

"My husband had always talked of his own readiness": C. S. King, *My Life With*

Martin, p. 296.

"Martin had felt a mystical identity with the spirit": Ibid.

"I would challenge you today to see that his spirit": C. S. King, cited in Burns, *To the Mountaintop*, p. 453.

"I'm hoping Easter Sunday he'll rise again!": cited in Schulke & McPhee, *King Remembered*, p. 259.

"there were so many parallels" between King and Jesus: Abernathy, *And the Walls Came Tumbling Down,* p.p. 619-620.

"You were our leader and we were your disciples": Ibid.

"When the masters left the disciples, they felt gloom at first": Ibid., p. 620.

The Poor People's Campaign was carried out by his disciples: McKnight, *The Last Crusade*.

How King Compared Himself to Jesus

""Gandhi's death at the hand of an assassin": King, cited in Ansbro, *Martin Luther King, Jr.*, p. 97.

"if physical death is the price that some must pay to free": King, "Facing the Challenge of a New Age," (1986), p. 143.

"You may even give your body to be burned, and die the death": King, "Paul's Letter to American Christians," (1998), p. 35.

"Once more it might well turn out that the blood": King, "Facing the Challenge of a New Age," (1986), p. 143.

"I feel, though, that my cause is so right": King, "*Playboy* Interview," (1986), p. 356.

"I may be crucified for my beliefs": C. S. King, *My Life With Martin*, p. 280.

if physical death is the price I must pay": cited in Schulke & McPhee, *King Remembered*, p. 69.

"We must not return violence under any condition": King, *Stride Toward Freedom*, (1958), p. 164.

"What is the cross but God's way of saying to a wayward child": King, cited in Cone, *Martin & Malcolm & America*, p. 127.

"The divine love, in short, is sacrificial in its nature": King, "A View of the Cross Possessing Biblical," (1992), p. 267.

"Christianity has always insisted that the cross we bear precedes": King, cited in Garrow, "Martin Luther King., Jr. and the Spirit of Leadership," p. 26.

"When I took up the cross, I recognized its meaning": King, cited in Garrow, *Bearing the Cross*, p. 564.

"the cross we must bear for the freedom of our people": King, cited in Cone, *Martin & Malcolm & America*, p. 127.

"made the incision over Martin's heart in the form of a cross": C. S. King, *My Life With Martin*, p. 156.

Historian Stewart Burns tells the story King's arrest during the boycott: Burns, *To the Mountaintop*, p. 106.

"The identification of King as a kind of savior": L. Baldwin, *There is a Balm in Gilead*, p. 246.

"I can't see what's the difference between him and the Messiah": cited in Schulke & McPhee, *King Remembered*, p. 273.

"the old folks saw in him a black Jesus": Ibid., p. 69.

"He lifted them so high, and they just can't help": Ibid.

"almost like a Messiah to them": C. S. King, *My Life With Martin*, p. 261.

One time she heard someone shout, "There he goes": Ibid., p. 207.

ANALYSIS: CHAPTER 8 NOTES

King and the Complexes

"He who was nailed to the cross for us this afternoon approaches"—cited in Burns, *To the Mountaintop*, p. 106.

Jung was careful when elucidating his theory on the complexes to state: Jung, "A Review of Complex Theory," (1969).

"felt compelled to rebut one particular rumor": King, *The Autobiography*, (1998), p. 138.

"A person who constantly calls attention to his trials": King, "Suffering and Faith," (1986), p. 41.

"archetypes are complexes of experience that come upon us like fate": Jung, "Archetypes and the Collective Unconscious," (1933), p. 62.

"We know the gods have claimed another victim": Ibid.

the grip of "the eternal laws" of the psyche: Jung, *The Essential Jung*, (1983), p. 124.

"Actually, I do not believe it can be escaped": Ibid.

"collective contents, such as religious, philosophical": Jung, *Flying Saucers,* (1978), p. 14.

"At times I think I'm a pretty unprepared symbol": King, cited in Cone, *Martin & Malcolm & America*, p. 170.

The Dangers to the Man Behind the Myth

"If I have to go through this to give the people a symbol": King, cited in Garrow, *Bearing the Cross*, p. 428.

"to act a part at the expense of one's humanity": Jung, *The Essential Jung*, (1983), p. 124.

Masking aspects of his humanity was just one of many personal sacrifices: Garrow, *Bearing the Cross*.

"the Cause had taken over his life" D. S. King, *Growing Up King*, p. 30

Whenever he wore his robe, I was happy": Ibid., p. 21.

"Martin Luther King the famous man [is] a kind of stranger to me": King, cited in Garrow, *Bearing the Cross*, p. 289.

The Dangers of Myth-Making to a Movement

"The people felt relatively secure as long as he": Fromm, *Ye Shall Be As Gods*, p. 111.

"If a relatively short absence of the leader results": Ibid., p. 112.

"They felt King's presence would elicit a 'Messiah Complex': Giddings, *When and Where I Enter*, pp. 282-283.

"that only a particular individual could save them": Ibid., 347.

"People have to be made to understand that they cannot look for salvation": Baker, "Developing Community Leadership," n. p.

"the thrust is to try and develop leadership out of the group": Ibid.

"I have always felt it was a handicap for oppressed peoples to": Ibid.

"tremendous outpouring of concern": C. S. King, *My Life With Martin*, p. 298.

"genuine love and brotherhood throughout the world": Ibid.

There were riots in sixty-three cities across the country: Burns, *To the Mountaintop*, pp. 452-452.

"the disintegration of everything that makes up the life of a civilized collectivity": Ibid.

who spoke over and over again. . .beseeching people to stay: Ibid., p. 452.

"an ironic tribute to the apostle of nonviolence": C. S. King, *My Life With Martin*, p. 299.

:If a relatively short absence of the leader results in making": Fromm, *Ye Shall Be As Gods,* pp. 111-112.

The slogan for the campaign was "Jobs or Income": McKnight, *The Last Crusade.*

"almost perfect failure: It was poorly timed, poorly organized": Ibid, p. 1077.

"Our leader is dead. In many respects I loved Dr. King more than Jesus": cited Burns, *To the Mountaintop*, p. 450.

"I have been to the top of the mountain. I have talked with God about it": Abernathy, *And the Walls Came Tumbling Down*, p. 459.

that "our 'sixteen months of wandering in the wilderness of mourning for Martin'": Abernathy, Ibid., p. 576.

Joshua was entirely different from Moses": Walker, cited in Abernathy, *And the Walls Came Tumbling Down*, p. 576.

"to press on until the walls [of Jericho] came": Ibid.

The Dangers of Myth-Making to History

"but emphasis on his charisma obscures other important": Carson, "Reconstructing the King Legacy," pp. 242-243.

"Directing attention to the other leaders who initiated and emerged from those struggles should not detract from our appreciation": Ibid., p. 246.

Carson contrasts the "great man perspective" with a "movement-centered perspective": Ibid.

"increasingly critical of [King's] leadership style, seeing it as the cause of feelings": Ibid., p. 245.

"To instill in members of local communities the confidence that they could lead their own struggles": Ibid.

"As the organizers put it, their job was to work themselves out of a job" Ibid., p. 246

"Christ, as a particular concrete manifestation of the Holy Spirit": Edinger, *The Christian Archetype*, pp. 126-127.

"The individual did not become the vessel for the Holy Spirit": Ibid., p. 127.

The notion that appearances by Great Men (or Great Women) are necessary: Carson, "Martin Luther King, Jr.: Charismatic Leadership," ¶19.

"The challenges we face will not be solved with one": Obama, 1998, n. p.

"Idolizing King lessens one's ability to exhibit some of his best attributes": Carson, "Reconstructing the King Legacy," p. 247.

The Dangers of Myth-Making to the Message

""America was on trial—self-consciously on trial, and America": C. E. Lincoln, Martin Luther King, Jr.," p. vii.

making him an "antiseptic hero,": Bond, "Remembering the Man and the Hero," n. p.

"Mythic characters personify intrapsychic processes, but there are many characters," Corbett, *The Religious Function of the Psyche*, p. 79.

"He wanted to have the right to have freedom from the white": Hayley Horan, cited in Selig, "America's Selective Remembering," p. 229.

"for the evils of racism, poverty and militarism to die, a new set of": King,

Where Do We Go From Here, (1967), p. 157.

"I have the reservations you have, but here the perception of too many": Reagan, *Reagan: A Life in Letters*, p. 634.

"Could it be that Mr. Reagan understood that the ease-ee-est way to get rid": Rangel, cited in Dyson, *I May Not Get There With You*, p. 283.

Lewis Baldwin who called King a great American gadfly: L. V. Baldwin, *There is a Balm in Gilead*, p. 251.

"If something doesn't happen soon, I'm convinced that the curtain of doom is coming down on the U.S.": King, cited in Albert & Hoffman, *We Shall Overcome*, p. 210.

America, I don't plan to let you rest until that day": Ibid.

"Millions of Americans are coming to see that we are fighting an immoral war": Ibid., p. 161.

Conclusion

"The whole future of America will depend upon the impact and influence of Dr. King": Heschel, "Conversation with Martin Luther King," p. 658.

INTEGRATION: CHAPTER 9 NOTES

In 1954, Dexter Avenue Baptist Church in Montgomery: King, *The Autobiography*, (1998), pp. 41-44.

Jung described this process using alchemy: Hopcke, *A Guided Tour*, pp. 161-166.

The Three Dimensions of Individual Individuation and Integration

"The Length of Life, as we shall use it": King, *The Autobiography*, (1998), p. 43.

"We are concerned with developing our inner powers": King, "The Three Dimensions," (1998), p. 123.

the "selfish dimension of life": Ibid.

"go through life with deep and haunting": Ibid.

"And we must pray, 'Lord, Help me": Ibid.

"The more I tried to do it in an hour, the more": Ibid., p. 124.

"I was not willing to accept myself. I was not willing": Ibid.

"the principle of self-acceptance is a basic principle in life": Ibid., p. 125.

Since the soul "stands between good and evil": Jung, "Mysterium Coniunctionis," (1970), p. 471.

"the attainment of full knowledge of the heights": Ibid., p. 474.

"Whenever you set out to build a creative temple, whatever it": King, "Unfulfilled Dreams," (1998), p. 194.

"Whenever we set out to dream our dreams": Ibid., p. 196.

"In the final analysis, what God requires is that your heart": Ibid.

"was not the culminating point but merely": Jung, "Mysterium Coniunctionis," (1970), p. 465.

"You know, a lot of people get no further in life": King, "The Three Dimensions," (1998), p. 126.

"A man has not begun to live until he can rise": Ibid., p. 127.

"The preacher must be concerned about the whole man": King, "Why Jesus Called a Man a Fool," (1998), p. 146.

It seems as if I can hear the Lord of Life saying: King, "The Three Dimensions,"

272

(1998), p. 131.
"the union of the whole man with the *unus mundus*":1058 534
Jung called a symbol of "unity *par excellence*": 1059 541
"move beyond humanity and reach up": King, "The Three Dimensions," (1998), p. 133.
"They deny the existence of God with their lives and they": Ibid., pp. 133-134.
"We were made for God, and we will be restless": Ibid;, p. 135.

The Three Dimensions of Cultural Individuation and Integration
"descending out of heaven, [came] a new heaven": Ibid., pp. 121-122.
"The length and the breadth and the height of it are equal": Ibid., p. 122.
"This new city of God, this new city of ideal humanity, is not": Ibid.
"transformation and change of heart": King, *The Autobiography*, (1998), p. 130.
"two hundred and fifty thousand people shouted in ecstatic": C. S. King, *My Life With Martin*, p. 223.
"the reunion of the spirit with the body": Jung, "Mysterium Coniunctionis," (1970), p. 475.
"A social movement that only moves people": King, *The Autobiography*, (1998), p. 220.
Jung called "the potential world": Jung, "Mysterium Coniunctionis," (1970), p. 534.
"the idea that all men have something within them that God injected": King, "The American Dream," (1998), p. 88.
Martin Buber's idea of the "I-Thou" relationship: Ibid., p. 89.
Often he described it in biblical language, calling it "the New Jerusalem": King, "The Three Dimensions," (1998), p. 122.
"the Promised Land": King, "I See the Promised Land," (1986), p. 286.
"God's kingdom on earth": King, "Loving Your Enemies," (1998), p. 59.
"In Christ there is no East or West/In Him no North or South": Ibid., p. 58
"one day all men everywhere will recognize": King, "The American Dream," (1998), p. 100.
"the morning stars will sing together": Ibid.
"every valley will be exalted, and every hill and mountain": King, "The Three Dimensions," (1998), p. 140.
"Well, I don't know what will happen now": King, "I See the Promised Land," (1986), p. 286.
"There is simply nothing the individual lacks": Raff, *Jung and the Alchemical Imagination*, p. 159.

Conclusion
"one of the great agonies of life": King, "Unfulfilled Dreams," (1998), p. 192.
"Your dream will not be fulfilled. The majestic hopes": Ibid.
"a voice crying through the vista of time": Ibid., p. 194.
"alchemists were consciously performing an *opus divinum*": Jung, *Flying Saucers*, (1978), p. 28.
"only love that can generate a peace that will": King, cited in Ansbro, *Martin Luther King, Jr.*, p. 34.
"For we are in the deepest sense the victims and the instruments of cosmogonic 'love'": Jung, *Memories, Dreams, Reflections*, (1989), p. 354.
"a beautiful symphony of brotherhood": King, "Remaining Awake During a Great Revolution," (1998), p. 224.

"the *summmum bonum* of life": King, "Paul's Letter to American Christians," (1998), p. 34.

REFERENCES

Abernathy, R.D. (1989). *And the walls came tumbling down: An autobiography.* New York: Harper & Row.

Albert, P. & Hoffman, R. (Eds.). (1990). *We shall overcome: Martin Luther King, Jr., and the Black freedom struggle.* New York: Pantheon Books.

Allport, G. W. (1979). *The nature of prejudice.* Reading, MA: Perseus Books.

Angelou, M. (1981). *The heart of a woman.* New York: Bantam Books.

Ansbro, J. J. (1982). *Martin Luther King, Jr.: Nonviolent strategies and tactics for social change.* New York: Orbis Books.

Baker, E. (1973). Developing community leadership: An interview. In G. Lerner *Black women in white America: A documentary history* (345-352). New York: Vintage.

Baldwin, J. (1955). *Notes of a native son.* Boston: Beacon Press.

Baldwin, J. (1962). *The fire next time.* New York: Dell.

Baldwin, L. V. (1991). *There is a balm in Gilead: The cultural roots of Martin Luther King, Jr.* Minneapolis, MN: Fortress Press.

Bennett, L. (1970). When the man and the hour are met. In C. E. Lincoln (Ed.), *Martin Luther King, Jr.: A profile* (pp. 7-39). New York: Hill and Wang.

Bond, J. (1993, April 4). Remember the man and the hero, not just half the dream. *The Seattle Times.* Retrieved from http://seattletimes.nwsource.com/mlk/legacy/bond.hmtl

Buber, M. (1965). *The knowledge of man: Selected essays* (M. Friedman, Ed.). New York: Harper & Row.

Buber, M. (1967). *A believing humanism: My testament, 1902-1965* (M. Friedman, Trans). New York: Simon and Schuster.

Burns, S. (2004). *To the mountaintop: Martin Luther King Jr.'s Sacred Mission to Save America 1955-1968.* San Francisco: HarperSanFrancisco.

Carson, C. (1987). Martin Luther King Jr.: Charismatic leadership in a mass struggle. Retrieved from http://www.stanford.edu/group/King/additional_resources/articles/charisma.htm

Carson, C. (1990). Reconstructing the King legacy: Scholars and national myths. In P. Albert & R. Hoffman (Eds.), *We shall overcome: Martin Luther King, Jr., and the Black freedom struggle* (pp. 239-248). New York: Pantheon Books.

Carson, C. (Ed.) (1992). *The papers of Martin Luther King, Jr.: Vol. I. Called to serve, January 1929-June 1951.* Berkeley: University of California Press.

Carson, C. (Ed.) (1994). *The papers of Martin Luther King, Jr.: Vol. 2. Rediscovering precious values, July 1951-November 1955.* Berkeley: University of California Press.

Carson, C. (1996). Transcendence. Retrieved from http://www.stanford.edu/group/King/additional_resources/articles/Transcendence.htm

Carson, C. (Ed.) (2000). *The papers of Martin Luther King, Jr.: Vol. 4. Symbol of the movement, January, 1957-December, 1958.* Berkeley: University of California Press.

Carson, C. & Holloran, P. (Eds.). (1998). *A knock at midnight: Inspiration from the great sermons of Reverend Martin Luther King, Jr.* New York: Warner

Books.

Chase, M. E. (1963). *The prophets for the common reader*. New York: Norton.

Cone, J. H. (1986). The theology of Martin Luther King, Jr. *Union Seminary Quarterly Review, XL* (4), 21-39.

Cone, J. H. (1990). Martin Luther King, Jr., and the Third World. In P. Albert & R. Hoffman (Eds.), *We shall overcome: Martin Luther King, Jr., and the Black freedom struggle* (pp. 197-221). New York: Pantheon Books.

Cone, J. H. (1991). *Martin & Malcolm & America: A dream or a nightmare*. Maryknoll, NY: Orbis Books.

The constitution of the United States of America. (1787). Retrieved from http://www.law.cornell.edu/constitution/constitution.overview.html

Corbett, L. (1996). *The religious function of the psyche*. London: Routledge.

Craigie, P. C. (1984). *Twelve prophets (Vol. 1)*. Philadelphia: Westminster Press.

The declaration of independence. (1776). Retrieved from http://www.1aw.indiana.edu/uslawdocs/declaration.html

Dyson, M. E. (2000). *I may not get there with you: The true Martin Luther King, Jr*. New York: The Free Press.

Early, G. (1996, August 28). Martin Luther King and the middle way. *The Christian Century, 113* (25), 816.

Edinger, E. F. (1987). *The Christian archetype: A Jungian commentary on the life of Christ*. Toronto: Inner City Books.

Fairclough, A. (2001). *To redeem the soul of America: The Southern Christian Leadership Conference and Martin Luther King, Jr*. Athens, GA: University of Georgia Press.

Friedman, M. (1985). *The healing dialogue in psychotherapy*. New York: Jason Aronson, Inc.

Franklin, R. M., Jr. (1986). An ethic of hope: The moral thought of Martin Luther King, Jr. *Union Seminary Quarterly Review, XL* (4), 41-51.

Fromm, E. (1955). *The sane society*. New York: Henry Holt and Company.

Fromm, E. (1956). *The art of loving*. New York: Harper Perennial.

Fromm, E. (1964). *The heart of man: Its genius for good and evil*. New York: Harper & Row.

Fromm, E. (1966). *You shall be as gods: A radical interpretation of the Old Testament and its tradition*. New York: Holt, Rinehart and Winston.

Fromm, E. (1976). *To have or to be?* Toronto: Bantam Books.

Fromm, E. (1994). *On being human*. New York: Continuum.

Garrow, D. J. (1981). *The FBI and Martin Luther King, Jr*. New York: Penguin.

Garrow, D. J. (1986). *Bearing the cross: Martin Luther King, Jr. and the Southern Christian Leadership Conference*. New York: William Morrow and Company.

Garrow, D. J. (1990). Martin Luther King, Jr. and the spirit of leadership. In P. Albert & R. Hoffman (Eds.), *We shall overcome: Martin Luther King, Jr., and the Black freedom struggle* (pp. 11-34). New York: Pantheon Books.

Gergen, K. J. (1989). The possibility of psychological knowledge: A hermeneutic inquiry. In M. J. Packer and R. B. Addison (Eds.), *Entering the circle: Hermeneutic investigation in psychology* (pp. 95-117). Albany, NY: State University Press.

Giddings, P. (1984). *When and where I enter: The impact of black women on race and sex in America*. Toronto: Bantam Books.

Gilligan, J. (1996). *Violence: Reflections on a national epidemic*. New York: Vintage Books.

Grier, W. H., & Cobbs, P. M. (1968). *Black rage*. New York: Basic Books.

Heschel, A. J. (1968). Conversation with Martin Luther King. In J. M. Washington (Ed.), *A testament of hope: The essential writings and speeches of Martin Luther King, Jr.* (pp. 657-679). San Francisco, CA: HarperCollins.

Hillman, J. (1975). *Re-visioning psychology*. New York: Harper Perennial.

Hillman, J., and Ventura, M. (1992). *We've had a hundred years of psychotherapy and the world's getting worse*. San Francisco: HarperCollins.

Hollis, J. (1998). *The Eden project: In search of the magical other*. Toronto: Inner City Books.

hooks, b. (2000). *All about love: New visions*. New York: Perennial.

hooks, b. (2001). *Salvation*. New York: William Morrow.

Hopcke, R. H. (1989). *A guided tour of the collected works of C. G. Jung*. Boston: Shambala.

Horney, K. (1937). *The neurotic personality of our time*. New York: W. W. Norton & Company.

Horney, K. (1939). *New ways in psychoanalysis*. New York: W. W. Norton & Company.

Horney, K. (1945). *Our inner conflicts: A constructive theory of neurosis*. New York: W. W. Norton & Company.

Horney, K. (1950). *Neurosis and human growth: The struggle toward self-realization*. New York: W.W. Norton & Company.

Huggins, N. I. (1990). Commentary. In P. Albert & R. Hoffman (Eds.), *We shall overcome: Martin Luther King, Jr., and the Black freedom struggle* (pp. 84-92). New York: Pantheon Books.

Ivory, L. (1997). *Toward a theology of radical involvement: The theological legacy of Martin Luther King, Jr.* Nashville, TN: Abington Press.

Jackson, J. (1999). Afterward. In M. L. King, Jr. *Why we can't wait* (pp. 144-153). New York: Signet Classic.

Johanssen, R. (1998). "A go-ahead nation." Retrieved from http://www.pbs.org/kera!usmexicanwar/dialogues/prelude/manifest/d2ben g.html

Jordan, J. (1994). *Moving towards home: Political essays*. London: Virago.

Jung, C. G. (1916). Seven sermons to the dead (H. G. Baynes, Trans.). Retrieved from http://gnosis.org/library/7Sermons.htm

Jung, C. G. (1933). The modern spiritual problem. In W. S. Dell & Cary F. Baynes (Trans.), *Modern man in search of soul* (pp. 196-220). San Diego, CA: Harcourt Brace.

Jung, C. G. (1933). Psychotherapists or the clergy. In W. S. Dell & Cary F. Baynes (Trans.), *Modern man in search of soul* (pp. 221-244). San Diego, CA: Harcourt Brace.

Jung. C. G. (1935). Archetypes and the collective unconscious. In R. F. C. Hull (Trans.), *The collected works of C. G. Jung* (Vol. 9, Part 1). Princeton, NJ: Princeton University Press.

Jung. C. G. (1963). The psychology of the transference. In R. F. C. Hull (Trans.), *The collected works of* C. G. *Jung* (Vol. 16). Princeton, NJ: Princeton University Press. (Original work published 1946)

Jung, C. G. (1969). A review of the complex theory. In R. F. C. Hull (Trans.), *The collected works of C. G. Jung* (Vol. 8, pp. 92-104). Princeton: Princeton University Press.

Jung, C. G. (1969). The transcendent function. In R. F. C. Hull (Trans.), *The collected works of C. G. Jung* (Vol. 8, pp. 67-91). Princeton, MA: Princeton

University Press. (Original work published 1916)

Jung, C. G. (1970). Mysterium coniunctionis. In R. F. C. Hull (Trans.), *The collected works of* C. G. *Jung* (Vol. 14). Princeton, NJ: Princeton University Press. (Original work published 1963)

Jung, C. G. (1975). Psychoanalysis and the cure of souls. In R. F. C. Hull (Trans.), *The collected works of* C. G. *Jung* (Vol. 11). Princeton, NJ: Princeton University Press. (Original work published 1932)

Jung, C. G. (1978). Flying saucers: *A modern myth of things seen in the sky* (R. F. C. Hull, Trans.). Princeton, NJ: Princeton University Press. (Original work published 1959)

Jung, C. G. (1983). *The essential Jung* (A. Storr, Ed.). Princeton, NJ: Princeton University Press.

Jung, C. G. (1989). After the catastrophe. In *Essays on contemporary events* (R. F. C. Hull, Trans.). (pp. 50-73). Princeton, NJ: Princeton University Press. (Original work published 1945)

Jung, C. G. (1989). Epilogue. In *Essays on contemporary events* (R. F. C. Hull, Trans.). (pp. 74-90). Princeton, NJ: Princeton University Press. (Original work published 1946)

Jung, C. G. (1989). *Memories, dreams, reflections*. New York: Vintage Books. (Original work published 1963)

Jung, C. G. (2010). *Answer to Job* (S. Shamdasani, Trans.), Princeton, NJ: Princeton University Press. (Original work published 1952).

King, C. S. (1969). *My life with Martin Luther King, Jr.* New York: Puffin Books.

King, D. S. (2003). *Growing up King: An intimate memoir*. New Yorks: Warner Books.

King, M. L., Jr. (1958). *Stride toward freedom: The Montgomery story*. New York: Perennial Library.

King, M. L., Jr. (1963). Antidotes for fear. In M. L. King, Jr., *Strength to love* (pp. 115-126). Philadelphia: Fortress Press.

King, M. L., Jr. (1963). Pilgrimage to nonviolence. In M. L. King, Jr., *Strength to love* (pp. 146-154). Philadelphia: Fortress Press.

King, M. L., Jr. (1963). A tough mind and a tender heart. In M. L. King, Jr., *Strength to love* (pp. 13-20). Philadelphia: Fortress Press

King, M. L. Jr. (1963). *Strength to love*. Philadelphia: Fortress Press.

King, M. L., Jr. (1967). *The trumpet of conscience*. San Francisco, CA: Harper & Row.

King, M. L., Jr. (1967). *Where do we go from here: Chaos or community?* New York: Bantam Books.

King, M. L., Jr. (1986). Black Power defined. In J. M. Washington (Ed.), *A testament of hope: The essential writings and speeches of Martin Luther King, Jr.* (pp. 303-312). San Francisco, CA: HarperCollins. (Original work published 1967)

King, M. L., Jr. (1986). The ethical demands for integration. In J. M. Washington (Ed.), *A testament of hope: The essential writings and speeches of Martin Luther King, Jr.* (pp. 117-125). San Francisco, CA: HarperCollins. (Original work published 1962)

King, M. L. Jr. (1986). Eulogy for the martyred children. In J. M. Washington (Ed.), *A testament of hope: The essential writings and speeches of Martin Luther King, Jr.* (pp. 221-223). San Francisco, CA: HarperCollins. (Original work published 1963)

King, M. L., Jr. (1986). Facing the challenge of a new age. In J. M. Washington (Ed.), *A testament of hope: The essential writings and speeches of Martin Luther King, Jr.* (pp. 135-144). San Francisco, CA: HarperCollins. (Original work published 1957)

King, M. L., Jr. (1986). I have a dream. In J. M. Washington (Ed.), *A testament of hope: The essential writings and speeches of Martin Luther King, Jr.* (pp. 217-220). San Francisco, CA: HarperCollins. (Original speech delivered 1963)

King, M. L., Jr. (1986). I see the promised land. In J. M. Washington (Ed.), *A testament of hope: The essential writings and speeches of Martin Luther King, Jr.* (pp.279-286). San Francisco, CA: HarperCollins. (Original speech delivered 1968)

King, M. L., Jr. (1986). Kenneth B. Clark interview. In J. M. Washington (Ed.), *A testament of hope: The essential writings and speeches of Martin Luther King, Jr.* (pp. 331-339). San Francisco, CA: HarperCollins. (Original interview published 1963)

King, M. L., Jr. (1986). Letter from Birmingham city jail. In J. M. Washington (Ed.), *A testament of hope: The essential writings and speeches of Martin Luther King, Jr.* (pp. 289-302). San Francisco, CA: HarperCollins. (Original work published 1963)

King, M. L., Jr. (1986). Love, law, and civil disobedience. In J. M. Washington (Ed.), *A testament of hope: The essential writings and speeches of Martin Luther King, Jr.* (pp. 43-53). San Francisco, CA: HarperCollins. (Original work published 1961)

King, M. L., Jr. (1986). "Meet the Press" television news interview. In J. M. Washington (Ed.), *A testament of hope: The essential writings and speeches of Martin Luther King, Jr.* (pp. 379-393). San Francisco, CA: HarperCollins. (Original interview televised 1966)

King, M. L., Jr. (1986). Nobel Prize acceptance speech. In J. M. Washington (Ed.), *A testament of hope: The essential writings and speeches of Martin Luther King, Jr.* (pp. 224-230). San Francisco, CA: HarperCollins. (Original speech delivered 1964)

King, M. L., Jr. (1986). Nonviolence and racial justice. In J. M. Washington (Ed.), *A testament of hope: The essential writings and speeches of Martin Luther King, Jr.* (pp. 5-9). San Francisco, CA: HarperCollins. (Original work published 1957)

King, M. L., Jr. (1986). Our struggle. In J. M. Washington (Ed.), *A testament of hope: The essential writings and speeches of Martin Luther King, Jr.* (pp. 75-81). San Francisco, CA: HarperCollins. (Original work published 1956)

King, M. L., Jr. (1986). *Playboy* interview: Martin Luther King, Jr. In J. M. Washington (Ed.), *A testament of hope: The essential writings and speeches of Martin Luther King, Jr.* (pp. 340-377). San Francisco, CA: HarperCollins. (Original work published 1965)

King, M. L., Jr. (1986). The power of nonviolence. In J. M. Washington (Ed.), *A testament of hope: The essential writings and speeches of Martin Luther King, Jr.* (pp. 12-15). San Francisco, CA: HarperCollins. (Original work published 1958)

King, M. L., Jr. (1986). Suffering and faith. In J. M. Washington (Ed.), *A testament of hope: The essential writings and speeches of Martin Luther King, Jr.* (pp. 41-42). San Francisco, CA: HarperCollins. (Original work published 1960)

King, M. L., Jr. (1986). A time to break silence. In J. M. Washington (Ed.), *A testament of hope: The essential writings and speeches of Martin Luther King, Jr.* (pp. 231-244). San Francisco, CA: HarperCollins. (Original speech delivered 1967)

King, M. L., Jr. (1986). Walk for freedom. In J. M. Washington (Ed.), *A testament of hope: The essential writings and speeches of Martin Luther King, Jr.* (pp. 82-84). San Francisco, CA: HarperCollins. (Original work published 1956)

King, M. L., Jr. (1986). Where do we go from here? In J. M. Washington (Ed.), *A testament of hope: The essential writings and speeches of Martin Luther King, Jr.* (pp. 245-252). San Francisco, CA: HarperCollins. (Original speech published 1972)

King, M. L., Jr. (1992). Application for admission to Crozer Theological Seminary. In C. Carson (Ed.), *The papers of Martin Luther King, Jr.: Vol. 1. Called to serve, January 1929-June 1951* (pp. 142-145). Berkeley: University of California Press. (Original application written 1948)

King, M. L., Jr. (1992). An autobiography of religious development. In C. Carson (Ed.), *The papers of Martin Luther King, Jr.: Vol. 1. Called to serve, January 1929-June 1951* (pp. 359-363). Berkeley: University of California Press. (Original paper written 1950)

King, M. L., Jr. (1992). Book review of *Personality, Its Study and Hygiene* by Winifred V. Richmond. In C. Carson (Ed.), *The papers of Martin Luther King, Jr.: Vol. 1. Called to serve, January 1929-June 1951* (pp. 357-358). Berkeley: University of California Press. (Original paper written 1950)

King, M. L., Jr. (1992). The Christian pertinence of eschatological hope. In C. Carson (Ed.), *The papers of Martin Luther King, Jr.: Vol. 1. Called to serve, January 1929-June 1951* (pp. 268-273). Berkeley: University of California Press. (Original paper written 1949-1950)

King, M. L., Jr. (1992). A conception and impression of religion drawn from Dr. Brightman's book entitled *A Philosophy of Religion*. In C. Carson (Ed.), *The papers of Martin Luther King, Jr.: Vol. 1. Called to serve, January 1929-June 1951* (pp. 407-416). Berkeley: University of California Press. (Original paper written 1951)

King, M. L., Jr. (1992). The humanity and divinity of Jesus. In C. Carson (Ed.), *The papers of Martin Luther King, Jr.: Vol. 1. Called to serve, January 1929-June 1951* (pp. 257-262). Berkeley: University of California Press. (Original paper written 1950)

King, M. L., Jr. (1992). Light on the Old Testament from the Ancient Near East. In C. Carson (Ed.), *The papers of Martin Luther King, Jr.: Vol. 1. Called to serve, January 1929-June 1951* (pp. 162-180). Berkeley: University of California Press. (Original paper written 1948)

King, M. L., Jr. (1992). The Negro and the Constitution. In C. Carson (Ed.), *The papers of Martin Luther King, Jr.: Vol. 1. Called to serve, January 1929-June 1951* (pp. 109-111). Berkeley: University of California Press. (Original paper written 1944)

King, M. L., Jr. (1992). The place of reason and experience in finding God. In C. Carson (Ed.), *The papers of Martin Luther King, Jr.: Vol. 1. Called to serve, January 1929-June 1951* (pp. 230-236). Berkeley: University of California Press. (Original paper written 1949)

King, M. L., Jr. (1992). The significant contributions of Jeremiah to religious thought. In C. Carson (Ed.), *The papers of Martin Luther King, Jr.: Vol. 1. Called to serve, January 1929-June 1951* (pp. 181-195). Berkeley: University of California Press. (Original paper written 1948)

King, M. L., Jr. (1992). The sources of fundamentalism and liberalism considered historically and psychologically. In C. Carson (Ed.), *The papers of Martin Luther King, Jr.: Vol. 1. Called to serve, January 1929-June 1951* (pp. 236-251). Berkeley: University of California Press. (Original paper written 1949)

King, M. L., Jr. (1992). A view of the cross possessing Biblical and spiritual justification. In C. Carson (Ed.), *The papers of Martin Luther King, Jr.: Vol. 1. Called to serve, January 1929-June 1951* (pp. 263-267). Berkeley: University of California Press. (Original paper written 1949-1950)

King, M. L., Jr. (1994). Notecards on books of the Old Testament. In C. Carson (Ed.), *The papers of Martin Luther King, Jr.: Vol. 2. Rediscovering precious values, July 1951-November 1955* (pp. 164-167). Berkeley: University of California Press. (Original cards written 1952-1953)

King, M. L., Jr. (1997). The "New Negro" of the South: Behind the Montgomery Story. In C. Carson (Ed.), *The papers of Martin Luther King, Jr.: Vol. 3. Birth of a new age, December 1955-December 1956* (pp. 280-286). Berkeley: University of California Press. (Original work published 1956)

King, M. L., Jr. (1997). "Non-aggression procedures to interracial harmony": Address delivered at the American Baptist Assembly and American Home Mission Agencies Conference. In C. Carson (Ed.), *The papers of Martin Luther King, Jr.: Vol. 3. Birth of a new age, December 1955-December 1956* (pp. 321-328). Berkeley: University of California Press. (Original address delivered 1956)

King, M. L., Jr. (1997). When peace becomes obnoxious. In C. Carson (Ed.), *The papers of Martin Luther King, Jr.: Vol. 3. Birth of a new age, December 1955- December 1956* (pp. 207-208). Berkeley: University of California Press. (Original address delivered 1956)

King, M. L., Jr. (1998). The American dream. In C. Carson & P. Holloran (Eds.), *A knock at midnight: Inspiration from the great sermons of Reverend Martin Luther King, Jr.* (pp. 85-100). New York: Warner Books. (Original sermon delivered 1965)

King, M. L., Jr. (1998). *The autobiography of Martin Luther King, Jr.* (C. Carson, Ed). New York: Warner Books.

King, M. L., Jr. (1998). The drum major instinct. In C. Carson & P. Holloran (Eds.), *A knock at midnight: Inspiration from the great sermons of Reverend Martin Luther King, Jr.* (pp. 169-186). New York: Warner Books. (Original sermon delivered 1968)

King, M. L., Jr. (1998). A knock at midnight. In C. Carson & P. Holloran (Eds.), *A knock at midnight: Inspiration from the great sermons of Reverend Martin Luther King, Jr.* (pp. 65-78). New York: Warner Books. (Originally published in 1963)

King, M. L., Jr. (1998). Loving your enemies. In C. Carson & P. Holloran (Eds.), *A knock at midnight: Inspiration from the great sermons of Reverend Martin Luther King, Jr.* (pp. 37-60). New York: Warner Books. (Original sermon delivered 1957)

King, M. L., Jr. (1998). Paul's letter to American Christians. In C. Carson & P. Holloran (Eds.), *A knock at midnight: Inspiration from the great sermons of Reverend Martin Luther King, Jr.* (pp. 25-36). New York: Warner Books. (Original sermon delivered 1956)

King, M. L., Jr. (1998). Remaining awake during a great revolution. In C. Carson & P. Holloran (Eds.), *A knock at midnight: Inspiration from the great sermons of Reverend Martin Luther King, Jr.* (pp. 205-224). New York: Warner Books. (Original sermon delivered 1968)

King, M. L., Jr. (1998). The three dimensions of a complete life. In C. Carson & P. Holloran (Eds.), *A knock at midnight: Inspiration from the great sermons of Reverend Martin Luther King, Jr.* (pp. 121-140). New York: Warner Books. (Original sermon delivered 1967)

King, M. L., Jr. (1998). Unfulfilled dreams. In C. Carson & P. Holloran (Eds.), *A knock at midnight: Inspiration from the great sermons of Reverend Martin Luther King, Jr.* (pp. 191-200). New York: Warner Books. (Original sermon delivered 1968)

King, M. L., Jr. (1998). Why Jesus called a man a fool. In C. Carson & P. Holloran (Eds.), *A knock at midnight: Inspiration from the great sermons of Reverend Martin Luther King, Jr.* (pp. 145-164). New York: Warner Books. (Original sermon delivered 1967)

King, M. L., Jr. (2000). "The birth of a new nation": Sermon delivered at Dexter Avenue Baptist Church. In C. Carson (Ed.), *The papers of Martin Luther King, Jr.: Vol. 4. Symbol of the movement, January 1957- December, 1958* (pp. 155-167). Berkeley: University of California Press. (Original sermon delivered 1957)

King, M. L., Jr. (2000). "Conquering self-centeredness": Sermon delivered at Dexter Avenue Baptist Church. In C. Carson (Ed.), *The papers of Martin Luther King, Jr.: Vol. 4. Symbol of the movement, January 1957-December, 1958* (pp. 248-259). Berkeley: University of California Press. (Original sermon delivered 1957)

King, M. L., Jr. (2000). "Facing the challenge of a new age": Address delivered at NAACP Emancipation Day rally. In C. Carson (Ed.), *The papers of Martin Luther King, Jr.: Vol. 4. Symbol of the movement, January 1957-December, 1958* (pp. 73-89). Berkeley: University of California Press. (Original speech given 1957)

King, M. L., Jr. (2000). "Loving your enemies": Sermon delivered at Dexter Avenue Baptist Church. In C. Carson (Ed.), *The papers of Martin Luther King, Jr.: Vol. 4. Symbol of the movement, January 1957-December, 1958* (pp. 315-324). Berkeley: University of California Press. (Original speech given 1957)

King, M. L., Jr. (2005). A creative protest. In C. Carson (Ed.), *The papers of Martin Luther King, Jr.: Vol. 5. Threshold of a New Decade, January 1959-December 1960* (pp. 367-370). Berkeley: University of California Press. (Original speech given 1960)

King, M. L., Jr. (2007). "Overcoming an inferiority complex": Sermon delivered at Dexter Avenue Baptist Church. In C. Carson (Ed.), *The papers of Martin Luther King, Jr.: Vol. 6. Advocate of the social gospel, September 1948-March 1963* (pp. 303-316). Berkeley: University of California Press. (Original speech given 1957)

King, M. L. Jr. (2013). *"In a single garment of destiny": A global vision of justice* (L. V. Baldwin, Ed.). Boston, MA: Beacon.

King, R. H. (1990). Martin Luther King, Jr., and the meaning of freedom: A political interpretation. In P. Albert & R. Hoffman (Eds.), *We shall overcome: Martin Luther King, Jr., and the Black freedom struggle* (pp. 130-152). New York: Pantheon Books.

King's "I Have a Dream" is the greatest political speech of the century. (2000, January 17). *Jet, 97,* 4.

Lewis, D. L. (1971). *King: A critical biography.* Baltimore: Allen Lane.

Lincoln, A. (1858). House divided speech. Retrieved from
http://www.historyplace.com/lincoln/divided.htm

Lincoln, A. (1863). The Gettysburg address. Retrieved from
http://eserver.org/history/gettysburg-address.txt

Lincoln, C. E. (1970). *Martin Luther King, Jr.: A profile.* New York: Hill and Wang.

Lomax, L. (1970). When "nonviolence" meets "black power." In C. E. Lincoln (Ed.),
Martin Luther King, Jr.: A profile (pp. 156-180). New York: Hill and Wang.
(Original work published 1968)

Lubragge, M. (1994-2003). "The components of Manifest Destiny." Retrieved from
http://odur.let.rug.nl/ usa/E/manifest/manif2.htm#rel

Martin Luther King, Jr.: Never again where he was. (1964, January 3). *Time.*
Retrieved from http://www.time.com/time/special/moy/1963.html

McKnight, G. D. (!998). *The last crusade: Martin Luther King, Jr., the FBI, and
the Poor People's Campaign.* Boulder, CO: Westview Press.

Meier, L. (1999). *Moses—the prince, the prophet: His life, legend, & message for
our lives.* Woodstock, VT: Jewish Lights Publishing.

Morris, A. D. (1990). A man prepared for the times: A sociological analysis of the
leadership of Martin Luther King, Jr. In P. Albert & R. Hoffman (Eds.), *We
shall overcome: Martin Luther King, Jr., and the Black freedom struggle*
(pp. 35-58). New York: Pantheon Books.

Oates, S. B. (1982). *Let the trumpet sound: The life of Martin Luther King, Jr.* New
York: Harper & Row.

Obama, B. (1998, Feb. 5). Super Tuesday speech. *New York Times* online edition.
Retrieved from http://www.nytimes.com/2008/02/05/us/politics/05text-
obama.html?pagewanted=all

Otto, R. (1958). *The idea of the holy* (J. W. Harvey, Trans.). Oxford, UK: Oxford
University Press. (Original work published 1917).

Packer, M. J. (1989). Tracing the hermeneutic circle: Articulating an ontical study
of moral conflicts. In M. J. Packer and R. B. Addison (Eds.), *Entering the
circle: Hermeneutic investigation in psychology* (pp. 95-117). Albany, NY:
State University Press.

Pearlman, Moshe. (1975). *In the footsteps of the prophets.* New York: Leon Amiel
Publisher.

Powers, G. D. (1995). *I shared the dream: The pride, passion and politics of the
first black woman senator from Kentucky.* Far Hills, NJ: New Horizon Press.

Prevost, J.P. (1997). *How to read the prophets.* New York: Continuum.

Raff, J. (2000). *Jung and the alchemical imagination.* York Beach, ME: Nicholas-
Hays.

Rauschenbusch, W. (1907). *Christianity and the social crisis.* New York: The
MacMillan Company.

Reagan, R. (2003). *Reagan: A life in letters.* New York: Free Press.

Schulke, F., & McPhee, P. (1986). *King remembered.* New York: Pocket Books.

Schwartz-Salant, N. (1995). *Jung on alchemy.* Princeton, NJ: Princeton University
Press.

Selig, J. L. (2007). America's selective remembering and collective forgetting of
Martin Luther King, Jr. *Spring: A Journal of Archetype and Culture, 78,* 219-
241.

Selig, J. L. (2012). "From the mountain of despair, a stone of hope": Reflections on
our next (?) civil rights movement. In Shapiro, J. & Partridge, R. (Eds.),
Occupy psyche: Jungian and archetypal perspectives on a movement (pp.
21-36). Journal of Archetypal Studies.

Shapiro, J. & Partridge, R. (Eds.). (2012). *Occupy psyche: Jungian and archetypal perspectives on a movement*. Journal of Archetypal Studies.

Sharp, D. (1987). *Psychological types: Jung's model of typology*. Toronto: Inner City Books.

Smith, K. L., & Zepp, I. G., Jr. (1998). *Search for the beloved community: The thinking of Martin Luther King, Jr*. Valley Forge, PA: Judson Press.

Stampp, K. M. (1956). *The peculiar institution: Slavery in the ante-bellum south*. New York: Vintage.

Steele, R. S. (1989). A critical hermeneutics for psychology: Beyond positivism to an exploration of the textual unconscious. In M. J. Packer and R. B. Addison (Eds.), *Entering the circle: Hermeneutic investigation in psychology* (pp. 223-237). Albany, NY: State University Press.

Steele, S. (1990). *The content of our character: A new vision of race in America*. New York: HarperPerennial.

Stein, H. T. & Edwards, M. E. (1968). Classical Adlerian theory and practice. Retrieved from http://www.adlerian.us/theoprac.htm

Tobin, L. M. (1992). Lucius M. Tobin to Charles E. Batten. In C. Carson (Ed.), *The papers of Martin Luther King, Jr.: Vol. 1. Called to serve, January 1929-June 1951* (p. 151). Berkeley: University of California Press. (Original letter written 1948)

Walker, A. (1983). *In search of our mother's gardens*. San Diego: Harcourt Brace Jovanovich.

Walker, A. (2000). *The way forward is with a broken heart*. New York: Ballantine.

Made in the USA
Lexington, KY
26 March 2017